Crime Prevention

Criminal Justice Series

Forensic Mental Health, by Mary McMurran, Najat Khalifa and
 Simon Gibbon

Crime Prevention, by Nick Tilley

Crime Prevention

Nick Tilley

WILLAN
PUBLISHING

Published by

Willan Publishing
Culmcott House
Mill Street, Uffculme
Cullompton, Devon
EX15 3AT, UK
Tel: +44(0)1884 840337
Fax: +44(0)1884 840251
e-mail: info@willanpublishing.co.uk
Website: www.willanpublishing.co.uk

Published simultaneously in the USA and Canada by

Willan Publishing
c/o ISBS, 920 NE 58th Ave, Suite 300,
Portland, Oregon 97213-3786, USA
Tel: +001(0)503 287 3093
Fax: +001(0)503 280 8832
e-mail: info@isbs.com
Website: www.isbs.com

First published 2009

ISBN   978-1-84392-394-7 paperback
       978-1-84392-395-4 hardback

British Library Cataloguing-in-Publication Data

A catalogue record for this book is available from the British Library

Mixed Sources
Product group from well-managed
forests and other controlled sources
www.fsc.org Cert no. TT-COC-2139
© 1996 Forest Stewardship Council

Project managed by Deer Park Productions, Tavistock, Devon
Typeset by Kestrel Data, Exeter, Devon
Printed and bound by T.J. International, Padstow, Cornwall

To Jenny

Contents

List of figures and tables

Figures

Tables

Preface

If you find this book browsing in a bookshop, or library, and are wondering whether or not to buy or borrow it, please do so! I hope you enjoy it, or at least are stimulated by it. If you have to read it for a course, I hope it is not too much of a chore. In either case, here's a reader's guide.

You should be able to read and understand each chapter as a self-contained unit without having read the earlier ones. There are, however, cross references and the later chapters do build on the earlier ones. You will, therefore, get more from the book if you read it all. It's quite short so not too much patience is needed. The most difficult chapter is probably Chapter 7. This is also liable to be the least interesting for the general reader. It talks about evaluation: an important and worthy issue that some of us are passionate about, but it may put others to sleep. The last chapter attempts some conclusions. Do have a look before investing in the whole book. Beware, though, that you may want to draw other conclusions, so you will need to read the rest and, unless you are a very fast reader, that will mean spending a little time and, perhaps, money to make a purchase.

You will see that at the end of each chapter there are exercises and suggested further reading. With luck some will want to look further afield and the readings will merely be a starting point. The exercises are presented as if the reader is part of a group. They have been designed to complement the text in a variety of ways, for example by looking things up, reflecting on your own experience, or doing some observations. I imagine most solitary readers will skip these.

Some of the points will, though, become more vivid if you pause to think about the exercises and in particular if you have a chance to talk to others about them too.

I should also issue you with a health warning. This book will contain errors. Smart readers will spot flaws. This is my first effort to write a textbook and will probably be my last. It's not, I have to say, been much fun, though it has been salutary. It has involved straying from familiar research territory, giving page space to views about which I had learnt to be sceptical, and leaving undeveloped sets of ideas that are presented only in embryonic form. I am reasonably content with what is presented here, at least for now, and hope it is read with more pleasure than was got in its writing. But I also hope that others will do better at what is attempted here and also that I do better in future too, if I am asked to and agree to go to a second edition. Kind readers will send me polite notes putting me right. Nasty ones will be more brutal, or sneer at the arguments in the privacy of their own back yards.

I should issue a few thank-yous to others who have, knowingly or otherwise, helped me with this work.

I wrote this at the invitation of my publisher, Brian Willan, and I think my thanks to him marginally outweigh my curses on him for getting me to do it. Thanks are certainly due for his patience as a series of deadlines for the text came and went.

You will not find a single mention of Karl Popper in the following chapters. He died in 1994, and I never met him. Yet Popper's influence has been profound. It even reaches into this preface! Popper advocated 'piecemeal social engineering'. This involves efforts to reduce specific harms, informed by social science, learning as we go through experimentation to make sure that we are being effective and not inadvertently causing harm. Popper was also a 'fallibilist': he stressed that we could all be mistaken in our thinking, and that one of the main tasks of science is to root out error through criticism. Yet he also emphasised the importance of imagination: the creation of those bold ideas that will almost certainly turn out to be mistaken, even if they are better than their predecessors. Popper explains my interest in crime prevention as an effort to deal with specific harms, my conviction that some of the material in this book will be seriously flawed despite my best endeavours, and my hope that improvements will be made in the future either by myself or others, including you.

Although this book includes a tricky chapter about evaluation,

evaluation is not the main topic. However, the influence of my long-time collaborator in writing on evaluation issues, Ray Pawson, will be clear to all who know our previous work. The motif that is returned to again and again, matching contexts, measures and mechanisms in the generation of outcomes, echoes Pawsonian themes.

I have worked with Gloria Laycock on and off for close to twenty years. During this time we have gently mocked one another's home discipline and habits of thought while collaborating on a variety of projects. We have also jointly taught bemused students, who are unaccustomed to seeing their teachers squabble in front of them. In spite of myself I've learned a lot from Gloria, which will doubtless be reflected in this book. She also kindly read it from start to finish and saved me from many errors of style and substance.

I am grateful to a number of colleagues and sometime PhD students who I bullied into reading and commenting on differing sections of the book. These include Jyoti Belur (Chapter 2), Karen Bullock (Chapters 6 and 7), Aiden Sidebottom (Chapters 1 and 5 to 8) and Gill Westhorp (Chapters 1 to 5 and 8). My daughter Alice, and her partner Cath Willis, who are both psychologists, read and commented (out of family duty) on Chapter 3. My wife, Jenny, read the whole manuscript from cover to cover – twice – to help me try to eliminate as many glitches as possible: what a star!

Finally, over more than two decades of work on crime prevention I have learned much from conversations with a wide range of practitioners, policy-makers and fellow academics. Among the most significant have been Mike Barton, Kate Bowers, Steve Brookes, Rick Brown, Karen Bullock, John Burrows, Sylvia Chenery, Pauline Clare, Ron Clarke, John Eck, Adam Edwards, Paul Ekblom, Graham Farrell, Marcus Felson, Herman Goldstein, Mick Gregson, Niall Hamilton Smith, Sarah Hodgkinson, Peter Homel, Ross Homel, Matt Hopkins, Mike Hough, Shane Johnson, Stuart Kirby, Johannes Knutsson, Gloria Laycock, Roger Matthews, Kate Painter, Ken Pease, Tim Read, Jackie Schneider, Mike Scott, Wes Skogan, Mike Sutton, Machi Tseloni, Barry Webb, Janice Webb, and the late Tom Williamson.

As ever, as author sadly I carry the can for all errors and misconceptions that remain. I'm pretty sure none of those acknowledged here would agree with all that is contained within this book, any more, dear reader, than you will.

Nick Tilley
Whitby

Chapter 1

Introduction:
what's to be done?

This book is about ways of preventing crime. It has been written with students, practitioners and policy-makers in mind, although some of the material may also be of interest to general readers. By the end of the book students should have a good idea of the major approaches used to try to prevent crime. They should also be able to reflect critically and constructively on the kinds of circumstances in which the various approaches might most fruitfully and ethically be applied. Practitioners and policy-makers should likewise have obtained a good grasp of major approaches to crime prevention. They should be better able to think through how, where and why differing methods of crime prevention can and should be used in developing policy and practice to deal with present and future crime problems. General readers may feel cheated. Many will already have strong, confidently-held views about the causes of crime and about what should be done about it. By the end of the book, I rather hope that they will feel less certain. I also hope they feel more informed in their thinking.

This book differs from sister texts that also discuss crime prevention. There is an important politics and sociology of crime prevention, which tries to explain why crime has come to be seen as a major issue and why particular policies and practices have come to be adopted to deal with it. This is not the subject of this short book. There are others that address crime prevention in these terms. There are also catalogues of 'what works' in crime prevention, which attempt to draw together robust research findings about what policies and practices have been found to work and not to work in preventing crime. Again this is not the focus of this book. Finally there are useful descriptions of what is done in policy and practice terms by way of crime prevention. This book has little to say on this. On the politics and sociology, interested readers are referred, for example, to Hughes (2007) and Koch (1998). For 'what works' catalogues and rationales, for them, readers are referred to Sherman *et al.* (1997) and Perry *et al.* (2006). For descriptions of what is and has been done in crime prevention policy and practice, see Hughes *et al.* (2002) and Tilley (2005).

I have written this book in the belief that students, policy-makers and practitioners need to have a strong grasp of the thinking behind the strategies and tactics that are used to try to prevent crime. The general reader, of course, helps shape orientations to crime policy through the ballot box. I hope that some will read this book in order that more ethical and effective preventive activity might emerge from a more informed public debate. Students need to be able to engage fully with the theories at work in crime prevention for obvious reasons. In order to assess, criticise, explain, interpret and apply crime prevention ideas they need to have a good understanding of them. This book aims to provide at least an overview, though it will become clear that students will need to look further if they are to appreciate the details. Policy-makers and practitioners also need to understand the ideas, but for more pragmatic purposes. As Kurt Lewin famously put it more than half a century ago, 'there's nothing so practical as a good theory' (1951: 169). This comprises a major premise behind the current text, to which I now turn.

Why does crime prevention need theory?

There are three answers to this question. First, theory is inescapable. Our every action is premised on assumptions and expectations about how the world works and how others will behave. These are 'folk theories' that we have to depend on to get by. Banks, telephones, police services, local authorities and universities, for example, all function in and through the assumptions that each working within them and each making use of them takes for granted. We work on the assumption (i.e. with the theory that) we will be paid. We pass over (and receive) money on the assumption that the tokens will have value and be exchanged for goods we wish to consume. We carry cards and use them in shops against assumptions about the operation of a banking system. When efforts are made to prevent crime they embody assumptions that may or may not be true, or true enough, to produce intended outcomes. And what may be true or true enough one day may not be so on another. This again reflects our experience in everyday life. Banking systems do not always work as expected. The theories they embody are not immutable or infallible. This shows when there are runs on them. Crime prevention activities likewise embody fallible theories that need to be explicated and made available for test and critical scrutiny if they are to be understood and improved.

The second reason theory is important is that in important respects crime problems are complex and changing. In unchanging conditions it might be possible to establish 'what works' and apply it in the reasonable expectation that what produced a preventive impact in one place and at one time would also produce the same effect at another place and at another time. For many crime problems this will not be the case. New motivations, new opportunities, new methods and new crime types mean that crime problems are apt to change by place and time. Even the same crime type may mask huge variations in method and motive. The types of people involved in crime vary widely. Moreover, in time both offenders and victims change and adapt to each other as well as to new conditions that emerge and furnish fresh crime and prevention opportunities. We will say much more about diversity and change in crime and its significance for prevention later in the book. Suffice it now to say that theory is needed to guide the policy-maker and practitioner towards what could be expected to produce preventive benefits in unfamiliar surroundings. Well-tested and well-formulated theories provide for informed thinking about what to do.

The third reason has to do with the values at stake in the policy and practice of crime prevention. This book begins by assuming that crime prevention is a worthwhile, not to say inescapable, concern. The very definition of crime implies classes of behaviour that are deemed so undesirable they are made unlawful. Efforts at preventing predatory behaviour by others who pose threats are not confined to humans and can be found throughout evolutionary history. Moulding people to conform to sets of expectations regarding what is deemed proper conduct has always formed part of social life, as has the issue of what to do when some fail to conform. For all these reasons crime prevention as an activity and interest is taken as a given. All methods used to prevent crime, however, raise normative questions that students need to understand, that policy-makers and practitioners need to recognise and consider, and that the traveller on the Clapham Street omnibus would do well to reflect on in coming to a view about what he, she, the government or any agency should do to try to prevent criminal behaviour.

In exploring the theories implicated in crime prevention, this book will pay particular attention to the *mechanisms* through which preventive outcomes are achieved, the means of their activation and the contexts needed for these preventive processes to operate. When we ask about 'mechanisms' we are asking about *how* interventions produce changes. This is not always obvious.

'Motor projects' were popular in the late-1980s and early-1990s. The details differ widely. Many involved the probation service (Martin and Webster 1994). These 'motor projects' were intended to prevent a range of car crimes. They involved providing young offenders with experience of working on 'bangers' and then driving them. What it was about them that could prevent which offenders from committing which crimes was not clear. Consider the following possible mechanisms:

- They provided a legitimate outlet for individuals who were determined to drive cars and who would otherwise steal them to do so;

- They provided a legitimate opportunity for individuals to drive cars who would otherwise drive illegally, for example without road tax or insurance;

- They provided contact with adult non-offenders who acted as mentors who attendees would not want to disappoint by offending;

- They provided skills and interests that offenders followed up at their leisure rather than committing crime;

- They provided pause for thought about the consequences of taking cars leading offenders to decide not to do so again. These consequences might include those for the offenders themselves, for example a criminal record or for others, for example pedestrians at risk from unskilled drivers of stolen vehicles;

- They provided a deterrent against future crime among those obliged to attend as part of a court order.

It is also possible that crime prevention measures might unintentionally promote crime. Thinking again about motor projects, another set of possibilities emerges.

- They appear so enjoyable that they encourage vehicle related crime as a means of obtaining a place in the project;
- They bring together groups of more and less experienced offenders who learn from one another and thereby become more skilful and more prolific offenders;
- They create groups whose members are able to work out better justifications for their criminal behaviour;
- They create peer groups whose members work together, learn to trust one another, and become better-networked offenders;
- They stimulate increased interest in cars and hence attendees' desires to drive them, which can only be satisfied through stealing them.

It may, of course, be that any or all of these crime-preventing and crime-producing mechanisms might be activated but that the mechanisms *actually* activated will depend on the nature of the attendees, and of the projects and the ways in which they are run. Those circumstances that are relevant to the mechanisms which are activated comprise the *context*. In any particular project the outcomes that are produced will be a function of the balance of mechanisms activated in that context among those touched by the intervention, some of which may be preventing crime and some of which may be fostering it.

Students of crime prevention need to be able to identify and analyse major crime prevention mechanisms and the kinds of condition required for their activation. In deciding what to do about existing and upcoming crime problems policy-makers and practitioners need to have a sufficient grasp of general intended and unintended context–mechanism–outcome patterns to make an informed judgement about what strategies and tactics to try. The general public may be less likely to endorse or resist proposals that have face validity if they have a better appreciation of the diverse ways in which crime prevention measures may produce wanted and unwanted effects. Students, policy-makers, practitioners and the public need also to recognise the values at stake in different forms of crime prevention. Given that there are no forms of crime prevention which pose no ethical challenges, all will need to recognise the need for trade-offs and for measures to minimise risks of injustice, inequity and divisiveness in the implementation of particular strategies, as well as their outcome effectiveness.

The term 'crime prevention'

This book is called *Crime Prevention*: but it is not the only term used to describe the matters covered in it. 'Public safety', 'crime reduction', and 'community safety' have also been used at various times and places to refer to similar concerns, although the meaning of these terms may also encompass fear of crime and sources of risk to person and property other than from crime, and these are not focused on here. This book is strictly about *crime* prevention. In Britain the designation 'crime prevention' has in the past conventionally been associated with the work of the police, the use of security measures recommended by the police, and neighbourhood watch schemes run by the police. Indeed in the past specialist police 'crime prevention officers' were trained at a police-run (though Home Office-funded) 'Crime Prevention Centre' to deliver this service[1]. For the purposes of this book, however, *prevention* is taken to refer to a much wider range of methods to try to avert crime, in several of which the police play either no part at all or only a very minor one. The preferred original title for this book was *Preventing Crime, Promoting Safety*. *Crime Prevention* was in the end chosen for its brevity, for its familiarity and for its common noun meaning.

Outline of the book

There are two key questions for crime prevention. The first relates to the focus of preventive efforts, 'where is crime prevention needed?' or 'where are crime prevention efforts likely to produce most benefits?' The second relates to what to do to address the identified needs or priorities, 'what measure or measures are most likely to deal with the issue most effectively, efficiently and ethically?' The remainder of this chapter briefly describes some major crime patterns that can inform decisions about where to direct crime prevention efforts. The following four chapters outline and discuss the main approaches to crime prevention, paying particular attention to the mechanisms, contexts and outcomes associated with them, and the ethical issues at stake with their use. Chapter 2 takes approaches associated with the criminal justice system. Chapter 3 takes approaches attempting to deal with individual criminality. Chapter 4 takes approaches that attempt to deal with social conditions producing criminal behaviour. Chapter 5 takes approaches that focus on reducing opportunities for crime.

Chapters 6, 7 and 8 move away from discussion of the differing approaches to crime prevention. Chapter 6 discusses the chronic problems encountered in implementing crime prevention initiatives. This is clearly important for policy-makers and practitioners, since many failures in prevention may be attributed to implementation weakness, and an understanding of the conditions for successful implementation should help strengthen what is put in place. There is a growing literature that tries to explain why implementation disappointments are widespread. Students need to be familiar with this if they are properly to understand what comes to be delivered in crime prevention and how this affects the results produced. The general reader may find implementation dull. Improved understanding of the challenges involved in implementing crime prevention programmes might, however, help set more realistic expectations about what can be achieved.

Chapter 7 discusses evaluation. The chapters leading up to it will make clear that our understanding of what works in what way, for whom, and in what circumstances in crime prevention, is quite limited. For some approaches the theory and research is much stronger than it is in others. Evaluation methodology is highly contested. Chapter 7 considers what kinds of evaluation activity are needed to improve the theories that are embedded in crime prevention programmes, on the grounds that only this can lead to better policy and practice. It is important that policy-makers and practitioners, who contract evaluations and develop and deliver projects and programmes that draw on their findings, understand methodology well enough not to be bamboozled by what is presented to them either by way of results or by way of proposals to conduct particular evaluation studies. Students need to have some grounding in evaluation methods if they are to be able sensibly to read, interpret and synthesise research literature relating to crime prevention strategies.

The final chapter of the book briefly draws together and recapitulates the main themes of earlier chapters in the form of twelve key propositions. The remainder of this introductory chapter is devoted to outlining major patterns of crime that suggest where

7

crime prevention interventions are likely to have their largest pay-off. These describe what have been referred to as the crime 'squeaks' which need greasing (Farrell and Pease 1993; Hough and Tilley 1998). To continue the metaphor, the chapters on approaches describe types of grease, the one on implementation methods of applying it, and that on evaluation finding out what kind of grease is needed for what type of squeak.

Crime patterns for crime prevention

Crime is highly patterned. It is not randomly distributed. Directing preventive efforts would be more difficult if this were not the case. The following briefly describes the patterns found in relation to space, time, victims, targets and offenders. A general description is provided in each case followed by some data that illustrate what tends to be found. Readers interested in more details on national patterns are referred to national and international statistics websites. For England and Wales, the Home Office has a wealth of data that can be downloaded.

Spatial patterns

Geographically, at whatever level crime patterns are looked at, crime tends to be highly concentrated in particular places. Crime levels vary by country. Within countries cities tend to have higher crime rates than elsewhere because they bring together large numbers of people, some of whom will wish to commit crime, large numbers of crime targets of various kinds, and a relatively high level of anonymity. Cities thus furnish many opportunities for the offender to act covertly, or without being noticed or disturbed, as they commit their crimes. Table 1.1 shows the prevalence rates for ten crimes combined by country and major city for ten countries. It shows substantial variations by country. It also shows that in almost all cases the major city has a higher rate than that found overall. The exception is Australia where only a small proportion of the population does not live in one city or another, and here it appears that Sydney's rate is very similar to the national rate.

Figure 1.1 shows the variations in recorded crime rates across 372 local authority areas in England and Wales in 2006–7, for comparable offences that are also measured in the British Crime Survey[2]. Nottingham had the highest rate at 138 per 1,000 residents.

Table 1.1 Overall annual ten-crime prevalence rates by country and major city 2004/5

Country	Capital/Major City	Country rate %	Capital rate %
Australia	Sydney	16.3	15.9
Belgium	Brussels	17.7	20.2
England and Wales	London	21.8	32.0
France	Paris	12.0	17.8
Hungary	Budapest	10.0	12.6
Ireland	Dublin	21.9	25.7
Italy	Rome`	12.6	16.6
Spain	Madrid	9.1	13.7
Sweden	Stockholm	16.1	22.6
USA	New York	17.5	23.3

Note: Data taken from van Dijk *et al.* (2007), based on international crime victimisation surveys in 2004 or 2005. The ten crimes include theft of a car, theft from a car, car vandalism, theft of a motorcycle, theft of a bicycle, burglary, attempted burglary, robbery, theft of personal property, sexual offences against women and assaults and threats.

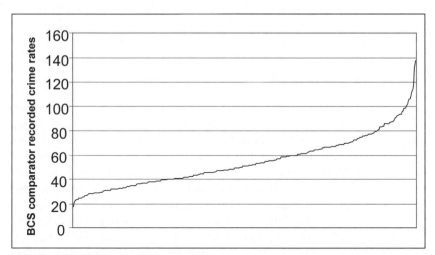

Figure 1.1 BCS comparator recorded crime rates per 1,000 population for 372 Crime and Disorder Reduction Partnership areas England and Wales 2006–7

Note: Comparator offences include those relating to violence against the person, sexual offences, robbery, domestic burglary, theft of and theft from a motor vehicle, and interference with a motor vehicle.

At the bottom was Teesdale at 17 per 1,000 residents. The national rate was 61 per 1,000. The ten per cent of local authority areas with the highest rates of crime accounted for a quarter of all crime in England and Wales. The ten per cent with the lowest rates accounted for only 2.5 per cent of the total.

Variations in levels are also found within local authorities. Crime is concentrated in particular wards. Figure 1.2 shows this for domestic burglary for all wards in Nottingham in 2006–7 (wards have an average population of 14,000). Figure 1.2 also shows the national rate and the rate for all of Nottingham[3]. It is clear that all Nottingham wards approach twice the national rate, but the highest wards have three times the rate of the lowest in the city. Within wards crime is concentrated in particular neighbourhoods, as shown in Figure 1.3 which indicates variations in rate for all wards with an overall rate of more that 25 per 1,000 residents (the 'superoutput areas' referred to in the figure have an average population of some 1,500 residents).

Within small areas crime is also concentrated in some locations and on some targets. Individual repeat victimisation is discussed below. For domestic burglary the heightened risk for the burgled property has been found to extend outward, but to diminishing degrees, to nearby properties (Bowers and Johnson 2005; Johnson *et al.* 2005; Johnson and Bowers 2007). Here patterns of concentration by place and time are predictable, which is clearly important for allocating preventive efforts.

While patterns of geographical concentration can be observed, it is important to unpack them and to realise that patterning at one level does not necessarily explain patterning at another. If a crime map is drawn of a city, it will generally be found that city centres have a high concentration of a wide range of offences. Across residential areas, neighbourhoods that are poorer generally tend to have higher levels of crime than those that are better off. But this does not mean that the relatively poor people within them are also at higher risk than their fellow residents who are rather richer. Rather, it may be, and is indeed found to be the case, that the better off living in poorer neighbourhoods suffer more crime than the poorer people within those neighbourhoods (Bowers *et al.* 2005; Tseloni *et al.* 2002). It is not hard to understand why: the better off in poorer neighbourhoods have more to steal. Both the city centre and poor area concentration patterns can be explained by the proximity of likely offenders to attractive crime targets.

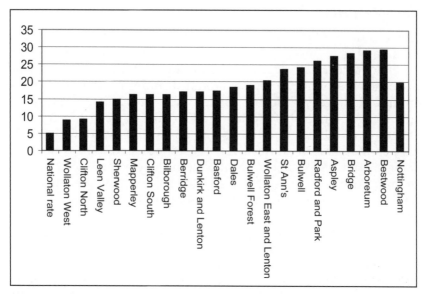

Figure 1.2   Rates of recorded burglary per 1,000 population by ward in Nottingham 2006–7

Source: Nottingham ward figures calculated from local city council data. Available at http://www.nomadplus.org.uk/newreportsxml.asp?report=Policing %20and%20 Public%20Saffety&sub=.

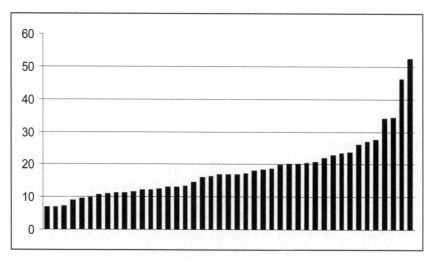

Figure 1.3   Census superoutput area variations in burglary per 1,000 population in the five highest burglary rate wards in Nottingham in 2006–7

Source: Calculated with data from http://www.nomadplus.org.uk/stats.asp.

Temporal patterns

Crime is unevenly distributed by time as well as by place. It varies by time of day, time of week and time of year. Motor mowers, for example, tend to be stolen in the spring. Children's bicycles tend to be stolen around Christmas. Youth disorder tends to take place around Hallowe'en. Alcohol related violence tends to take place late at night. Shop thefts often tend to take place at lunch times. Domestic burglaries through open doors and windows tend to happen in hot weather. Relatively few crimes tend to be committed between 4am and 12 noon. Local patterns may be produced by local circumstances. In some university towns, for example, there are traditions of end of year celebrations that include drinking, disorder and minor vandalism.

Temporal patterns are produced in various ways: by the supply of and demand for stolen goods (for example stolen lawn mowers), by seasonal events (for example Christmas, Hallowe'en), by weekly leisure patterns (for example drinking at weekends), by work patterns (for example fewer shop workers during many other workers' lunch times), by the weather (for example domestic burglary through insecure doors and windows), and by sleep patterns (the relative lack of crime incidents when most have gone to bed and few offenders are ready to begin their days).

As an example, Figure 1.4 shows the temporal patterns for street robbery and snatch theft for under and over sixty-year-olds in Nottingham for the three years from October 1999. It is clear that few offenders or victims are about during the early morning. Older victims are more readily available during the day and younger ones at night when there are relatively fewer old people available from whom to steal.

Victim patterns

Across a wide variety of crime types, those who have been victims of crime once have been found to be at heightened risk of a further crime. If they experience two crimes, they are at still higher risk of a third. And so on. The risks increase with the number of crimes experienced. Moreover the risks are at their highest in the immediate aftermath of a crime. They then fade.

This general pattern has been found for both property crime and personal crime. It has been found for individuals, households and businesses. It has been found for high-volume crimes and for low-

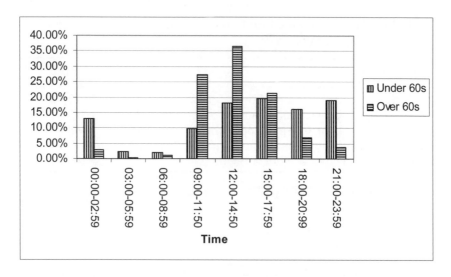

Figure 1.4 Times of street robberies and snatch thefts in Nottingham, October 1999–September 2002

Source: Nottingham recorded crime data.

volume crimes. It has been found in rural areas as it has in urban areas. It has been found for all countries where the research has been undertaken.

Table 1.2 shows, as an example, the pattern of repeat commercial burglaries in Hartlepool, in North-East England, using a rolling year beginning January to December 1990, each first incident at an address being tracked forward for twelve months to see whether and how many further incidents took place. This shows that of the 1,125 businesses identified, 22 per cent suffered at least one commercial burglary. Of those who suffered one commercial burglary, 40 per cent suffered at least one more and so on. It is clear that risk increases with the number of incidents. Figure 1.5 shows the time course for the repeat incidents in Hartlepool, dividing the year during which repeats could occur into five equal periods. In accordance with the pattern found in many other places and for many other offences the initial risk is high but then falls over time.

As a rule, if we want to predict where and when a particular crime will take place our best bet is to look at those who have suffered one or more crimes in the days and weeks immediately after they experienced that crime. This still does not necessarily

Table 1.2 Hartlepool recorded business burglary repeat patterns
January 1990–December 1991

All businesses	1125	*100%*
Businesses having one or more burglary/ies	250	22%
Businesses having two or more burglaries	97	40%
Businesses having three or more burglaries	47	48%
Businesses having four or more burglaries	27	57%
Businesses having five or more burglaries	17	63%

Note: Data drawn from Tilley (1993c).

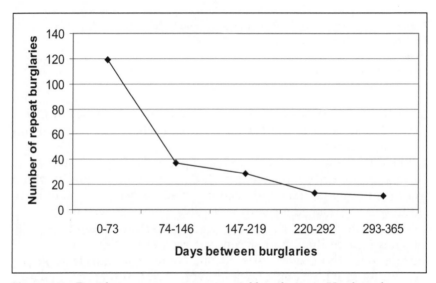

Figure 1.5 Days between repeat commercial burglaries in Hartlepool,
January 1990–December 1991

Note: Data drawn from Tilley (1993c), recorded crime data.

make a particular crime at a particular time and place very probable, however. Suppose that there is a one in twenty chance of experiencing a burglary in a given year. Suppose that in the week following the burglary the probability of being burgled increases by a factor of ten. This would yield a one in two chance of being burgled over the year. However, a one in two chance over a year amounts to roughly a one in a hundred chance over the week. For that week those who had not experienced a burglary would face a burglary risk of around one in a thousand.

There are two broad ways in which repeat patterns may be generated. The first is that the crime event itself increases the risk of a subsequent crime. The second is that those who are repeatedly victimised have some attribute that makes them at especially high risk of being targeted by offenders.

One crime can precipitate another in a variety of ways: the offender can go back to take goods he or she was unable to take the first time; the offender knows how to commit the crime and get away with it so returns to a known opportunity; the offender may tell another criminal about the opportunity for the crime; the offence may have left a property insecure in a way that renders it open to further crime; the crime may have been intrinsically rewarding thus reinforcing the offender's behaviour which is repeated (as, for example, in domestic violence); or the crime may spark a feud in which two parties offend against one another, turn by turn.

It is clear that risks of crime victimisation vary quite widely. Some are at much higher risk than others because of who they are, what they do, or where they are. Those who are young, sharing tenanted accommodation, male, single, unemployed, and living in deprived areas of cities, for example, live much crime-riskier lives than those who are older, owner-occupiers, female, gainfully employed, married and living in the country. Clearly, vulnerability within the relatively high-risk group could be substantially increased by more particular aspects of individual members' lifestyles. In relation to domestic burglary, for example, these aspects of lifestyle could include: living in a particularly crime-prone property and neighbourhood, being careless about security, owning the kinds of goods that offenders look out for, providing open-house for parties attracting those known to be offenders, leaving the property empty for long and predictable stretches of time, and so on. We would expect not just that more of those living the riskier lives experience crime but that more would also be repeat victims.

Table 1.3 Household types with high rates of domestic burglary, 2006/7 BCS

	All burglary	With entry[1]	Attempts[2]	Unweighted base
		% victims once or more		
Age of household reference person				
16–24	6.7	4.0	2.9	1,604
25–34	3.7	2.0	1.8	6,021
35–44	2.8	1.6	1.2	9,463
45–54	2.9	1.7	1.3	8,953
Household type				
Household reference person under 60:				
Single adult and child(ren)	5.5	3.3	2.5	2,422
Adults and child(ren)	2.6	1.5	1.2	10,391
No children	3.1	1.8	1.4	17,595
Household income				
Less than £10,000	3.4	2.1	1.4	8,095
Tenure				
Social renters	4.1	2.4	1.9	7,883
Private renters	3.9	2.3	1.8	5,463
Household reference person employment status				
Unemployed	6.0	3.2	3.3	500
Economically inactive	2.5	1.6	1.0	17,955
Student	6.4	4.7	1.9	403
Looking after family/home	5.4	3.3	2.2	1,793
Long-term/temporarily sick/ill	5.1	2.8	2.4	2,186
Other inactive	4.4	3.2	1.6	451
Household reference person occupation				
Never worked and long term unemployed	3.4	2.3	1.2	1,063
Full-time students	5.1	3.1	2.1	740
Not classified	4.7	2.1	2.8	523
Accommodation type				
Terraced house	3.1	1.9	1.4	12,294
Flat or maisonette	3.2	1.8	1.6	5,186
Other accommodation types	3.9	3.3	0.6	232
Area type				
Urban	2.8	1.7	1.2	35,407
Number of years at address				
Less than 1 year	4.6	2.6	2.2	4,579
1 year, less than 2 years	3.2	1.9	1.4	2,962
Level of physical disorder				
High	5.1	3.2	2.1	2,572
Level of home security				
None	22.5	16.4	6.9	181
ALL HOUSEHOLDS	**2.5**	**1.5**	**1.1**	47,027

1 'Burglary with entry' refers to cases where premises were entered whether or not anything was stolen.
2 'Attempts' refer to cases where there was clear evidence of a physical effort to enter but it was unsuccessful.
Source: Adapted from Nicholas *et al.* (2007: 89).

Table 1.3 shows the attributes of households that are at higher than national risk of domestic burglary, according to British Crime Survey findings.

It is perfectly possible that high rates of repeat victimisation result both from links between series of events and from variations in susceptibility to crime of the sort captured in Table 1.3. Research findings, however, indicate that repeat events are very often linked to one another. One event leads to another, in particular as prolific offenders return to familiar crime haunts: why look elsewhere when there are known rewards and proven methods? The implications of repeat patterns for crime prevention and detection are clear. These include the allocation of limited preventive resources to those who have already been victimised and some direction of proactive efforts at detection on those premises that are, for a short while, at especially high risk (Farrell and Pease 1993). We return to this in later chapters.

Target patterns

Some goods are stolen at a much higher rate than others. Cash is always popular. Jewellery is generally also well-liked by thieves. Large refrigerators and washing machines are not stolen in large numbers. Thieves take what they can transport inconspicuously and either use themselves or dispose of easily. This explains why small, accessible, lightweight, high-value, anonymous goods that can be sold on to consumers, who either do not know or do not care that they are stolen, are taken at a high rate. Mobile phones are a good example at the time of writing. But any new good that comes on to the market that has the right attributes will be stolen in large quantities. Once the market is saturated, rates of theft will fall. As portable, high-value, anonymous goods become aspirational, especially to the young and impecunious, they become ideal targets for theft. At a point when they cease to be fashionable, or once they become commonplace, thefts of them will decline. Think, historically, of silk handkerchiefs and pocket watches.

Table 1.4 shows the goods stolen in domestic burglaries in 2006–7, according to the British Crime Survey. It shows that small, anonymous, and high-value items tend to be preferred presumably because they are relatively easy to carry and dispose of.

Table 1.4 BCS findings on items stolen in domestic burglary 2006/7

Items	Percentage of burglaries with loss where item taken
Purse/wallet/money etc.	45
Jewellery	25
Electrical goods/cameras[1]	24
Computer/computer equipment	23
Mobile	16
Handbag/briefcase/shopping bag	12
CDs/tapes/videos/DVDs	12
Clothes	8
Documents	7
House keys	7
Car keys	5
Food/toiletries/cigarettes	5
Vehicle/vehicle parts	4
Tools/work materials	3
Bicycle/bicycle parts	2
Garden furniture	1
Sports equipment	1
Household items/furniture	1

[1]'Electrical goods/cameras' includes televisions, videos, stereos, cameras, MP3 players and DVD players.
Note: Unweighted base 509.
Source: Crime in England and Wales 2006/07: Supplementary Tables: Nature of burglary, vehicle-related theft, personal and other household theft, vandalism, and violent crime. Available at: http://www.homeoffice.gov.uk/rds/crimeew0607_tables_bvv.html.

Offender patterns

Men commit crime at a much higher rate than women. A low level of criminal behaviour is quite normal among males in early adolescence. As the title of one volume states, *Everybody Does It*, where the 'it' is crime (Gabor 1994). Loosening of direct parental control and oversight, biological development, and increasing amounts of time spent with peers who are in a similar situation conspire to create a context in which some degree of criminal behaviour is very widespread, though continuing ties to school and home for most mean that the volume of crime committed is modest.

At the same time, a relatively small number commit a very large number of crimes, and a few have extended criminal careers. Higher-rate offenders and those with longer criminal careers tend to start their criminal careers earlier than more occasional offenders. For these there are more deep-seated sources of criminality.

The 2003 Crime and Justice Survey took a random sample of around 12,000 people aged ten to 65 in England and Wales and asked them about their offending behaviour (Budd *et al.* 2004). This found that just over four in ten reported having committed at least one of a selection of twenty 'core offences'[4]. Four per cent had committed a 'serious offence' (see Note 4 in the Endnotes). Men were found to commit crime at a higher rate than women: for example thirteen per cent of males as against seven per cent of females had committed a core offence in the previous year. The peak age for offending was 14–17 for males and females for both property offences (17–25% of males and 10–13% of females in this age-range had committed one or more property offences in the previous year) and violent offences (30–33% of males and 15–18% of females had committed one or more violent offences in the previous year). The rate of involvement in crime dropped dramatically as age increased (three and one per cent prevalence rates respectively for property crime for men and women aged 46–65, and one per cent for both for violent offences). Of the large numbers committing offences only a very small proportion were found to commit crime prolifically. The research concluded that two per cent of the sample and 26 per cent of the previous year's offenders accounted for 82 per cent of all the offences included in the research.

A variety of 'risk factors' are associated with higher probability of significant levels of involvement in criminality. These include:

- Poor concentration;

- Poor school attainment;

- Poor parental supervision, erratic and harsh discipline, and child abuse;

- Broken homes, especially without affectionate mothers;

- School disorganisation;

- Criminal, antisocial and alcoholic parents;

- Socio-economic deprivation, notably large families, low family income and poor housing;

- Opportunities to offend;

- Taking drugs;

- Regularly drinking alcohol;

- Exclusion from school;

- Friends or siblings who offend;

- Living in a disorganised and deprived neighbourhood;

- Poor social skills.

The more risk factors that are present the greater likelihood of criminal involvement, and in particular participation in violent crime. This issue will be returned to in some detail in Chapter 3.

Changes in patterns

Many crime patterns are fairly constant. Those relating to age and sex of offenders, repeat victimisation, target choices for theft, and spatial offending patterns appear to be universal. They help make sense of some longer term crime trends. In most industrialised societies there was a steady increase in property crimes from the end of the Second World War till the early- to mid-1990s. This can largely be explained in terms of the increasing supply of those kinds of goods that are especially popular among thieves, and alterations in patterns of everyday life. Increases in wealth, alongside technological developments, created a proliferation of relatively small, anonymous, high-value, portable items, that were either intrinsically enjoyable or were craved by those who were finding them hard to afford. Increases in female participation in the labour market, growing levels of urbanisation, increases in numbers of single-parent families, improvements in personal transportation, and decreases in the need for domestic chores as a result of labour saving devices freed those most liable to be involved in crime from those controls that may have inhibited them in the past, or provided protection to otherwise vulnerable property. In short, more goods to pinch, fewer controls on those most apt to take them, and reduced oversight of possessions that are attractive to thieves will, other things being equal, produce more crime. The implication of this paragraph is that crime levels increased in response to social and technological developments that were, in many other ways, highly desirable.

There are, however, also quite sudden changes in pattern, some of which have obvious sources, and some not. Panel 1 of Figure 1.6 shows rather stark recorded bigamy trends in England and Wales from 1898–2005. The spikes clearly coincide with the two world wars where the results of temptation and opportunity created by the movements of many men are quite obvious. Panel 2 shows growth and then decline of the US homicide rate from 1950–2005. The normal age curve for criminal behaviour is shown in Panel 3, which shows the ages of all known homicide offenders from 1980–2004. There is a massive spike in the late teens and early twenties. Panel 4 distinguishes changes in rates of homicide from 1980–2004 for three age bands: those aged fourteen and under; those aged fifteen to 22; and those aged 23 and over. Panel 4 shows that, while rates for the younger and older age bands remain much the same, there is a substantial rise in the middle group from the later 1980s to early-1990s, followed by a fall through the mid- to late-1990s. This accounts for much, though not all, of the change in the latter part of the trend shown in Panel 2. As with bigamy, the trends are marked. Yet the explanation is not nearly so obvious, and is much debated.

Conclusion

The latter part of this chapter has described, in rather broad terms, some major patterns showing where crime problems are concentrated. It has also shown that these patterns can change. Within local areas, analysts look at these patterns in much greater detail, drawing on a range of local data, some from the police and some from other agencies, to identify particular local crime and disorder problems to decide where, when and in relation to whom preventive efforts are most needed. Nationally, analysts may track changes in crime problems to identify emerging issues that call for preventive attention at a national level. We return to the identification of problems calling for preventive attention in the final chapter. Meanwhile in the next four we explore different approaches to prevention, which suggest what can be done in relation to identified problem patterns.

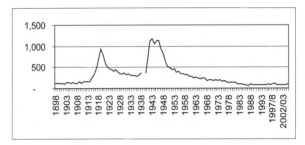

Panel 1: Bigamy in England and Wales 1898–2005

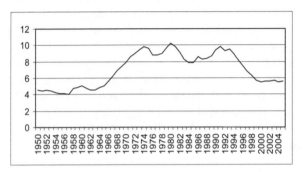

Panel 2: US homicide rate 1950–2005

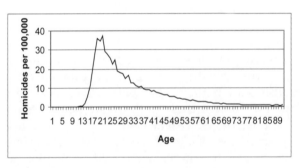

Panel 3: US homicide rate by age 1980–2004

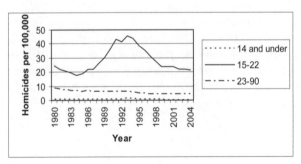

Panel 4: US homicide rates by age group 1980–2004

Figure 1.6 Changes in crime patterns

Exercises

1 Take any crime prevention measure, for example increased lighting, CCTV, burglar alarms or mentoring for young offenders, and list as many mechanisms that you can think of that might increase or reduce crime. Try to think through the circumstances in which the positive and negative effects are most likely to be produced.

2 Take any crime problem that is of particular interest to you, for example shootings, shop theft, commercial robbery, or drug trafficking and, using internet sources, try to find as much as you can about patterns that might inform the targeting of preventive efforts.

3 Write a brief crime biography or autobiography. An example is given in Appendix A, where Norman Storey's tale is told. You, or your subject, cannot, of course, be treated as representative of any group. However, the exercise will help you develop a better feel for crime and crime prevention, especially if you make comparisons with the crime (auto)biographies of others in your group and return to your account as you read later chapters of this book.

Further reading

For an overview of international crime patterns using sweeps of the International Crime Victimisation Survey (ICVS), see Van Dijk, J., van Kesteran, J. and Smit, P. (2007) *Criminal Victimisation in International Perspective: Key Findings from the 2004–2005 ICVS and the EU ICS*. The Hague: Boom Juridische Uitgevers.

For recent British Crime patterns, see Nicholas, S., Kershaw, C. and Walker, A. (2007) *Crime in England and Wales 2006/7*. Home Office Statistical Bulletin 11/07. London: Home Office.

On repeat victimisation, see Farrell, G. and Pease, K. (2001) *Repeat Victimization*. Crime Prevention Studies Volume 12. Monsey, NY: Criminal Justice Press.

On offender attributes, see Budd, T., Sharp, C. and Mayhew, P. (2004) *Offending in England and Wales: First Results from the 2003 Crime and Justice Survey*. Home Office Research Study 275. London: Home Office.

For methods of examining patterns of crime, in particular those that are spatial and temporal, see Chainey, S. and Ratcliffe, J. (2005) *GIS and Crime Mapping*. Chichester: John Wiley and Sons.

Websites

Home Office Research Development Statistics (RDS) http://www.homeoffice.gov.uk/rds/

Scottish crime data http://www.scotland.gov.uk/Topics/Statistics/15730/3320

US Bureau of Justice Statistics http://www.ojp.usdoj.gov/bjs/

Australian crime data http://www.aic.gov.au/stats/

New Zealand crime data http://www.stats.govt.nz/people/justice-crime/crime.htm

Canadian crime data http://dsp-psd.pwgsc.gc.ca/Collection-R/Statcan/85-205-XIE/85-205-XIE.html

Many police services around the world also publish data on local crime patterns on the internet.

Notes

1 This Home Office Crime Prevention Centre was initially based at Staffordshire Police Headquarters, and ran from 1963. The operation moved to Easingwold in North Yorkshire as the Crime Prevention College in 1996. It ceased specifically to be a police training facility and came also to serve many other agencies. It then became the Crime Reduction College and was finally re-named the Crime Reduction Centre in 2003. It was closed in 2005.
2 Comparator offences include those relating to violence against the person, sexual offences, robbery, domestic burglary, theft of and theft from a motor vehicle, and interference with a motor vehicle.
3 Nottingham had not only the highest rate of recorded crime for all BCS comparator crime. It also had the highest rate specifically for domestic burglary.
4 The core offences were domestic burglary*, commercial burglary*, theft of a vehicle*, attempted theft of a vehicle, theft from the inside of a vehicle, theft from outside a vehicle, attempted theft from a vehicle, thefts from

work, from school, from the person*, other theft and shoptheft, criminal damage to a vehicle and other criminal damage, robbery of an individual* or a business*, assaults with injury* and without injury and selling class A* and other drugs. The eight marked with an asterisk were deemed serious for the purpose of the research.

Chapter 2

Criminal justice measures and mechanisms

Through most of history (and pre-history) the prevention of predatory actions towards property and people has not been seen to be the responsibility of criminal justice agencies. Rather, individually and collectively, potential victims have assumed that it is up to them to take steps to reduce their own risks. In many places and for quite a long period police, courts, prisons and physical punishment have existed, of course, but have not comprised the major means by which protection is provided. Moreover, the population at large has not expected this to be the case. It is only relatively recently, perhaps over the last century, that many have come to believe that they have a reasonable right to expect protection from the formal organisations and processes of criminal justice. Over the past thirty years or so, many have come to doubt that criminal justice systems have the potential to prevent crime or promote safety. Equally, what is arguably the primary concern of criminal justice agencies as a whole, the delivery of criminal justice to individuals, has not always been seen to sit easily alongside utilitarian concerns with reducing crime and its harms. Against that background this chapter considers what criminal justice agencies can and should do to prevent crime and promote safety. We return to general issues of criminal justice agency roles and responsibilities at the end of the chapter.

There are five major mechanisms through which criminal justice agencies can directly reduce crime and promote safety and five in which they can do so indirectly.

Direct crime prevention

1 Incapacitation

Incapacitation is the most obvious means by which the criminal justice system may prevent crime. Those who are incarcerated, transported, executed or otherwise physically treated (for example by castration, drugs or dismemberment) in ways that disable crime, cannot commit it, in some cases indefinitely and in others for a given duration. The obviousness of the incapacitation mechanisms helps explain their popular appeal.

'Selective' incapacitation is advocated for those who are thought to pose a particular risk because of their mental or moral states or because of their track records as probable or potential prolific offenders.

There are at least six problems with incapacitation as a crime prevention strategy (Zimring and Hawkins 1995). The first is that it risks committing an injustice on the perpetrator. Punishments are backwards-looking, imposed on the basis of what the offender deserves for what he or she has done, not for what they might do in the future. Second, even if it were to be accepted that incapacitation for expected future behaviour were to be sanctioned in the interests of the safety of others rather than the deserts of those incarcerated, predicting individuals' future criminal behaviour is notoriously difficult. Many would suffer an unjust harm by being incarcerated (or otherwise incapacitated) for an act they would not commit in any case. Insofar as this was the case, the state too would unnecessarily bear the costs of applying the incapacitation. Third, insofar as this incapacitation were meted out by criminal justice agencies, to the extent that they were seen to be behaving unjustly the criminal justice system itself would lose credibility and citizens' motivations to support it would be undermined. Fourth, the overall evidence for its effectiveness where it has been practiced is equivocal. Moreover the fact that much crime is committed in groups means that stopping an individual through incapacitation is not equivalent to stopping the offence in which he or she would otherwise have participated. Fifth, specifically in relation to imprisonment as a means of incapacitation, the experience is liable to increase rates of criminality on release in ways discussed in the next section of this chapter. Sixth, again in relation to imprisonment, it must not be forgotten that the state is generally believed to have responsibility for inmates as well as those in the community and prisons are themselves hotspots of crime bringing together habitual criminals who frequently offend against one another. Unsurprisingly, prisons are crime hotspots.

Notwithstanding these objections to incapacitation as a crime prevention strategy, there can be no denying that those incarcerated are unable while inside to commit crimes directly on those in the outside community (though of course they may orchestrate offences from their cells using their aptly-named cell phones, as well as offend against each other or prison staff). Similarly those executed and suffering some forms of physical treatment will, as a result, be unable to commit at least some crimes. In this sense a by-product of some forms of punishment will be to incapacitate offenders who might otherwise be committing crimes. Moreover, insofar as policies are directed at selective incapacitation and successfully identify and target prolific offenders they may reduce crime. In some cases, even in face of the objections listed here, it might be decided that the balance of the argument favours mobilising the criminal justice system to incapacitate known offenders. We should probably not, however, use the term 'punishment' to describe these practices, and reserve it instead to sanctions applied in response to and justified only by offences that have actually been committed and for which those to whom the sanctions are applied have been found guilty following due process.

It should also be noted that in decisions about early release of those sentenced by the court to custody (or any other relevant sentence), it is of course sensible to consider the probability that the individual will reoffend, using the best evidence available.

On the basis of an exhaustive study, mostly based on the US, Zimring and Hawkins (1995: ix) conclude that, 'the amount of crime prevented through incapacitation is both variable and contingent, varying in relation to different social circumstances and under different criminal justice policies. No prospect exists of discovering a unitary level of crime prevention that might be achieved by penal restraint'. A British based study suggests that as an overall crime reduction policy, increasing incarceration is not a promising policy: Tarling, using a range of data sources, concludes that a 25 per cent change in levels of incarceration produces a one per cent change in crime level (Tarling 1993: 138–60).

2 Specific deterrence

Specific deterrence is probably the second most commonly assumed mechanism whereby the criminal justice system is deemed to have a crime prevention impact. Specific deterrence refers to the preventive effects sanctions may have on those who are punished. Offenders are deterred from committing future crimes by the unpleasantness of the punishment and their decision not to risk more of it in the future. They are 'taught a lesson' by punishment and the lesson is, 'don't do it again!'

As with incapacitation there are a number of rather basic objections to using specific deterrence as a crime control strategy. In practice punishments through the criminal justice system may activate crime-promoting mechanisms on some of those punished that more than counterbalance those inhibiting further crime. One such crime promotion mechanism refers to the bestowal of a criminal identity on those affected (Box 1971; Lemert 1972). While the original crime may be quite normal among those of the sex, age, and background from which the individual comes, most of them soon grow out of crime. The consequence of the deviant identity bestowed is that the individual may embrace it: it may become his or her master-status. Moreover, this may be further encouraged as a consequence of becoming a formally identified offender so that doors to certain jobs may become harder to open and socialising with non-offending others may become more difficult, channelling the individual towards others in a similar position, reinforcing one another's deviant status and disposition to commit crimes. A second mechanism may relate to that criminal learning that is fostered in the company of other offenders. Techniques, opportunities to collaborate in crime and means of justifying offending behaviour can all be picked up during those punishments applied in group settings. In these ways specific deterrence is liable to be off-set in its effects by other mechanisms promoting criminal behaviours that are inadvertently activated among those punished. A third mechanism that operates for some, specifically in regard to fines, relates to the means for discharging the penalty. Those unable to pay may commit more crime in order to raise the necessary funds, a process that has been notorious in the case of prostitutes.

The foregoing points do not mean that specific deterrence never takes place. They refer to mechanisms that *may* be activated to counterbalance deterrence. Some people may indeed be deterred from future crime. One group comprises those who have suffered repeated bouts of imprisonment and reach a point where they feel they can no longer face more of it. The prospect of further time behind bars comprises one factor leading them to decide to try to desist from future offending. A second group, at the other end of the spectrum, comprise those on the fringes of criminal careers. For these individuals a 'brush with the law' may 'bring them to their senses'. It becomes a turning point where the prospects of reduced life chances and further shame in the eyes of significant others outweighs the attractions of further offending in the company of a delinquent peer group.

Many crime reduction projects and routine practices attempt to activate the deterrent crime reduction mechanisms. These initiatives adopt stepped interventions in relation to the many who have misbehaved but who are not known yet to have become immersed in routine criminal behaviour as a way of life. As we saw in Chapter 1 many commit a few crimes in their youth and cease doing so spontaneously. The idea behind the stepped interventions is to avoid the risk of unintentionally bestowing a deviant identity and instead to increase the chance that, where necessary, deterrence mechanisms will be activated. Official sanctions that risk unintentionally bestowing a deviant identity are treated as a last resort. Lancashire Constabulary has operated a 'Juvenile Referral' scheme based on these principles. If a juvenile is found to be involved in disorder or antisocial behaviour their details are entered into a database and a letter sent to their parents in an effort to deter the child and alert the parents so that they can provide necessary care and control. If the child is found again to be involved within six months of the first instance a further letter is sent to their parents, as well as to the child's school and the education welfare services to alert them to the need to look out for the child to meet any needs the child might have, and to apply any controls necessary. If a third incident occurs, a multi-agency meeting is convened to try to work out what has been producing the repeated behaviour and what might be done to divert the child away from it. Finally, if the behaviour persists only then are enforcement options considered as a last resort. These might initially include parenting orders or Anti Social Behaviour Orders (Bradbury 2001).

The same criminal justice intervention may activate a deterrence mechanism amongst some and a provocation mechanism among others. Famously, the suite of projects in the US that aimed to reduce repeat domestic violence by arresting the perpetrator produced mixed effects across the different cities in which it was implemented. In some cities repeat incidents seemed to be reduced by the arrest policies and in others they were increased (Sherman 1990). The post hoc explanation was that among well-integrated employed persons living in stable communities arrest engendered shame and thereby inhibited further violence. Contrariwise, among the unemployed living in marginal and unstable communities, the experience of arrest engendered anger with increased chances that repeat domestic violence incidents would follow. Large cities are made up of differing community and employment conditions. Here a mosaic of differing effect patterns would be generated and the net outcome would be a consequence of summing these. More detail on this example is found in Chapter 7.

The policy and practice consequences of variations in deterrent and incitement effects of arrest for domestic violence among differing sub-populations are far from clear. Would the police officer be in a position realistically to make an informed case by case decision to arrest or not to arrest? Even if the police officer were able to do this, and thereby maximise benefits and minimise costs in terms of repeat incidents, could a differentiated criminal justice response to the same act be justified? If the answer to either or both of these questions is no, then whatever the potential deterrent benefits from selective arrest practices, such a general policy would be untenable.

3 General deterrence

Criminal justice agencies are also often deemed to deliver general deterrence. General deterrence refers to the preventive effects sanctions (or the prospects of them) have for those who are not the direct target of criminal justice efforts. The idea is that seeing others being investigated, tried or punished by the police, courts and penal institutions encourages the rest of us to behave better than we otherwise would. The potential loss of face, freedom or physical well-being is sufficient to persuade many of us who might otherwise offend to remain reasonably honest. There is little doubt that deterrence operates for many of us most of the time (Kennedy 2008).

There is some evidence that crime levels have increased where policing has been suspended for some reason, for example through strike action (Sherman 1992a). This is not because everyone then commits crime. Rather for a proportion of the population the active operation of agencies of the criminal justice system is sufficient to deter them from committing crime. This suggests that a degree of general deterrence is provided by a functioning criminal justice system. On the other hand marginal changes in police strength do not appear on their own to have a corresponding impact on crime levels (Clarke and Hough 1984).

There is, however, evidence from police crackdowns that crime can be reduced through general deterrence mechanisms, when there is targeted and concentrated police (and other enforcement agency) action on some particular location (Sherman 1990; Farrell *et al.* 1998; Tilley 2004b). Indeed the deterrence effects can be made to outlast the crackdown itself, where high levels of publicity precede the crackdown and where its completion is unannounced. Crackdowns can also produce effects beyond their geographical scope. Many potential offenders are liable to overestimate the risks of capture created for them, although this will not be the case for all crimes and all offenders. Moreover, the effects of increased police attention are apt to fade as offenders come to understand and adapt to the new circumstances.

The deterrent effects of crackdowns appear to work by creating uncertainty about the level of risk offenders face (Sherman 1990; Homel 1995; Tilley 2004b). The police have been able to create uncertainty over risk and consequent deterrent effects through quite concentrated randomised attention to potential offenders. This has been shown most vividly in the use of randomised breath tests on drivers in New South Wales. These were conducted at a sufficiently high rate that drivers felt they faced a real and unavoidable risk of being caught if they drank alcohol and drove. They were uncertain about the level of risk they faced on any given occasion and were unable to control it. The introduction of random breath testing was followed by a steep and sustained fall in the numbers of deaths caused by drinking and driving (Homel 1988, 1995).

In addition there have been rather more subtle efforts to target general deterrence towards those believed to be likely to commit crimes, making use of crackdowns (Kennedy 2008). The best known of these is probably the Boston Gun Project's Operation Ceasefire (Kennedy *et al.* 2001). This had a very specific focus: the reduction of youth gang-related shootings in Boston. Gang members were told that if they committed firearms-related offences not only would the gang-members committing the offences be targeted, so too would all other gang members. The idea was that this would not only directly deter the offences in question, but it would also activate internal social control within the gang to discourage gun-related crime. In concert with this, a reduction in gun-crime related injury would then reduce the incentive to carry weapons for self-protection. In this instance general deterrence by formal criminal justice agencies, including police and probation, was used deliberately to activate other more informal crime reduction mechanisms among those whose behaviour was at issue. The interventions involved well-targeted high levels of publicity to ensure that the consequences of behaving in the specified ways were clear. These consequences would include concerted attention to all infractions of whatever kind by a wide range of agencies with enforcement powers. Substantial effects on youth gang related homicides are claimed in the evaluations of the Boston project. Figure 2.1 shows the change in levels of youth homicide in Boston associated with the introduction of Ceasefire. The general strategy used in the Boston project may be applied much more widely in targeted efforts to deal with specific problems (Kennedy 2008).

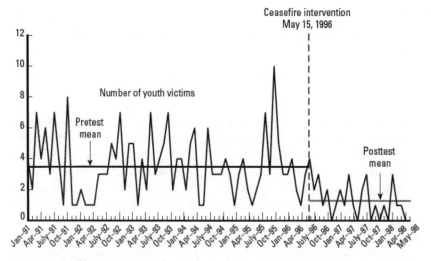

Figure 2.1 Changes in numbers of youth homicide victims associated with Operation Ceasefire in Boston, US

Source: Kennedy *et al.* 2001: 58. Originally published by the National Institute of Justice, U.S. Department of Justice.

In Britain the Street Crime Initiative of 2002–2005 focused enforcement attention on robbery and snatch theft at a period when it had been rising rapidly. Police patrol was targeted at hot spots and substantially increased efforts were made to detect cases and bring them before the courts. The effects were marked, though they also faded quite rapidly once the special efforts drew to a close, as shown in Figure 2.2.

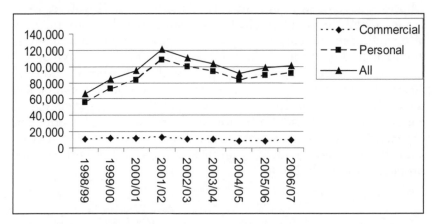

Figure 2.2   Personal and commercial robbery in England and Wales 1998–2007

Source: Data from Nicholas *et al.* 2007.

One advantage that a crackdown strategy has, according to Sherman (1990), is that it can enable attention to some offences that would not ever ordinarily become a sufficient priority to warrant police attention. Rather than always prioritise the most serious or widespread offences using standard means, a revolving crackdown strategy would involve sporadic concentrated attention to different places and offence types. There would be no safe place or offence type where a criminal could be confident of police inattention. They could never know whether they could proceed without significant risk. They could never proceed with known risk. Such a strategy might be a more effective way of deploying limited police resources to maximise deterrent effects than a continuous focus on more serious or more common crimes, where offenders can adjust and adapt their actions to known police practices and priorities. This strategy has not, to my knowledge, yet been attempted.

There are various downsides of crude crackdowns. They may provoke crime. The most notorious example comprises Operation Swamp in Brixton in 1981 reported on by Lord Scarman (Scarman 1982). Here resentment and riot were stimulated by the crackdown.

Crackdowns also risk criminalising occasional offenders caught up in the crackdown processes. They are liable to be treated more formally than would be the case if a crackdown were not in place and this may involve injustice as well as assignment of a criminal label that would otherwise not be applied. In addition to this, of course, those targeted may come to resent the police for their inconsistent and unsympathetic actions. Much policing depends on community trust in the police. Crackdowns, unless they have very widespread public support in advance, jeopardise this.

Crackdowns of various kinds can, thus, produce crime falls through general deterrence mechanisms. They do not, however, invariably do so. Table 2.1 summarises the patterns that emerge in terms of conditions, forms of crackdown, deterrence mechanism activated and outcomes.

Other efforts to mobilise general deterrence effects of the criminal justice system have met with more disappointing outcomes. 'Scared Straight' projects have taken youngsters on the fringes of criminal behaviour to prisons, where they are confronted with the reality of the experiences they risk if they follow criminal careers. Typically they meet offenders who highlight the unpleasantness of the consequences of their own past criminal behaviour. It is assumed that this will lead those exposed to rethink their way of life and instead to go straight. This has some surface plausibility. Many of us avoid behaviour we believe puts our futures in jeopardy. The results of evaluations have, however, been disappointing. They have not found any net benefits. Indeed, if anything the net effects seem to have been negative (Petrosino *et al.* 2002). What is less clear is whether there have been impacts that push in different directions. For some, perhaps, risk is alluring, seeing prison may demystify it, or the exposure to prison as a spectacle may be largely forgotten and irrelevant when they return to their peer groups. For others, the exposure to prison may indeed lead them to reflect on the course their lives might take. It could, thus, be a turning point (Tilley 2006). The net impact evaluations are unable to sort these issues out. It would be surprising if all reacted to the initiative in the same way. Likewise it seems unlikely that brief exposure to the eventual downsides that a criminal career might bring will be sufficient to inoculate many against the more immediate temptations of criminal behaviour to which they may more routinely be subject.

Even more disappointing are those cases where the criminal justice system inadvertently creates incentives for others to commit offences, while aiming at their deterrence. This happens when

Table 2.1 Types of crackdown: context, methanisms and outcomes

Intervention	Context	Mechanism	Outcome
Sudden unannounced high police presence in area	Marginal groups, with low levels of police trust, but some internal cohesion	Indignation; provocation; police delegitimation and mistrust	Resistance and riot, reduced co-operation with the police
Well publicised high initial police presence in area, with quiet withdrawal	High crime area	Increased risk perception; uncertainty over risk	Rapid initial crime fall
	High-rate offenders	Innovation and speedy re-estimates of changed risk	Early resumption of crime as revised risk estimates made; some innovation in Modus Operandi; quick initial and residual deterrence decay
	Low-rate offenders	Non-innovation and slow re-estimate of risk; slow realisation of crackdown withdrawal	Gradual initial and residual deterrence decay
Area crackdown on property crimes	Offenders needing high-crime proceeds (perhaps because of drug dependency)	Adaptation to offending patterns to yield equivalent returns	Displacement of offending by place, type or method
Time limited crackdown on specific behaviour	'Respectable' offenders	Anxiety over apprehension; uncertainty over risk, inability to control risk	Quickly reduced offending; residual deterrence decay
Publicity announcing crackdown	Plausible messages to offenders	Perceived increase in risk; uncertainty over level of risk increase	Rapidly reduced offending pre (or without actual) crackdown, residual deterrence till reduced risk realised

Measure	Target	Mechanism	Outcome
Randomised enforcement/ crackdowns on individuals, with minor penalties	Members of groups wanting to be deemed 'respectable'	Anxiety about uncertain and uncontrollable risk of exposure to shame	Rapid fall in targeted behaviour and slow resumption
	Members of 'marginal' groups	?Anger at arbitrary, unexpected detection OR resignation at penalty	?Violence, compensatory crime, compliance with punishment
Conditional crackdowns, applied to membership group following specified behaviours	Offenders belonging to loose groups engaged in diverse behaviour open to enforcement activities	Perceived heightened group risk and costs of generalised enforcement on members; informal social control within target group	Reduced behaviour that activated crackdown
Sustained low publicity, low dosage crackdown over large area	Typical offender population	Crackdown not noticed, lacks/quickly loses credibility	No change
Crackdown targeted on suspected prolific offenders	Large proportion of offences committed by known regular, high-rate offenders	Incapacitation; general deterrence	Reduction in crime proportionate to supply of high-rate offenders at any given time

Note: Except for entries marked '?', these are rooted in some evidence, though it is far from conclusive.

Source: Tilley (2004b).

'martyrdom' makes the offender a hero in the eyes of members of his or her community, rather than someone who is disgraced. Examples include prosecution of those refusing to pay poll tax and of political protesters (Pawson 2006). Here offenders can claim the moral high ground and the use of the criminal justice system is often construed as further evidence vindicating and giving further publicity to the stands they take. The criminal justice system in these cases incites rather than deters.

4 Restorative justice

The downsides of the ways in which the formal criminal justice system ordinarily works have been widely noted. Restorative justice has been advocated instead not only as a means of avoiding some of the unintended criminogenic consequences of the traditional system, but also as a means of providing more effective closure for victims (Johnstone and Van Ness 2007). We concentrate here mainly on crime prevention, the focus of this book.

The main crime reduction thinking behind restorative justice is that it provides a means whereby many unintended crime causation mechanisms are replaced with ones that will reduce the probability of future crime. As with the Boston Gun Project informal social control mechanisms are mobilised and the downsides of formal ones are avoided. The term often used to capture this is 'reintegrative shaming' (Braithwaite 1989). Processes of reintegrative shaming are akin to, indeed continuations of, those that will be familiar to many readers from seeing or experiencing what happens when young children misbehave in families. Childhood infractions bring disapproval but not rejection by parents. The child is often required to acknowledge and make amends for what they have done. This helps them appreciate that they have acted wrongly. However, once the child has admitted what they have done, shown remorse and made amends they are 'reintegrated'. The unconditional love provided for children does not mean that misbehaviour is disregarded. Instead it means that the child is forever accepted, is open to forgiveness and is actively encouraged to play a full and constructive part in family life.

Restorative conferencing, as it is sometimes called, involves bringing offender (and supporters) and victim (and supporters) together. It is a managed process where the offender must admit to the offence and listen to the victim. He or she is expected to acknowledge the harm done and agree some form of restitution.

The offender is also expected to give an account of their action. Support by those accompanying victim and offender is both moral and practical. The conclusion of the conference is not a sentence but an agreement about the future and the agreement includes (conditional) restoration of the status of the offender as a person: someone to be trusted and accepted rather than mistrusted and shunned. Restorative conferences can be emotionally charged events. The offender's conscience is pricked. Their shame is seen and felt by them and by their supporters alike. The offender should become subject to internal and informal external control. In this way it is hoped that their offending will reduce or cease.

The process is facilitated by avoiding the ways in which western, adversarial court systems typically pitch offender and victim against one another, leading the offender to deny either the action of which he or she is accused, or responsibility for it, thus preventing the victim from playing an active part in effecting closure to what will often have been a traumatic experience. Most victims are evidently more satisfied and less fearful following restorative conferencing than they are following conventional court proceedings (Green 2007).

The term 'restorative justice', however, has been applied to quite a wide range of practices, not simply conferencing. They have in common efforts to move beyond the formal criminal justice system to bring victims, community members and offenders together in a reparative relationship. The offender is confronted with the consequences of his or her act and is expected to acknowledge wrong-doing and show some remorse, to the victim in particular but also to the community. In this way it is hoped that the social breach can be healed. In some cases restorative justice replaces formal criminal proceedings and the downsides they bring. In others it supplements them and restorative efforts may even be undertaken while the offender is serving his or her sentence in custody (see Johnstone and Van Ness 2007).

While studies suggest that restorative justice brings substantial benefits in terms both of victim satisfaction and rates of reoffending, it is no panacea. Not all victims want it and not all offenders who go through it cease their offending behaviour. Nevertheless, for many offenders preventive mechanisms appear successfully to be activated. In a review of research on reoffending following restorative justice interventions Hayes (2007) identifies variable but on balance positive preventive benefits.

One downside of restorative justice, when it replaces formal proceedings, is the possibility that justice will be sacrificed, if by justice we mean consistent and deserved treatment of those who have been found guilty through due process. There is a risk that those not guilty will go for restorative conferencing in spite of their innocence, in the (often flawed) belief that it will be a softer option. Moreover, insofar as the conclusions of conferences are dependent on the settlements agreed in their course, the 'same' act may lead to quite different outcomes from one occasion to the next. This seems unfair to those whose conditions for reintegration are relatively more severe than those applied to others.

5 Disruption

'Intelligence-led policing' tries to reduce crime and promote safety by keeping track of criminals and their plans, and disrupting them (see Ratcliffe 2008). It involves the systematic and continuous effort by enforcement agencies, principally the police, to trace criminal organisations, associations, collaborations, plans and behaviour patterns. These efforts have been facilitated by a variety of technological developments, including: improvements in forensic techniques; the development of computerised databases; the refinement of CCTV (closed-circuit television) systems, including automated number plate recognition; improved techniques for covert observation; dedicated software allowing quick and relatively straightforward processing of information for crime analysis purposes; and cheap, powerful and user-friendly GIS (geographic information systems).

Intelligence officers compile and interpret information from a variety of overt and covert sources and convert that information into plausible accounts of what is currently happening. These accounts are then used to plan operations designed to thwart the criminals. Intelligence-led policing is applied to local offending as well as to offending patterns at regional, national and international levels.

Disruption to thwart offending can take many forms and activate a variety of crime control mechanisms, some of which have already been touched on in this chapter. Techniques for disruption have not so far been codified. Table 2.2 comprises a preliminary attempt to identify the main kinds of mechanism that may be activated within intelligence-led policing to reduce crime. It suggests that intelligence-led operations as a means of crime reduction operate by disabling offenders and offences, disinforming those who might otherwise commit crimes, or by undermining the interpersonal trust that

Table 2.2 A typology of disruption mechanisms

Aspects of crime business	Main methods of disruption		
	1 To disable	2 To (dis)inform	3 To seed distrust
a. Crime events	Crime event interruption	Offender misdirection or misinformation on crime opportunities	Entrapment at point of event
b. Recruitment of offenders	Targeted arrest on offenders who recruit others	Publicity of potential entrapment	Entrapment at point of recruitment
c. Criminal organisations	Co-ordinated arrest and imprisonment of key network members	Use of informants to feed back (dis)information; publicity for (alleged) use of informants	Publicity for successful use of informants
d. Illicit markets	Closure of businesses dealing in illicit goods	Claims for closure of stolen goods markets and penalties for taking part in them	Use of and publicity for use of sting shops
e. Individual offenders	Targeted enforcement on known prolific offenders	Messages to potential offenders about attention paid to them	Public use of unknown informants
f. Community tolerance	Witness protection; professional witnesses	Publicity for use of unnamed community sources; promotion of images mocking/discrediting offenders	Rewards for information that will help convict offenders; concerted, concentrated and credible policing at neighbourhood level

will be needed in order to commit a crime. These form the three main columns in Table 2.2, and are numbered respectively 1, 2 and 3. The six rows (labeled a–f) describe major aspects of successful crime business that may be undermined by being disabled, by disinformation and by seeding mistrust. The rows refer to actual crime events; to the recruitment of new generations of offenders either to offending or to participation in more serious or organised offending; to the organisations and often rather looser networks of collaboration and co-operation within which offending takes place; to the market in illicit (stolen, counterfeit or smuggled) goods on which many benefits from offending ultimately depend; to the individual offenders committing the criminal acts; and lastly to the communities that actively or passively, knowingly or unknowingly play host to the offenders and allow them to operate.

Eighteen types of intelligence-led crime preventive mechanisms emerge, which may be activated, for example, in the ways shown in the individual cells of the table. They all disrupt crime activity and crime business, though in different ways. Their application depends on a close and contemporary understanding of emerging patterns of criminal behaviour and collaboration, and on smart decisions about what will be most promising in any given situation.

The simplest and possibly one of the first intelligence-led operations occurred in 1606 when information received was used to interrupt the Gunpowder Plot before the damage was done (1a in Table 2.2). Even where intelligence is more systematically sought and analysed and hence there is greater foreknowledge of upcoming planned criminal events, intelligence-led authorities may postpone action in order more comprehensively to dismantle the organisation or network that is implicated and might thus be expected to commit further crimes.

Intelligence-led policing as a means of disrupting and hence reducing crime has high surface plausibility and as a result has been widely embraced internationally. In the face of this it is at first sight surprising that there has not been more development of its underlying theory and that there is so far little by way of systematic assessment of its crime reduction impacts. One problem with the evaluation of intelligence-led policing is that its outcomes will depend in part on the quality of information sought, the skills of the analyst, and the abilities of those receiving the information to come to good conclusions about which interventions to put in place in the specific circumstances. It may not make much sense to ask whether or nor intelligence-led policing per se reduces crime. A better set of questions would relate to the circumstances in which the preventive mechanisms targeted as a result of intelligence-led policing do or do not reduce or increase crime.

Let us consider one technique listed in Table 2.2: the use of sting shops. These are evidently fun to run for those operating them, though hugely expensive. They involve a covert operation in which the police (from another area) set up and operate a shop in or near an area where offenders committing property crimes are known to operate. They buy and sell the kinds of goods that are characteristically stolen. Those running the shops know the going price for stolen goods. They attempt to identify offenders who come in and sell goods that are known to have been stolen. The idea is that after a period of a few months the shop closes and a large number of thieves are arrested, prosecuted and convicted. The expectation then is both that a large number of active criminals are punished and in being punished may be incapacitated or deterred, and also that other offenders will lose confidence in their ability conveniently to dispose of and hence benefit from selling stolen goods locally through shops. Apart from the very high cost, one major weakness is that the establishment of a shop taking stolen goods makes property crime more likely. It incites crime. Crimes that might otherwise not be committed are committed. Moreover, those drawn into crime are criminalised. In addition to this the compensating benefits are uncertain. They depend on alternative outlets for stolen goods not being readily available. If there are plenty of equally attractive alternative outlets then no subsequent effect may be expected. If there are no equally attractive alternative outlets, then that strengthens the probability that the establishment of a sting shop will stimulate crime.

This is not, of course, to gainsay the potential benefits from attempting to disrupt the market in stolen goods nor is it to disparage intelligence-led policing more generally. It is simply to say that the effective application of intelligence-led policing depends on a good grasp of the local setting and sensitivity to the possibility that unintended and unwanted side-effects will be produced which may more than outweigh potential crime reduction benefits. These side-effects may be quite subtle. It may also be decided that their risk is worth taking for longer term and larger benefits. A case in point arises where local criminal families or other criminal networks effectively provide informal (if brutal) control over local youth nuisance and petty crime within a neighbourhood, while using it as a base from which more serious crime, such as armed robbery or organised drug trafficking, is committed elsewhere. Intelligence-led operations against such a local network may succeed in disrupting and disabling its serious offending but at the expense of increases in the local nuisance it controlled and also, of course, the possible unbalancing of drugs markets where the removal of one group may open the door to others or to violent turf wars as they compete to take over.

Indirect mechanisms

Crime is a 'wicked issue'. It has diverse and complex causes as we saw in Chapter 1, and as will become even clearer in the following chapters. Many methods of its prevention will therefore require interventions by agencies that do not form part of the criminal justice system. We turn now to the contributions criminal justice agencies can make even when not directly delivering interventions that on their own reduce crime.

1 Collaboration: crackdown and consolidation strategies

The need for collaboration in preventing crime and promoting safety has become a contemporary nostrum. Central and local government departments, schools, businesses, individuals, and communities themselves can all affect crime and the conditions for it. They will sometimes need to work in concert with one another to maximise their impact.

Crackdown and consolidation strategies describe one form in which collaboration can take place. This chapter has already referred to the ways in which crackdowns can have an impact and that that impact can extend beyond its operational range. The crackdown, nevertheless, is a resource-intensive preventive measure that produces only temporary benefits (though even here providing short-term respite may be worthwhile). Consolidation measures are designed to build on and complement the crackdown effects to create sustainable falls in crime.

Crackdowns are often applied in very high-crime neighbourhoods where those who are not involved in crime are in thrall to those who are and are incapable of controlling them. Residents are reluctant to intervene directly or to call the police for fear of recrimination. Service providers may be unwilling to enter the area because they are not prepared to risk harm to themselves or their property. Those residents able to go elsewhere are inclined to move out. Replacements are reluctant to move in and only the desperately needy do so. Increasing numbers of houses are boarded up. The criminal and vulnerable remain, with the former preying on the latter. It is a familiar and rather depressing scenario. Problems of crime, social disorganisation and physical decline are intimately related to one another. None is likely to be addressed effectively unless the others are too. Crackdown and consolidation strategies blend different forms of intervention to address this suite of interconnected problems. The crackdown creates a window of opportunity for building community confidence and effecting improvements in the physical fabric of the area. A series of crackdowns may be needed as crime levels begin to rise following the swift fall that can be achieved following concerted enforcement attention. Against this background non-enforcement public, private and voluntary sector agencies can move in to work with community members to increase their confidence in one another and in external organisations, and to remedy the physical structures and appearance of the area. Eventually, improvements in the reputation of the area and hence its attractiveness to future (non-criminal) residents can then be expected. A virtuous circle of increasing confidence, reducing crime and improvements in physical conditions is stimulated by strategically co-ordinated crackdown and consolidation activity. Successful examples are rare but can be found (see Farrell *et al.* 1998; Tilley and Webb 1994). Figure 2.3 shows the logic of a crackdown and consolidation strategy.

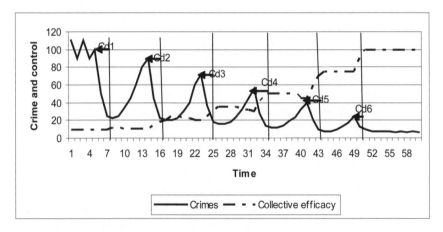

Figure 2.3 Crackdown and consolidation strategy

Notes: 'Cd' refers to Crackdown; the first crackdown in indexed at 100 and subsequent ones are set at 80% of the previous rate: the drop lines refer to the end of the crackdowns; the horizontal lines at the top of the drop lines point to the start point of the crackdowns. The residual deterrence explains the time taken before the crime climbs following the end of each crackdown. 'Collective efficacy' refers to an amalgam of social cohesion and informal social control. (See Sampson *et al.* 1997.)

2 Information and expertise

Even if reducing crime requires action by others, criminal justice agencies are the largest custodians of data relating to crime and criminality. The police, probation service, prisons and courts all hold data that may be drawn on locally to identify crime patterns, to identify offender and victim attributes, and to track known offenders. Of course not all crime is reported, not all of that reported is recorded, and only a minority of offences are detected. The picture obtained from criminal justice agencies is, thus, partial. Moreover there are other sources, for example health bodies on non-accidental injuries and drugs, and local authorities on graffiti, fly-tipping, and truancy. Furthermore, victimisation and self-report surveys of various sorts may tell us about crime patterns that are reported to no-one and about patterns of crime involvement that are never detected. Yet, in practice the most comprehensive and most readily used local data sources tend to come from the police. This is then fed into decisions that help prioritise preventive efforts and work out which organisations need to be involved, often using means that are not available to those within the criminal justice system and that are discussed in other chapters in this book.

The potential for data properly to inform prioritisation and intervention depends, of course, on their quality and availability. This in turn depends on practices within contributing agencies, of which the police are the most important. In practice, data quality and data flows have been rather poor in the past in most jurisdictions, but are improving.

In addition to providing information the police, in particular, have often comprised major sources of expertise in local areas about ways of reducing or pre-empting crime, even when these means are not under their direct control. They have fed this expertise into decisions about plans for future developments and into decisions about ways in which crime problems might most effectively be addressed. In British police services specialists who have variously been called crime prevention officers, crime reduction officers, architectural liaison officers and crime prevention design advisers have undertaken this work.

3 Leverage

The potential use of leverage on those able to implement crime prevention measures complements police access to data and the expertise police services often have in the prevention of crime by non-enforcement as well as by enforcement means. The police have a range of options at their disposal to persuade those able to prevent crime that they should do so: everything from polite requests backed by evidence of the size and nature of the problem to efforts to have legislation put in place that would force those reluctant to introduce measures to do so. One example of leverage relates to a scrap metal merchant near to which the police found that there had been a large number of petty crimes. The police also believed that stolen property was often received at the site. The owners were reluctant to co-operate with the police. Eventually, in concert with the Environmental Agency which found that there had been some seepage of toxic materials into the nearby ground, the police were able to have the site closed and the problems then ceased. In this case the police were not directly preventing the crime. Rather, they were using their information to apply leverage through a collaborating agency to effect a change that would lessen local crime and nuisance. For further examples of the ways in which leverage may be applied and cases where this has occurred see Scott (2005). We return to issues of leverage more generally in Chapter 6.

4 Victim services

Chapter 1 included a discussion of repeat victimisation patterns: the substantially increased risk of further crime faced by victims. The police have been able to forewarn victims of their increased risk and advise them of measures they can take to reduce their risks. In some instances, in particular in relation to domestic burglary, they have also been able to channel free or subsidised security upgrades to reduce vulnerability, and to mobilise close neighbours to watch over victimised properties during their period of highest risk. Moreover, the tendency of repeats to be committed by the same offenders, and the fact that those offenders tend to be prolific, has provided a basis for proactive efforts (for example use of alarms triggering swift police response) to catch them. The offenders can then be processed in ways designed either to deter or to incapacitate them, at least for a while, from further crime. Repeat victimisation focused crime prevention efforts run by the police alone or in concert with other agencies have a strong track record in effecting reductions in crime (Forrester *et al.* 1988, 1990; Hanmer *et al.* 1999; Chenery *et al.* 1997). They often include the police motivating or channelling crime prevention efforts that are under the control of or directly delivered by third parties. They do not solely involve the specific use of police powers.

5 Setting incentives for treatment

In Chapter 3 we turn to measures aimed at reducing the disposition for or need to commit crimes. For the moment it needs only to be pointed out that these measures are often put in place within, or by, elements of the criminal justice system. Once offenders have been convicted and sentenced by the courts, then probation services, prison services and parole officers may all either be directly involved in providing treatments that are designed to help avert reoffending, or may contract others to provide them. In addition to this, the police have also applied leverage to those leaving prison to accept services that aim to reduce their dependency on drugs. The police are informed when those who are known to commit crimes due to their drug dependency leave prison and are coming to live in their neighbourhood. The police then explain that unless the drug services are accepted by the ex-inmates they will become targets of concentrated police attention (Lancashire Constabulary 2003).

Roles and responsibilities

This chapter raises important issues concerning the roles and responsibilities of criminal justice agencies. One view would be that they should all be concerned with the delivery of justice to individuals and that concerns with the prevention of crime or promotion of safety are secondary. According to this the primary responsibility of the criminal justice system and its agencies is to bring to book as many of those who are guilty as possible and at all costs to avoid penalising the innocent. Any crime reduction consequences are essentially beneficial side effects that might reasonably be expected or hoped for. More strongly, it might be expected that failures to deliver just treatment to individuals caught up in the criminal justice system will be deeply resented and might precipitate failure to co-operate with criminal justice agencies and even provoke criminal behaviours of various kinds, as occurred in the Brixton riots.

There is much to agree with in this argument. Failure to make equitable and lawful behaviour a cardinal principle for those working within criminal justice agencies does risk discrediting them (Hough

2004). It does not, however, mean that justice is the sole objective of the criminal justice system. Protection, reform and rehabilitation are long term concerns that few would contest, even though many would agree that there would have to be very strong particular grounds for any ever to trump the imperative of providing justice for individuals suspected of criminal behaviour.

Finally, special consideration needs to be given to the police. Since the Metropolitan Police Act of 1829 it has repeatedly been reiterated that the chief function of the police is not to feed the courts and prisons but rather to secure safety and public tranquility. It has also repeatedly been noted that the police have lost sight of this. To be sure, it has also often been assumed that security can be achieved through the detection and prosecution of offenders, but the latter comprise a means, not the chief end of policing. Teasing out how and in what conditions these means do and do not prevent crime has been a major concern of this chapter. Moreover this chapter has also shown that there is much that the police can do and indeed do do to prevent crime and promote safety that does not simply involve catching and convicting villains. Where catching and convicting criminals is seen as the main method of crime prevention and crime prevention the main objective of the criminal justice agencies, there is a risk that justice is the casualty.

Conclusion

There is little doubt that the criminal justice system as a whole and the separate parts of it can contribute to crime prevention. It cannot be assumed, however, that it will automatically do so or do so through the traditional enforcement-related mechanisms that many assume to be at work. Incapacitation, specific deterrence and general deterrence, in particular, do not always work and can sometimes backfire. They can, nevertheless, also sometimes prevent crime. Careful attention to how and when this will be the case is necessary if preventive benefits are to be maximised. There are also other ways in which criminal justice agencies, working alongside other organisations, can feed into or stimulate effective crime prevention. At the same time there are risks that pursuing a crime prevention agenda alone might compromise other key values of criminal justice, in particular fair treatment for all, and this needs to be considered and taken into account.

Exercises

1 Devise a strategy through which criminal justice agencies could reduce the rate of racial attacks on small shops, or of robberies of supermarkets, or of burglaries of student properties.

2 In what ways might justice be jeopardised by crime prevention as aims of the criminal justice system? How would you reconcile the two?

3 How can deterrence be delivered equitably and effectively in the service of crime prevention?

4 Think back to a time when you were unfairly accused, told off or punished. How did you feel? How did it affect your attitudes or future behaviour? Compare your responses to those of others.

5 Which of the following would most affect your decision to commit a minor crime, say pick-pocketing: the size of the penalty (say £250 fine as against £50); the chances of being caught by the police (say one in two as against one in ten); or the chances that your mother would find out (say one in two as against one in ten)? Compare your answer to those of others in your group.

Further reading

For a discussion of the effectiveness of traditional policing, see Clarke, R. and Hough, M. (1984) *Crime and Police Effectiveness*. Home Office Research Study 79. London: HMSO.

For a classic discussion of shaming and reintegrative shaming which draws on a wide range of criminological theory and findings see Braithwaite, J. (1989) *Crime, Shame and Reintegration*. Cambridge: Cambridge University Press.

For a very modern discussion of ways in which deterrence may be used imaginatively, effectively and ethically in crime prevention see Kennedy, D. (2008) *Deterrence and Crime Prevention*. London: Routledge.

For a wide-ranging discussion of the nature and potential of intelligence-led policing see Ratcliffe, J. (2008) *Intelligence-Led Policing*. Cullompton: Willan Publishing.

For ways in which the police can persuade others competent to prevent crime that they should do what they can see Scott, M. (2005) 'Shifting and sharing police responsibility to address public safety issues,' in N. Tilley (ed.) *Handbook of Crime Prevention and Community Safety*. Cullompton: Willan Publishing.

Chapter 3

Individual measures and mechanisms

Chapter 1 highlighted the high proportion of crimes that can be attributed to a relatively small number of prolific offenders. As we saw most offenders have quite short offending careers. Moffitt describes those as 'adolescent-limited offenders', in contrast to the much smaller number of what she refers to as 'life-course persistent offenders' who start earlier and continue their crime careers later than their adolescent limited counterparts. She refers to the two types in the following terms,

> Adolescent newcomers (to antisocial ways) had not formerly exceeded the normative levels of antisocial behavior for boys at ages 3, 5, 7, 9, or 11. Despite their lack of prior experience, by age 15, the newcomers equaled their preschool-onset antisocial peers in the variety of laws they had broken, the frequency with which they broke them, and the number of times they appeared in juvenile court. . . . Unlike their life-course-persistent peers, whose behavior was described as inflexible and refractory to changing circumstances, adolescence-limited delinquents are likely to engage in antisocial behavior in situations where such responses seem profitable to them, but they are also able to abandon antisocial behavior when prosocial styles are more rewarding. They maintain control over their antisocial responses and use

antisocial behavior only in situations where it may serve an instrumental function. (Moffitt 1993: 678, 686)

One form of crime prevention attempts to target those at high risk of sustained crime involvement either by diverting them before they become prolific offenders or by promoting desistance once they have embarked on their crime careers. It is to this that the present chapter turns. We begin by looking at 'risk factors' that are used both to identify those who can be expected to turn into prolific offenders and as targets for intervention. We then move on to the dynamics and situational contingencies of crime careers and efforts to find means of diversion from the criminal path and attraction to the law-abiding one.

Following these discussions of general orientations to prolific offenders, we move to one approach to dealing with high-rate offenders: cognitive-behavioural therapy, and one specific source of high-rate offending: drug-dependency.

Risk factors and crime reduction

The risk factors approach to reducing crime has gained ground over the past two decades. It has been fed by a mix of common sense, self-report offending studies, longitudinal studies tracking the behaviour of samples of folk from early childhood onwards, and a number of promising projects that have targeted risk factors. The idea is a simple one: find robust correlates of offending behaviour, preferably antecedents; hope that some of these comprise causes; effect changes that remove some of these correlates; and hope that real causes have been undermined leading to reduced levels of criminality. The risk factors approach to reducing criminality also draws on and has affinities with a counterpart public health model.

The British Prolific and Persistent Offenders (PPO) scheme has risk and risk factors for criminality at its heart as illustrated in Figures 3.1 and 3.2:

What is advocated here is a strategy that sorts individuals out on the basis of the risk factors they exhibit and the stage they are at in their criminal careers. Those showing large numbers of childhood risk factors are picked out for attention. Early interventions are made in the lives of those individuals or groups bearing patterns of

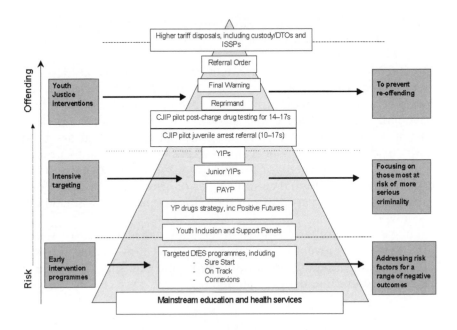

Figure 3.1   Dealing with the many potential and few actual prolific offenders

Note: DTO refers to Detention and Training Order (a custodial sentence for those aged 12–17); ISSP refers to Intensive Supervision and Surveillance Programme (the most rigorous non-custodial intervention for young offenders, aged 10–17); CJIP refers to Criminal Justice Intervention Programme (focused on crime-related problem drug-taking); YIP refers to Youth Inclusion Programme (for those identified as at high risk of criminal involvement, aged 8–17); PAYP refers to Positive Action for Young People (for those at risk of social exclusion, crime or antisocial behaviour, aged 8–19).

Source: Home Office (2004).

risk factor that suggest that, in the absence of intervention, they are liable to become heavily involved in crime. A variety of programmes supplementing universal provisions for children and young people are focused on the relatively high-risk populations. The risk factors that predict higher probability of criminal involvement also predict other negative outcomes such as school failure, teenage pregnancy, unemployment and poor health. Addressing the risk factors associated with criminality is therefore thought likely to produce multiple benefits.

For those who do go on to engage in risk-related behaviour and who begin to engage in antisocial and criminal behaviour, more intensive targeting may follow. Those believed to be on the brink

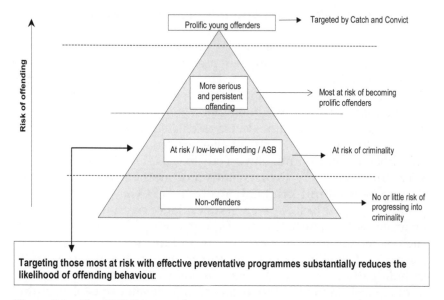

Figure 3.2 The PPO Framework

Source: Home Office (2004).

of significant involvement in criminal behaviour are thus targeted with interventions that aim to pull them back.

Finally, for those who behave in ways that are taken to indicate that they are embarking on what might turn out to be significant criminal careers, stepped criminal justice interventions are put in place to try to steer them towards more law-abiding lives. These begin with low-level, low-tariff measures and only move on to heavier and more punitive interventions among those who are unresponsive to the lower-level measures.

What Figures 3.1 and 3.2 show is an approach to reducing criminality which sees a continuum between those who are at little or no risk of becoming involved in criminality (at the bottom of the pyramid) to those who are heavily involved in crime (at the top). The underlying theory is: a) that we can be most effective and efficient in criminality reduction by providing strong universal services; b) that we then need to target, as early as we can, populations that are at risk of becoming involved; and c) that growing intensity in our interventions is called for as involvement in criminality begins and continues. Punitive measures and (costly) personalised treatments are reserved for those who have become immersed in crime careers.

The logic of risk factors and intervention targeting

To make the logic of risk-factors interventions clear it is helpful to distinguish markers for the presence of causes from causes themselves (cf Farrington 2007). Think of frequency of visits to the dentist and involvement in criminal behaviour. There is no reason to believe that the one causes the other. However, we might expect an association, if childhood neglect is associated with both infrequency of visits to the dentist and involvement in crime. But even here childhood neglect is unlikely directly to cause criminal involvement. What, then, might be the mechanism or mechanisms leading from neglect to youthful criminal involvement? They could, at least plausibly, include lack of parental surveillance creating opportunities or incentives to join delinquent groups offering extrinsic rewards such as money from property crime and intrinsic rewards such as a sense of belonging to a caring primary group. Equally, they could include patterns of eating sugary foods that create fast but short-term rewards (and also dental caries), that create habits of pursuing short-term rewards, such as those furnished by crime, as against slower but possibly longer-term, rewards from obedience to the law and hard work. It could be that lack of routine dental care would act as a flag for heightened risk of criminal involvement. It would not mean that it comprises a cause of crime, nor that a programme providing, say, regular, accessible dental surgeries with higher rates of attendance by those who might otherwise not see a dentist often, would make attendees less liable to be involved in crime. Any association between frequency of dental check-ups and crime involvement would, at best, help identify sub-populations that were at higher and lower risk of criminal involvement.

The relationship between these markers and causes is shown in Figure 3.3.

For the most part the risk factors approach to reducing criminality homes in on generic risk factors. This is presumably because there is some intuitive connection between these and criminality, though this is seldom articulated in the risk factors literature. It is, however, implicit in the notion that policies and practices that address these generic risk factors will somehow deal with underlying causal mechanisms.

David Farrington (1996, 2007), reviewing a wide literature, identifies a number of risk factors for criminality, including the following:

```
┌─────────────────────────────────────────┐
│                                         │
│          Specific surface marker        │
│                                         │
└─────────────────────────────────────────┘
```

(e.g. failure to have regular dental check-up)

```
┌─────────────────────────────────────────┐
│                                         │
│              Generic marker             │
│                                         │
└─────────────────────────────────────────┘
```

(e.g. childhood neglect; high rates of sugar consumption)

```
┌─────────────────────────────────────────────┐
│                                             │
│        Underlying (real) causal mechanisms  │
│                                             │
└─────────────────────────────────────────────┘
```

(e.g. lack of parental surveillance; learned habits of
dependency on short-term rewards)

Figure 3.3 Markers for and underlying causes of criminality

- Poor concentration, impulsivity and daring;
- Low intelligence and attainment;
- Poor parental supervision, erratic and harsh discipline, and child abuse;
- Broken homes without affectionate mothers;
- Parental conflict;
- Criminal, antisocial and alcoholic parents;
- Socio-economic deprivation, notably large families, low family income and poor housing;
- Opportunity.

Loeber *et al.* (2006) count numbers of standard risk factors in their longitudinal Pittsburgh study and find that the more any individual has the more likely they are to behave violently. By the time

Table 3.1 Risk factors for male and female persistent youth offending

	Ratio of risk factor present to risk factor absent*	
	Male	Female
Drug use in last 12 months (age 12–17)	5.4	5.0
Friend or family offenders (age 12–17)	3.6	6.0
Regular drinking (age 12–15)	3.0	5.7
School exclusion (age 12–16)	2.2	2.2
Lone parent	1.6	1.0
Step-family	1.5	2.3
% serious and persistent offenders (all ages)	12%	4%

*This means, for example, that those males aged 12–17, who had used drugs in the past year, were 5.4 times as likely to be persistent offenders as those in that group who had not used them.

Source: Flood-Page *et al.* (2000).

individuals have picked up nine or more, it appears that they are almost certain to be violent.

Drawing on a self-report study, Flood-Page *et al.* (2000) compare risk factors for serious and persistent youth offending among males and females. Their findings are shown in Table 3.1.

By far the most influential British study of criminal careers, which has done much to highlight risk factors, is a longitudinal study of 411 males born in 1953 in a working class area in South London. The first contacts for this cohort were made when the boys were 8–9 years old and the most recent when they had reached the age of about 55 (Farrington *et al.* 2006). This study does much to reveal the possibilities as well as some of the key limitations of risk-focused efforts at reducing criminality.

Key risk factors at age 8–9 are said to include the following mix of individual, familial, school and economic attributes:

- Disruptive child behaviour (e.g. troublesomeness);

- Criminality in the family (e.g. a convicted parent, a delinquent sibling);

- Low IQ or low school attainment;

- Family factors, including poor child-rearing, a disrupted family and a young mother;
- High daring, impulsiveness, or poor concentration;
- Economic deprivation (e.g. low income, poor housing, large family size).

These are related to crime career patterns, of which four broad types are identified: 'persisters' (those convicted both before and after their 21st birthday), 'desisters' (those convicted only before their 21st birthday), 'late onset' (those only convicted at age 21 or older), and unconvicted (those with no convictions up to the age of 50).

Table 3.2 shows the four types of crime career pattern followed by the South London sample up to the age of 50, in relation to the numbers of risk factors they exhibited when they were 8–9 years old (the 'vulnerability score') as well as their level of 'troublesomeness' at that time.

Table 3.2 Risk factors and crime careers

Vulnerability score	Unconvicted	Desisters	Late onset	Persisters	Total
0	110	13	13	16	152
1	68	18	15	11	112
2	44	8	2	18	72
3	9	8	4	9	30
4–5	6	6	4	16	32
Troublesomeness					
Low	111	8	11	12	142
Low average	64	12	13	17	106
High average	31	13	7	14	65
High	31	20	7	27	85
Total	237	53	38	70	398

Data calculated from Farrington *et al.* (2006: 60).

This table brings out the problem of 'false positives' and 'false negatives'. False positives comprise those who are identified as being at risk of serious crime careers, and hence to warrant intensive preventive attention, but who would not go on to follow them. False negatives comprise those who do go on to a serious crime career but are not identified as being at risk of following one. The table shows that of the 398 individuals whose crime careers were tracked to age 50, there were 70 persisters who might profitably have been targeted early to prevent them from following long-term crime careers. If the 32 most at risk, that is showing four to five risk factors, were to have been used to inform the targeting of preventive services then exactly half of them would have comprised 'false positives' in the sense that they did not go on to persistent crime careers. Only sixteen are shown to have had persistent crime careers. These sixteen make up only 23 per cent of the 70 persisters. This means that targeting them alone in an effort to pre-empt persistent offending would miss over 75 per cent of the persisters, the false negatives.

The lower the number of risk factors chosen to select targets in order to reduce the number of false negatives for intervention, the higher the number (and proportion) of false positives. Thus if the threshold were set at three risk factors, 62 individuals would be the focus of attention. To have done so would have included 25 who went on to be persisters (just over a third of the 70 persisters identified, meaning there were two-thirds rather than three-quarters false negatives), but that would have meant also intervening with 37 who did not go on to persistent crime careers. Some 60 per cent of the 62 focused on would thus comprise false positives.

Equally Table 3.2 shows that a third of the persisters (27 of 70) showed no risk factors or only one of them at age 8–9. Hence, realistically any risk-based criminality reduction programme would miss a substantial rump of 'false negatives'.

Figure 3.4 shows the distribution of true positives, false negatives and false positives at different thresholds for targeting interventions on the basis of numbers of risk factors shown at aged 8–9, using the data from Farrington et al. (2006). With one risk factor many are targeted but the majority would not go on to become persistent offenders anyway, though most persistent offenders would be included. In practice only a third of the total South London sample did not exhibit a single risk factor. With 4–5 risk factors as the threshold, far fewer are targeted but the costs in terms of false negatives are high. Moreover even here half the positives are false.

False positives and false negatives raise a number of problems. It is inefficient to target false positives. Potential effectiveness in crime reduction is limited by false negatives. With a given resource the

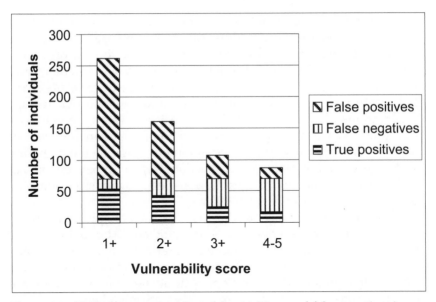

Figure 3.4 Targeting, true positives, false positives and false negatives in risk-based criminality reduction interventions

Data calculated from Farrington *et al.* (2006: 60).

higher the number of false positives tolerated the lower the dosage in relation to true positives; the lower the number of false positives the higher the dosage for true positives but the larger the number left out. In the case of risk factors as revealed in the South London cohort study the identification of those to target is, as we have seen, pretty rough and ready. Moreover, of course, it is assumed that there are measures available that will reduce entry into persistent crime careers and also avoid unintentionally steering some into them. Many worry about labelling effects, whereby those picked out for intervention come to assume the attributes bestowed on them (Bullock and Tilley 2003a). There is always the risk that some of the false negatives will become true positives as a result of inclusion in targeted services. Finally, it is important to recognise the limitations on the impact that risk-focused interventions can have on overall crime levels. Persisters may comprise the group of individuals committing most crime, but this does not mean that they commit a high proportion of all crime that is committed. Much is committed by occasional offenders or those with only short-term crime careers. Preventing their crime involves rather different strategies, that do not target on the basis of risk factors.

In practice where targeting occurs, as called for in the PPO scheme, it rarely if ever adopts the research-based risk factors method of selecting individuals for intervention. Professional judgement is used instead, though it is not known whether or to what degree this produces fewer false positives or false negatives than methods mechanically measuring numbers of risk factors. Observations of a gang-focused initiative attempting to target those belonging to or at risk of being drawn into gangs on the basis of professional judgement found acrimonious disagreement among workers involved in making the selection, large numbers deemed at some risk and some arbitrariness in the selection of those eventually focused on (Bullock and Tilley 2003a).

It is also important to note that the risk factors approach can be adopted in the interests not only of reducing crime but of improving life chances for young people more generally. Here, the focus tends to be on at-risk populations of young people and on helping them achieve their potential in the hope that at the same time they are less likely to become seriously involved in criminal behaviour.

'Communities that Care' (CtC) comprises a risk-focused preventive programme that is widely used internationally. It is described as a 'long-term programme for building safer neighbourhoods where children and young people are valued, respected and encouraged to achieve their potential' (Langman 2005: 5). It aspires to be research-based, targeting risk and protective factors in order to reduce school failure, school-age pregnancy and sexually transmitted disease, and involvement in drug abuse, violence and crime.

Its (British) *Guide to Promising Approaches* (Langman 2005) lists quite a wide range of risk factors under several headings, relating to different 'domains' of influence, including the family, school, community and individuals, friends and peer groups:

Family risk factors

- Poor supervision and discipline;

- Family conflict;

- Family history of problem behaviour;

- Parental involvement in/attitudes condoning problem behaviour;

- Low income and poor housing.

School risk factors

- Low achievement beginning in primary school;
- Aggressive behaviour, including bullying;
- Lack of commitment, including truancy;
- School disorganisation.

Community risk factors

- Disadvantaged neighbourhood;
- Community disorganisation and neglect;
- Availability of drugs;
- High turnover and lack of neighbourhood attachment;
- Low 'collective efficacy' (social cohesion/informal social control)..

Individuals/friends/peer risk factors

- Alienation and lack of social commitment;
- Attitudes that condone problem behaviour;
- Early involvement in problem behaviour;
- Friends involved in problem behaviour;
- Low intelligence;
- Anxiety and social awkwardness.

This is a miscellaneous group of factors that cover individual attributes (such as intelligence), economic and social conditions (such as low income and poor housing), background social experiences (such as parental involvement in criminal behaviour), immediate circumstances (such as availability of drugs) and actual antisocial behaviour (such as aggressive behaviour). These simply describe a set of variables plausibly associated with criminality for which there is some evidential support, without reference to or consideration of the causal mechanisms whereby they individually, jointly or in interaction produce these effects. The approach is atheoretical.

The counterparts to these risk factors are 'protective' factors. These are negative correlates with involvement in criminality, whose introduction is deemed to include attention to causal mechanisms that inhibit crime or promote lawful behaviour. Protective factors relate in general terms to the following:

- Healthy behaviours (that help develop healthy, responsible adults);
- Clear standards (from parents, teachers and community);
- Social bonding (attachments to those who set clear standards and motivate adherence to them);
- Protective processes:
  - Opportunities for involvement, to feel valued by family, school and community;
  - Social and learning skills, to take advantage of opportunities on offer;
  - Recognition and praise for positive behaviours, to incentivise their continuation.

'Communities that Care' promotes programmes that promise to reduce the supply of risk factors and increase the supply of protective factors. Mentoring, for example, is said to reduce the following identified risk factors:

- Low income/poor housing;
- Low achievement beginning in primary school;
- Aggressive behaviour, including bullying;
- Attitudes that condone problem behaviour;
- Early involvement in problem behaviour;
- Friends involved in problem behaviour.

Mentoring also evidently may supply the following protective factors:

- Social bonding;
- Healthy standards;
- Opportunities for involvement;
- Social/learning skills;
- Recognition/praise.

For each risk factor in each domain, evidence of the efficacy of varying interventions is reviewed to produce what aims at being an evidence-based guide to crime risk-factor reduction. Table 3.3 reproduces a summary extract from the CtC overview of interventions in relation to risk and protective factors within the family domain, where there are evaluated 'promising approaches' in place in the UK.

One advantage of broad programmes such as CtC is that they have the potential to draw in a range of agencies and organisations which can contribute and also potentially achieve some of their own targets through taking part. Health, education, and social services, for example, all clearly have potential contributions to make to delivering tested risk and protective factors focused interventions in the family domain as shown in Table 3.3. Moreover, each presumably is helped in achieving its mission by working in concert with others contributing to the same or complementary integrated local programmes.

Trajectories and turning points

Although there has been a great deal of interest in risk-factor focused criminality prevention, its ascendancy has not remained unchallenged. Just as there have been critiques of the atheoretical 'risk factorology' that has prevailed in public health, so too there has been increasing skepticism over hunting down criminality risk factors and focusing on them for crime prevention (Homel 2005: 86).

Doubts have been cast on the view that risk factors encountered early tend to set individuals in one direction or another and that the job is therefore to deal with them to redirect those who would otherwise succumb to criminality. Instead, developments in criminality (and lawfulness) are seen to occur more stutteringly in response to various contingencies that are encountered. Those who seem to be set fair to obey the law may be thrown off course as may those who seem set on a life course that will lead them to a sustained career in crime. This is not, of course, to suggest that early risk factors have no predictive value, only that they may work though the differential probability of being in later situations whose immediate effects produce (or inhibit) criminal behaviour.

Laub and Sampson (2003) report what is probably the longest

Table 3.3 Evaluated promising programmes in the UK addressing family risk factors

Risk factor addressed	Type of programme	Protective factors*					Developmental period
		HS	SB	OP	SK	RE	
Poor parental supervision and discipline	Prenatal services	✓	✓	✓	✓	✓	Prenatal
	Early detection and treatment of postnatal depression	✓	✓	✓	✓	✓	Prenatal–2
	Early detection of speech and language delays	✓		✓	✓	✓	2–6
	Family support using home visiting	✓	✓	✓	✓	✓	Prenatal–2
	Parenting information and support	✓	✓	✓	✓	✓	All
	Helping children with specific learning difficulties	✓	✓	✓	✓	✓	2–11
Family conflict	Early treatment of speech and language delays	✓	✓	✓	✓	✓	2–6
	Family support using home visiting	✓	✓	✓	✓	✓	Prenatal–2
	Parenting information and support	✓	✓	✓	✓	✓	All
	Helping children with specific learning difficulties	✓	✓	✓	✓	✓	2–11

	HS	SB	OP	SK	RE	
Family history of problem behaviour						
Prenatal services	✓	✓	✓	✓	✓	Prenatal–2
Family support using home visiting	✓	✓	✓	✓	✓	Prenatal–2
Pre-school education	✓	✓	✓	✓	✓	3–5
Involving the family in education	✓	✓	✓	✓	✓	0–6
Parental involvement/ attitudes condoning problem behaviour						
Prenatal services	✓	✓	✓	✓	✓	Prenatal
Family support using home visiting	✓	✓	✓	✓	✓	Prenatal–2
Parental information and support	✓	✓	✓	✓	✓	All
Involving the family in education	✓	✓	✓	✓	✓	0–6
Low income/ poor housing						
Prenatal services	✓	✓	✓	✓	✓	Prenatal
Family support using home visiting	✓	✓	✓	✓	✓	Prenatal–2
Pre-school education	✓	✓	✓	✓	✓	3–5
Involving the family in education	✓	✓	✓	✓	✓	0–6

* HS refers to Healthy Standards, SB to Social Bonding, OP to Opportunities; SK to Skills and RE to Recognition

Source: Adapted from Langman (2005: 109). The chart from which this is drawn also lists other programme types where there are promising evaluated programmes in other countries or where only practice guidance was available at the time the publication appeared. There are parallel charts for the school, individuals/friends/peers and community domains.

term and most detailed longitudinal study of beginning, continuing and desisting from criminal behaviour. They pick up a large sample of Bostonians that had originally been tracked by Sheldon and Eleanor Glueck. The Gluecks had identified 500 male delinquents and 500 male non-delinquents aged 10–17, born between 1923 and 1932. The Gleucks tracked their lives and kept detailed records over 25 years. Laub and Sampson picked up the delinquent group in the mid 1990s, traced as many as they could and collected further data on them for statistical analysis. They also interviewed 52 of the men in depth, often over several sessions.

Laub and Sampson conclude that 'turning points', 'linked to the interactions of human agency, lifecourse events, situations and historical contexts', are crucial to the crime trajectories that individuals follow (Laub and Sampson 2003: 36). They stress the significance of intentionality: the men, they find, made choices (sometimes unconsciously) about what to do in the situations they met; they were not passive objects of early childhood experiences and biological attributes that drove them through their crime careers. Laub and Sampson are especially critical of the view that it is possible to distinguish one small set of youngsters destined to be 'life-course persistent' offenders from the larger number of 'adolescent-limited' offenders, as had been proposed by Moffitt (1993), for which they find no evidence. Pretty much all offenders desisted in the end. Moreover, Laub and Sampson found that contingencies played a major larger part in producing diverse crime career paths. These formed part of the situations in which choices were made: becoming employed, getting married and or joining the military for these men comprised major broad changes in context for the choices made by them. Their experiences of these differed as did their patterns of choices made. The major mechanisms through which these led to the patterns of choice made had to do with the types of social bond created, the everyday routine activities established, the direct social controls experienced, the normative assumptions in place and the personal identities fostered for and by the men. Changes in employment and marriage conditions provided a basis for a new situation in which previous choices over involvement in criminal behaviour might be substituted by new ones.

In regard to crime desistance, Laub and Sampson state:

> Overall it appears that successful cessation from crime occurs when the proximate causes of crime are affected. A central element in the desistance process is the 'knifing off' of

individual offenders from their immediate environment and offering them a new script for the future. (Laub and Sampson 2003: 157)

The trajectories and turning points approach focuses on and attempts to explicate the mechanisms at work in the crime-related situated choices made, as against the risk factors approach which focuses on associations between offending and other variables without the same concern for the mechanisms whereby they are connected.

Ross Homel (2005) considers the preventive strategies that follow from a trajectories and turning points method of understanding crime careers. He shows how the patterns of transition vary by individual but also how there are common transition points. Each transition point offers the possibility of continuity along an existing path or a turn. The turn may be either towards crime involvement or away from it. Transitions and the associated potential turning points can be occasioned in many ways: for example through divorce, death of a parent or sibling, moving house, starting playgroup or school, the arrival of a new teacher, attending summer camp, changing school, leaving home, beginning or ending a relationship with a partner, the experience of sexual abuse, serious illness, arrest for a criminal offence, joining a club or entry to or departure from residential care. Each provides new opportunities and fresh choices. What happens depends on the details of the transition and the choices of the person involved.

There are a number of characteristic transitions, in particular going to school, changing school, leaving school, starting work and embarking on an intimate relationship. The direction taken as these transition points are met is not, of course, unaffected by what went before but neither does what went before determine what path is necessarily taken at transition points. Transitions are important as points at which there are both risks that those encountering them will turn towards increasing crime involvement, and opportunities for those already involved to turn away from criminality. The policy and practice implication is that close attention should be paid to what is experienced at transition points. In particular efforts should be made to forestall slippage towards criminality for those not already involved and to facilitate redirection towards lawful behaviour for those who are already involved in crime and antisocial behaviour.

What Homel is not advocating is a standard set of interventions for all potential transition points but a tailored effort to deal sensitively and in an informed way with young people, in particular those showing signs of criminal involvement. For these individuals, heightened sensitivity to and systematic attention to the potential risks and opportunities at transition points offer promising points of intervention. This would be to plan and try to make positive what would otherwise be accidental and potentially hazardous. Where particular experiences suggest especially dangerous potential turning points, for example being taken into care or the experience of sexual abuse, then routine attention to what happens is, of course, implied.

Have a look at the tale of Norman Storey (Annex A). Norman exhibited few risk factors, but was on the fringe of a deviant lifestyle. It was arrest that triggered a decision to turn away from the trajectory towards crime on which he seemed to have embarked. Norman's background will have affected the choices he made. Others with a different background and with different family reactions to the arrest might have responded very differently: their crime careers might have been reinforced.

The transitions and turning points approach to understanding crime careers and working out potential intervention points is theoretically sophisticated and rooted in some strong research. At least so far the effective practice dividends, however, are less clear. In comparison to the risk-focused preventive initiatives, a body of well-researched past practice is not available to draw on.

Cognitive-behavioural treatment[1]

Cognitive-behavioural therapy has come to be widely used to deal with a range of problem behaviours, including those related to crime. It emerged in the mid-1970s, drawing on two contrasting and competing traditions in psychology, one relating to behaviour and behaviour modification and the other to cognition. Each tradition is internally very varied. In broad terms, however, the former tended to take little interest in internal processes: the emphasis was on the behaviour of animals and people. The latter was principally concerned with how people perceived and understood themselves and the world around them, with much less interest in what they did. The former tended to be self-consciously scientific, with a strong emphasis on observation. The latter tended to be much more humanistic, emphasising hermeneutic methods. The former was sceptical of introversion and of anything that could not be seen and measured. The latter was sceptical of accounts of human beings that failed to recognise that there is an internal side to them: people do not just react mechanically; instead crucially they are thinking, feeling beings. The therapeutic emphasis of the former was on changing the environment acting on people, which elicited recurrent unwanted ('maladaptive') behaviours. The therapeutic emphasis of the latter was on improving unhappy people's sense of self by helping them change it.

Cognitive behavioural theory takes from behaviourism the notion that the environment affects behaviour and from cognitive psychology the notion that that influence is mediated by intra-psychic mechanisms. That is, the environment is crucial but how it has its influence is a function of the ways it is processed by the person. In simple terms, thoughts and feelings are at work in responding to experience.

Many chronic offenders will have learned habits of responding to problem situations by committing crime, drinking heavily and/or acting violently. Cognitive-behavioural approaches attempt to deal with the flawed and faulty reasoning which is deemed to explain such patterns of criminal behaviour. Offenders are taught, for example, how better to read the situations they encounter, problem-solving skills, and anger management in order that they respond more appropriately and, for example, less aggressively, to circumstances they encounter. They learn thereby not to misconstrue others' actions as insulting, to control anger before it spills over into aggressive behaviour and to resolve difficult circumstances with strategies that do not involve the use of violence.

A variety of techniques are used in cognitive behavioural treatment of offenders. These include, for instance, 'systematic desensitisation' which involves presenting the subject with arousing stimuli that have previously provoked crime and then relaxing them in order that those stimuli no longer stimulate feelings leading to the unwanted behaviour; teaching 'perspective taking', an ability some offenders lack, to understand how others may perceive situations so that this can be taken in account; 'modelling' appropriate responses to situations to which the offender has previously responded in inappropriate criminal ways (perhaps in response to earlier criminal modelling); and 'coaching' in suitable as against unsuitable behaviour, with feedback to the subject on their efforts.

Different offenders have different cognitive shortcomings, so the therapy needed to correct their faulty thinking would not be identical. It appears also that levels of motivation vary in ways that are important to the receptiveness of subjects to the treatment provided.

In practice in England and Wales several standard programmes rooted in cognitive-behavioural principles were put in place through the Probation Service during the Crime Reduction Programme (1999–2002). These included 'Think First', 'Reasoning and Rehabilitation', 'Enhanced Thinking Skills', 'Priestly One-to-One' and 'Addressing Substance-Related Offending' (Hollin et al. 2004). Most were for groups and included a standard number of standard sessions. For example Think First involved 22 two-hour sessions, Reasoning and Rehabilitation involved 38 two-hour sessions, and Enhancing Thinking Skills involved 10 two-hour sessions. Priestly One-to-One was for individuals deemed unsuitable for group work (or in locations where no group work was available) but used the same kind of cognitive-behavioral principles in 20 one-hour sessions. The completion rates were low for all group-work programmes (from 21–38%), but reached 70 per cent for the individual programme. The aggregate outcomes from comparing the 2,230 members of the experimental group with the 2,645 members of the comparison group across the five programmes were disappointing. The completers had only a marginally lower reconviction rate than the comparison group for males and a higher one for females (males 54% as against 60%, and females 56% as against 50%). Non-completers had a much higher reconviction rate (68% for males and 77% for females). Overall findings for cognitive-behavioural programmes are mixed (see Friendship and Debidin 2006; McDougall et al. 2006).

A summary of a recent Cochrane review of the use of cognitive behavioural interventions to prevent youth gang participation could do no more than advocate further evaluative research, presumably of the sort it was unable to find. It said:

Research indicates that youth who join gangs are more likely to be involved in delinquency and crime, particularly serious and violent offences, compared to non-gang youth and non-gang delinquent youth. Research also has found that both delinquent youth and youth who join gangs often show a range of negative thoughts, feelings and beliefs compared to non-delinquent peers. Cognitive-behavioural interventions, designed to address these deficits, have had a positive impact on a variety of behavioural and psychological disorders among children and youth. This systematic review was designed to assess the effectiveness of such cognitive-behavioural interventions for preventing youth gang involvement. A three-part search strategy found no randomised controlled trials or quasi-randomised controlled trials of the effectiveness of cognitive-behavioural interventions for gang prevention; four excluded studies examining the impact of Gang Resistance Education and Training (GREAT) were of too poor a quality to be included in analysis. The only possible conclusions from this review, therefore, are the urgent need for additional primary evaluations of cognitive-behavioural interventions for gang prevention and the importance of high standards required of the research conducted to provide meaningful findings that can guide future programmes and policies. (Fisher *et al.* 2008)

A basic failing in the cognitive-behavioural approach may be its notion that repeated offending follows from flawed thinking. This may not be so for many criminals. Even where it is the case changing thinking may be tricky, especially where standard sessions are offered to all members of a group. A key attraction of the cognitive behavioural approach is that it is relatively quick and inexpensive, though nothing much is gained if it is not effective.

Drug treatment

The theory behind drug treatment as a crime prevention strategy (as against other rationales for drug treatment) is that drug taking drives crime in various ways. There are three basic drug-taking crime generation mechanisms. The first relates to the way some drugs may dispose the individual to behave criminally, most particularly by being violent. The second relates to the need drug dependency creates for substantial sums of money to buy the drugs that many users can only raise through crime. The third relates to the market supported by drug-takers which produces drug trafficking, and associated criminal activities including serious violence to protect and pursue business and violence at the point of drugs sale.

Illicit drug-taking is quite commonplace among those at peak offending ages. The 2005/6 British Crime Survey (BCS) found that in England and Wales, some 45 per cent of 16 to 24-year-olds had taken one or more illicit drugs at some point in their lives, 25 per cent in the last year and fifteen per cent in the last month. Notwithstanding this general pattern, there is also ample evidence not only in Britain but in other countries also of an association between illicit drug taking and property crime (Office of National Drug Control Policy [ONDCP] 2000; Makkai and Payne 2003; Flood-Page *et al.* 2000). Table 3.4, for example, is taken from Holloway and Bennett (2004) and shows the results of drug tests made on a sample of arrestees in England and Wales. This shows some variation by crime type. For example, cocaine/crack was found at almost twice the rate as opiates among robbery arrestees (30% as against 17%), but opiates were found for almost twice as many arrestees for shoplifting as crack cocaine (63% compared to 32%). Overall two-thirds of shoplifting arrestees were found to have taken heroin and/or cocaine and/ or crack, but only a quarter of those arrested for theft of a motor vehicle had done so.

What is not quite so clear is that the relationship is a simple causal one, wherein drugs generate crime. Crime may also produce the drug-taking: the resources provided by crime provide the wherewithal to become involved in drug-taking. And regular drug-taking may be part of a general chaotic lifestyle for a minority that also includes involvement in crime: it is not the drugs per se that are responsible for the crime but a broader way of life that includes much else besides (McSweeney and Hough 2005: 571–2).

Table 3.4 Drug tests results for arrestees in England and Wales

Reason for arrest	Number of arrestees	Opiates %	Cocaine/Crack %	HCC* %
Shoplifting	468	63	32	67
Burglary	193	38	26	47
Theft from person	12	25	33	42
Drugs possession	231	25	28	42
Drugs supply	59	24	29	39
Handling stolen goods	35	34	20	37
Theft from motor vehicle	31	29	19	36
Robbery	60	17	30	35
Deception/fraud	100	23	18	28
Theft of motor vehicle	143	15	15	24

*Heroin and/or Cocaine and/or Crack
Source: Holloway and Bennett (2004: 12).

More complex drug-crime causal relationships are now widely believed to be at work (Makkai and Payne 2003; McSweeney and Hough 2005; Seddon 2007). Occasional drug taking (especially cannabis) and property crime are quite normal in adolescence. More regular minor property crimes may enable increased and more serious drug usage because drugs become affordable. High rates of drug usage eventually produce dependency among some individuals. Drug dependency brings with it a need to raise regular and large sums of money. One key method of raising this money may then include a high rate of property crime as well as participation in low-level drug trafficking. Many of those involved become members of peer groups with common deviant and self-destructive lifestyles which support, normalise and reinforce high levels of drug-taking and the crime surrounding it. In addition, some of the drugs taken (including alcohol which is of course not generally illicit for those over a given age) may engender aggressiveness and hence violent crime. The need to acquire drugs can also provoke violent behaviour towards suppliers. Moreover the illicit drugs market, which is sustained by both occasional and high-rate users, draws in serious criminals whose efforts to protect and take over supply routes involve major organised crime. Once established those benefiting from local markets have an interest in maintaining it with new cohorts of customers, who can be attracted by cut-price offers that help foster dependency.

Those who are drug dependent have diverse attributes and needs (Marsden and Farrell 2002; National Institute on Drug Abuse 2006; Audit Commission 2002). Motivation to stop, pattern of multiple drug use, medical and psychological problems, economic and social circumstances, and level of dependence all vary widely. There is no standard treatment that is believed to be appropriate for all. Tailoring to need is therefore required.

Where treatment is offered and taken up among those who commit crime, levels of offending have been found to fall, though the 'same' treatment has been found to have widely varying outcomes (Audit Commission 2002). Treatment has to be sustained if those receiving it are not to revert to their drug-taking and crime habits (Marsden and Farrell 2002). What is required is often initial detoxification followed by maintenance (for example with methadone as a substitute for heroin), followed by dose reduction and, after that, services aimed at relapse prevention since, for example, under the influence of peers drug-taking may easily be resumed. Cognitive-behavioural methods of the sort discussed in the previous section are often used (National Institute on Drug Abuse 2006).

A major problem in treatment at all stages and of all types has been the high rates of drop-out, especially among those with chaotic life styles (McSweeney and Hough 2005; Harper and Chitty 2005; Skodbo *et al.* 2007). Because of this and the high rates of offending associated with drug-taking, elements of coercion or compulsion have been introduced to motivate offenders' entry into, participation in and completion of sustained courses of drug treatment (Seddon 2007; National Institute on Drug Abuse 2006; Skodbo *et al.* 2007). These have been found in some studies to be able to produce better retention in treatment and likely drops in drug-taking and in crime (Skodbo *et al.* 2007), though findings across the board are neither consistent nor unequivocal (Seddon 2007). The underlying theory is that at each stage the benefits of participation in treatment and behaviour in accord with it outweigh the costs in terms of the forgone benefits from the drugs and from acquiescence to temptations that follow from the groups with which criminal drug users typically associate (Frisher and Beckett 2006)[2].

Ethical issues

Treatment of offenders raises a number of ethical issues, especially where that treatment is compelled or coerced. The utilitarian argument for compulsory treatment is that it is justified to the extent to which the outcomes produce net benefits. If it does not do so then that treatment is not justified. There are two problems with this argument. The first is that though there is evidence that some benefits can be produced the evidence is far from unequivocal. The second is that it involves disregarding the subject's status as a moral agent with rights and responsibilities. Individuals decide what to do and are to be judged and treated on the basis of the decisions they take. They may deserve punishment, but their status as moral agents is denied if they are treated compulsorily. They may choose treatment. They may even be persuaded to accept treatment. But the respect due to them as persons is disregarded if it is imposed on them.

It might be claimed that the status of some offenders as moral agents is overridden if their actions are involuntarily caused by some internal or external force that renders them incapable of choosing to act in any different way. There appears, however, to be little or no evidence that this is the case, except for a tiny minority of offenders. While it might be plausible to medicalise some offenders for whom some specific, identified physiological abnormal causal agent is at work, inferring a medical condition from behaviours is much more problematic since it may merely mask moral judgements in the language of pseudo-science, moral judgements that would require the individual to be treated as a moral agent. Where there is some specific physiological cause, difficulties may arise when the imposed treatment may not be in the interests of the subject, even though it is in the interests of the rest of the community. To impose it would seem to run foul of the normal requirement for informed consent in medical treatment. In this context drug addiction raises difficult problems. Does addiction imply that the capacity for moral agency has been lost, even though the actions leading up to the addiction have at some point been chosen by moral agents? This may be the case for some, although for many others some level of choice presumably remains, as it does for many other categories of persons whose choices are constrained in one way or another.

Allowing offenders to choose treatment as against the punishment they would otherwise be deemed to merit in the interests of the social benefits that are expected raises fewer problems. Threatening more punishment than would otherwise be deserved does, however, raise problems of treating the individual as a means to a social end rather than an end in him or herself warranting fair treatment and respect as an agent.

Finally, problems of distributive justice may arise in relation to treatment provided for offenders, where treatment is in scarce supply (see Seddon 2007). If the offender chooses treatment, is there any reason why they deserve to take priority over others who may have similar needs and preferences but have not committed the crime that provides access to the treatment? There is a risk here, of course, also of providing perverse incentives to offend in order to obtain access to services that would otherwise either not be available at all or only available in the more distant future. It is not clear that the offender has any greater entitlement to treatment than others. Indeed perhaps less.

Conclusion

Though much crime is committed by occasional offenders, especially during adolescence, much is also attributable to prolific offenders.

Their prolific offending is produced by a mix of predisposing social conditions, personal attributes and biographical contingencies. They are a far from homogenous group. Predicting who will come to be a prolific offender is fraught with difficulty. There are so far no silver bullets that will reduce the level of crime of prolific offenders and the heterogeneity of the groups makes it unlikely that any will be found. Looking for silver bullets does not appear to be a fruitful direction for policy, practice or research. Focusing on the varying needs of significant subsets of prolific offenders, identifying members of those subsets, and devising and delivering ethical pre-emptive services tailored to them would appear to be the most promising preventive strategy and agenda for improving strategies. For those who are immersed in high levels of offending, hastening desistance (that appears in almost all case to take place eventually) in informed ways tailored to individual needs may be the current best policy and practice buy.

Exercises

1 When, if ever, is compulsion justifiable in treating individuals in the interests of crime prevention?

2 Find out about services for drug-related offenders in your area. Explain and critically assess their theoretical assumptions.

3 Do the patterns of false positives and false negatives undermine the case for risk-factor criminality prevention? If not, how would local services in your area need to change to deliver it?

4 Outline what you believe would be an ideal evidence-based short-, medium- and long-term research, policy and practice agenda to deal with future and existing high-rate offenders.

5 Look back at your crime autobiography (Chapter 1), and relate it to the material discussed in this chapter.

Further reading

For a strong overview of developmental crime prevention, see Homel, R. (2005) 'Developmental crime prevention', in N. Tilley (ed.) *Handbook of Crime Prevention and Community Safety*. Cullompton: Willan Publishing.

For a strong overview of drugs and alcohol problems and responses, see McSweeney, T. and Hough, M. (2005) 'Drugs and alcohol', in N. Tilley (ed.) *Handbook of Crime Prevention and Community Safety*. Cullompton: Willan Publishing.

For more extensive discussion specifically of drugs and drug-treatment theory and practice see Audit Commission (2002) *Changing Habits: The Commissioning and Management of Community Drug Treatment Services for Adults*. London: Audit Commission.

On cognitive-behavioural theory and practice see Maguire, J., edited by Furniss, J. M. (2000) *Cognitive Behavioural Approaches: An Introduction to Theory and Research*. Available at: http://inspectorates. homeoffice.gov.uk/hmiprobation/docs/cogbeh1.pdf?view=Binary accessed June 2008.

For a wide-ranging review of what's known about risk and protective factors see Langman, J. (2005) *A Guide to Promising Approaches*. London: Communities that Care.

Notes

1 Maguire (2000) provides a much fuller and very accessible account of the origins, assumptions and uses of cognitive-behavioural approaches to crime.
2 Frisher and Beckett (2006) suggest that the natural desistance in drug-taking widely found in the general population is not so much found in criminal, problematic drug-taking populations, where dependency has set in and where external persuasion is therefore needed to alter the balance of rewards in favour of treatment and desistance in drug-taking.

Chapter 4

Social measures and mechanisms

There are many senses in which crime is fundamentally a social phenomenon. 'Crime' is socially constructed. Rather than a consistent class of behaviours, it describes a variable set of socially defined categories (Curra 2000). Most criminal behaviour involves social relationships: between offenders, victims, members of the criminal justice system, and the general public (Young 1991). Crime tends to be committed socially, by offenders working in association with one or more others or as parts of loose networks or (more rarely) as organised groups (Felson 2006). Patterns of criminality vary by the communities and networks that offenders inhabit: for example poorer, relatively disadvantaged neighbourhoods are associated with much higher rates of participation in high-volume acquisitive crime than better off ones (Wilson 1987). As shown in Chapter 3, routes into and out of criminal involvement are to a large extent a function of sets of social relationships and opportunities that respectively propel or attract individuals into an offending lifestyle and drive or pull them out of it (Laub and Sampson 2003; Homel 2005). Social responses to criminal acts involving the media and criminal justice agencies can precipitate spirals of increasing levels of offending, as criminal identities are bestowed and reinforced (Wilkins 1964). Social policies, for example to do with housing allocation methods, can unintentionally create concentrations of offenders with consequences for the production of mutually supporting networks of criminals and weak social controls over them (Bottoms and

Wiles 1986, 1997; Bottoms *et al.* 1992). Commercially competitive practices lead to opportunities (for example car design), temptations (for example supermarket lay-out) and provocations (for example happy hours in bars), that generate criminal behaviour (Homel *et al.* 1997; Wortley 2001). Obtaining the fruits of offending very often depends on a compliant or collusive market for the distribution and consumption of stolen or otherwise illicit goods (Sutton 1998; Sutton *et al.* 2001).

Likewise, crime control is fundamentally social. Taken-for-granted norms and values that inhibit much criminality are absorbed from others (see Wikström, forthcoming). Informal social controls on potential offenders are operated with varying levels of intensity in families, peer groups, schools, neighbourhoods, and in public places (Sampson *et al.* 1997; Kennedy 2008). The establishment of obligations to non-offending third parties, notably partners and children, is frequently the occasion for withdrawing from or reducing rates of offending (Laub and Sampson 2003). Those who are socially integrated (and hence subject to control by others) behave less criminally than those who are poorly integrated (Hirschi 1969). Collective responses to offending can help reintegrate those who offend back into law-abiding ways through sensitising them to the harms they have done and by bringing them back into the orbit of effective social control (Braithwaite 1989). The priorities for and delivery of crime prevention public policy and practice turn on complex sets of social relationships involving, among others, politicians, government departments, local authorities, police departments, courts, members of the public, and the mass media (Hughes 1998, 2007; Gilling 1997; Garland 2001). The priorities and delivery of private sector crime prevention policy and practice likewise turn on complex sets of social relationships involving those in public policy as well as customers, owners/shareholders, competitors and company directors (Hardie and Hobbs 2005).

In some cases the social dynamics of prevention and offending interact with one another. Criminal justice processes designed to prevent crime at the same time produce it through processes of labeling and social exclusion (see Young 1999). 'Stranger danger', discussed further as a form of situational crime prevention in Chapter 5, is designed to protect children from the predatory stranger but may also inhibit their protection (and control) by the solicitous stranger. The informal social controls that are applied to control one form of criminal behaviour may involve the commission of another form of criminal behaviour, as with knee-cappings for vehicle theft in Northern Ireland.

Some of these senses in which crime is a social issue and the implications for prevention are picked up in other chapters. This chapter is concerned with preventive efforts aiming directly to activate social and community crime prevention mechanisms or to deactivate social and community crime generation mechanisms. Much crime prevention aimed at tackling 'root causes' of crime is targeted at the underlying social sources of criminality of the kind sketched at the start of this chapter.

The community dynamics generating high rates of crime in some neighbourhoods are often deep-seated, and can be produced as the unintended consequences of economic and social change. William Julius Wilson (1987), for example, gives a classic account of the race, gender, unemployment, migration, and family pattern interactions producing high levels of crime in certain black neighbourhoods in Chicago in the 1980s. He highlights the heavy concentration of murder and robbery, among black men in particular, in highly disadvantaged areas. In 1984 over half the city's murders were committed in seven of the 24 districts with a heavy concentration of poor blacks and Latinos. One predominantly black-populated police district, Wentworth, had 3.4 per cent of the city population but 11 per cent of the murders and 13 per cent of the aggravated assaults in the city.

Wilson's explanation for the mix of poverty, lack of two-parent families and crime focuses on quite complex causal processes. Historical discrimination had left 'a large black underclass in central cities in 1983' (1987: 33). The flow of young black people into the inner city areas had led to their geographical concentration in particular neighbourhoods. Changes in the economy had shrunk the supply of accessible unskilled manual jobs for men. Better off residents migrated to the suburbs. Those remaining lacked contacts or networks that could help them find work. Work-related norms therefore withered. Joblessness as a way of life set in, 'the development of cognitive, linguistic, and other educational and job-related skills necessary for the world of work in the mainstream economy (was) thereby adversely affected' (1987: 57). Teachers became frustrated and did not teach, and children did not learn. Few marriageable men became available and hence more families were headed by single-mothers. In Chicago Housing Authority projects in 1983, of 25,000 families with children only eight per cent included married couples, and 89 per cent received aid to families with dependent children

(AFDC). Good, employed male role models became scarce. Wilson argues that in the resulting massive, segregated, ghettoised public-housing projects and neighbourhoods, 'residents have difficulty identifying with their neighbors. They are, therefore, less likely to engage in reciprocal guardian behavior. Events in one part of the block or neighborhood tend to be of little concern to those residing in other parts' (1987: 38).

He concludes,

'In short the communities of the underclass are plagued by massive joblessness, flagrant and open lawlessness and low-achieving schools and therefore tend to be avoided by outsiders.' (Wilson 1987: 58)

The details of Wilson's analysis are likely to vary by country and community, but the general structure is likely to remain much the same for very high crime neighbourhoods. External conditions trigger a suite of internal processes the upshot of which is to generate high levels of criminal disposition, accompanied by low levels of informal social control. There is liable also to be a complex of other complementary, mutually reinforcing social problems, including social and physical disorganisation, problem drinking and drug-taking, poor school performance, relatively low levels of male employment, low levels of family formation and high levels of family breakdown, out-migration by many when the opportunity is available, and tendencies to housing take-up by the vulnerable and/ or criminal unable to find accommodation elsewhere. Life chances tend to be low and rates of mortality and morbidity high. Crime is just one of a constellation of interrelated and interdependent community problems, but one that is likely to hit hard both on remaining law-abiding residents and on offenders themselves, who not only commit crimes but are also disproportionately victimised. In the kind of community described by Wilson, numbers of risk factors of the sort described in Chapter 3 will be high.

From this point of view situational crime prevention, traditional enforcement responses to offending individuals and groups, and treatment of the sort described in Chapters 2, 3 and 5 might seem to make little sense. They all fail to attend to the underlying (often termed 'root') causes of crime and criminality, and at best provide short-term palliatives. Attacking the 'root causes' involves much more ambitious efforts at re-setting the causal dynamics in ways that will produce long-term and sustainable improvements in diverse social outcomes including levels of crime and criminality alongside education, health, employment, and child welfare.

Various large-scale government-funded programmes and projects in Britain have attempted to address suites of interrelated and mutually reinforcing social and community problems. These have included, for example, Community Development Projects (1969–1977), Estate Action (1985–2005), Action for Cities (1988–1994), City Challenge (1994–1998), the Single Regeneration Budget (1994–2001), New Deal for Communities (1998–) and the Neighbourhood Renewal Fund (2001–). Success has been patchy and crime has never been the sole or major focus. These initiatives have been ambitious, complex and broad-based, aimed at reversing long-term spirals of social, physical and economic decline. Many areas have repeatedly been included in successive programmes, suggesting that even with the very substantial investments made, the 'root causes' have been resistant to well-meaning interventions. Detailed attention to these broad-based efforts where crime is but one concern lies beyond the scope of this book, which is concerned specifically with crime prevention.

Many of us might sympathise with wide-ranging community-based programmes with multiple aims. They are admirably ambitious. This book, however, has more modest aims. It is concerned specifically with crime prevention. It might be tempting to dismiss community-based efforts at this alone as superficial tinkering that fails to tackle much more fundamental problems. Before doing so, however, the following arguments should be considered:

1 Despite very high levels of expenditure, large-scale programmes have had limited success in producing regeneration and the expected associated reductions in crime and criminality.
2 The most convincing arguments for trying to deal with the complex and interrelated underlying causes of patterns of dysfunction in highly disadvantaged communities are not that they may reduce crime and criminality, but that they address wider issues of social inequality and inequity. Suppose, for example, that reducing levels of relative inequality were to be associated with increases in rather than reductions in crime, would that count in favour of maintaining or increasing inequality? For most, crime is a secondary issue, at best part of the rhetoric that may be used for funding or policy developments with quite different objectives.
3 A precondition for addressing root causes of complexes of problems in deeply problematic neighbourhoods may be that (surface) crime

and physical disorder issues are contained first. Few residents and members of public and private sector organisations, for example, will be willing to invest in community development activities if they perceive crime risks to be very high.

4 Much crime is committed by and suffered by those not living in areas of multiple deprivation. It will not be prevented or reduced through attention to the kind of deep-seated suites of 'root causes' referred to here.

Assuming for the moment that it is reasonable to try to prevent crime short of bold programmes that have tried to target root social causes of multiple problems, let us turn our attention to community focused initiatives that have a specific crime prevention concern.

Community crime prevention

Three main approaches to community crime prevention effort can be identified, Neighbourhood Watch, community policing, and community engagement. Each will be discussed in turn.

Neighbourhood Watch

Neighbourhood Watch has been operating in Britain for over a quarter of a century. The first scheme was set up in the affluent village of Mollington in Cheshire in 1982, following a spate of burglaries. A newspaper article reports that it was still in operation in 2007 (Edge 2007). The local co-ordinator is quoted as saying,

We had a spate of trailers, bikes and stone troughs stolen, but of late it has been fairly quiet . . . There were a few eggs thrown at Hallowe'en. It's just petty crime, really. We're lucky like that. I suppose it shows that our long-established Homewatch scheme works.

From its small Mollington origins, Neighbourhood Watch grew very rapidly. The British Crime Survey found that, in 2000, 27 per cent of households belonged to a Neighbourhood Watch scheme (Sims 2001). The National Neighbourhood Watch Association estimated that that over 155,000 schemes were operating at that time. The BCS found that among non-member households 78 per cent would join if there were a scheme in their area (Sims 2001).

Neighbourhood Watch has clearly enjoyed wide public support. It evidently has high surface plausibility. Neighbourhood Watch does not aim to deal with underlying causes of crime and criminality of the sort sketched earlier in this chapter. Rather it focuses specifically on reducing crime and the fear of crime. The theory behind Neighbourhood Watch is that:

- Members act as the eyes and ears of the police. They report suspicious behaviour to the police. They may sometimes be asked to look out for particular people or activities following alerts of local criminal behaviour. The police then act. In this sense Neighbourhood Watch is an adjunct of the enforcement approaches to crime discussed in Chapter 2.

- Signs and stickers indicating that Neighbourhood Watch is operating in an area act as a credible deterrent to offenders, who believe that their risks are increased if they offend there. It thus comprises one form of situational crime prevention, which is discussed in Chapter 5.

- Members are given advice on ways in which they can improve the security of their persons and property. In this sense Neighbourhood Watch provides a medium for spreading some further techniques of situational crime prevention.

- Members are mobilised to look out for one another and to apply informal social control on those who might otherwise offend in their communities.

Neighbourhood Watches have consistently been over-represented in more affluent low crime, low disorder areas, and under-represented in high-crime, high-disorder neighbourhoods. The British Crime Survey of 2000, for example, found that 32 per cent of households belonged to Neighbourhood Watch in low burglary areas, 23 per cent in medium burglary areas and thirteen per cent in high burglary areas. Likewise 32 per cent belonged in areas with low levels of disorder, 24 per cent in areas with medium disorder and sixteen per cent with areas of high disorder (Sims 2001; see Laycock and Tilley 1995a for earlier evidence). Neighbourhood Watch seems therefore to have been more easily seeded in areas where additional crime controls are least needed. The reasons are not difficult to understand. In low crime neighbourhoods, there are often already those with the social capital to set up new organisations. There is far less social capital in poor and disorganised areas, of the sort described earlier in this chapter. The social capital in low-crime neighbourhoods also delivers much that Neighbourhood Watch promises without the need for Neighbourhood Watch as such: for example trusted networks of residents capable of exerting informal social control, trusted relationships with the police, mutual surveillance etc., as well as the basis for establishing new organisations. Moreover there can also be high levels of intimidation in high crime neighbourhoods, making residents reluctant to participate in organisations linked to the police. Finally, Neighbourhood Watch has been a police performance indicator in relation to which it may have been tempting to focus on areas where they are more easily set up!

Because the underlying rates of crime are low in areas where Neighbourhood Watch most easily flourishes there is less far for crime to fall and hence evidence of effectiveness is more difficult to find. Indeed there is little evidence that Neighbourhood Watch reduces either crime or fear of crime (see the evidence summarised to 1995 by Laycock and Tilley 1995a, supported later in Sims 2001). At worst, police services necessary to support Neighbourhood Watch are drawn from higher-crime to lower-crime neighbourhoods. Insofar as Neighbourhood Watch does impact on crime levels in low-crime neighbourhooods, any that is displaced is liable to flow from low-risk areas to high-risk areas, reinforcing existing patterns of unequal crime distribution.

Neighbourhood Watches tend, as in Mollington, to be established following crimes of concern to local residents. Unlike Mollington, however, they have tended to become more or less moribund when the crime levels fall back to normal levels (Laycock and Tilley 1995a). Regression to the mean (whereby unusually high, or low, measurements tend to be followed by a move towards the average) is liable, of course, to produce an illusory impression of effectiveness as are the generally low-crime levels that tend to be found in Neighbourhood Watch areas.

In 1995 Laycock and Tilley highlighted the patterns outlined here: the lack of evidence on effectiveness, the tendency of schemes to be more easily seeded in low-crime areas, and the decline in activity that normally quickly follows the setting up of schemes (Laycock and Tilley 1995a). Their report suggested that differential strategies were needed depending on the nature of communities and the levels of crime experienced. The report, however, was met with a stinging attack in the *Sunday Mail* by the late Alan Clarke MP. Vested interests in prevailing patterns of Neighbourhood Watch were well-defended, and the 2000 BCS found patterns strikingly similar to those found earlier. Once the Neighbourhood Watch cat was let out of the bag it seemingly became impossible to put it back in. The Neighbourhood Watch movement was, and apparently still is, unstoppable.

This should not be taken to suggest that Watch schemes can never be of any value. In relation to domestic burglary and domestic violence, for example, neighbours have been mobilised to deal with the relatively acute risks of repeats experienced by victims following incidents during periods when risks are highest (Forrester *et al.* 1988, 1990; Hanmer *et al.* 1999), with some evidence that this has contributed to effective prevention. Neighbourhood Watch has also spawned a multitude of other watch schemes, for example street watch, pub watch, farm watch, forecourt watch, shop watch, fish watch, car park watch, school watch, beach watch, allotment watch, betting shop watch, boat watch, campus watch, chemist watch, office watch, and business watch. Some of these may be more promising than many Neighbourhood Watches, especially where the rationale for membership is sustained by relatively high risks of crime and where watch schemes are associated with the delivery of specific measures targeting identified problems.

Community policing

Community policing has its origins less as a vehicle for crime prevention than one for public confidence building (Tilley 2003). It began in response to perceived weaknesses in police–community relations in the 1970s and early 1980s. The idea was that the police needed to forge stronger relationships with those they were there to serve, since some sections of the public, in particular members of ethnic minority groups, appeared to feel disenchanted with the police service. Though the thinking behind community policing has a longer history, the Brixton riots of 1981 and the Scarman report that followed them strongly suggested the need for the police to work more closely with the community and to be more responsive to its views and interests (Scarman 1982). The concerns with community confidence continue. The agenda, however, has become a much broader one that is also concerned with crime prevention and problem solving within communities.

The idea of community policing is that police priorities should be set in consultation with the public, that the public should play a part in working out what is to be done to address priority problems and that where possible the public should play a part in helping to address local problems. This does not mean abandoning the eyes and ears role stressed in Neighbourhood Watch. It does, however, suggest rather more: a police service that is accountable to local people for what it tries to achieve and for the means used, and a police service that involves the public not only in fulfilling an agenda set by the police but in informing that agenda and delivering on it. Public safety is thereby co-produced, and policing is sensitive to community variation.

In the US community policing has become the 'national mantra of the police' (Greene 2000: 301). The most elaborate and most fully documented effort to bring in community policing has been in Chicago (the Chicago Alternative Policing Strategy – CAPS), where Wesley Skogan has led an unprecedented research effort to track in detail what has happened over more than a decade (Skogan and Hartnett 1997; Skogan 2006).

The original vision for community policing in Chicago was set out in a Chicago Police Department document entitled *Together We Can*. (Rodriguez 1993). This slogan captures well the aspiration of the police to work with the community effectively to address the crime and disorder problems facing the city and its several communities. The document begins with a quotation on the role of the police from Sir Robert Peel:

To maintain at all times a relationship with the public that gives reality to the historic tradition that the police are the public and that the public are the police: the police being only the members of the public that are paid to give full-time attention to duties which are incumbent on every citizen in the interest of community welfare and existence.

Together We Can goes on to state that:

[The new policing strategy] mobilizes both government and community resources in a new and constructive partnership toward reducing crime, fear, and neighborhood disorder. It is, in short, Chicago's own vision of community-based policing.

So, community policing is a new strategy that is rooted in traditional conceptions of the way the police and community should work together. Previous developments in policing had drawn the police from those they are there to serve, and community policing represents a reversion to an historical conception of its nature and purpose.

Broad research findings are drawn on in laying out the departmental mission:

> What we have learned from . . . research are some wide-
> ranging and fundamental truths not just about police work,
> but about the nature of crime and police-community relations
> as well. Perhaps more than anything else, this research
> revealed a fatal shortcoming of the traditional model: the
> forced isolation of the police from the community prevented
> police from meeting their expectations of preventing (or at
> least controlling) crime.

The need for the whole police department to be drawn into developing a changed relationship with the community is stressed:

> As part of our new strategy, we have made a commitment
> to establish a relationship between the community and the
> police that will break down longstanding barriers, reduce
> community tensions, open up avenues of information, and
> provide constructive and meaningful opportunities for
> collaboration. Responsibility for forging this partnership
> cannot be assigned to a select few individuals in the
> Department. It must be pervasive: every Department member
> – but especially those at the most basic operational level –
> must see community outreach as an important and ongoing
> element of their jobs.

Problems will be identified and solved alongside the community:

> Under this new alliance, both partners must share
> responsibility for identifying and solving problems. Just as
> the public empowers government through the democratic
> process, government (through the Police Department) must
> empower the community by getting them actively involved
> in the job of creating and maintaining neighborhood order.
> The police cannot be everywhere, but the community can.
> Together, then, we can improve the quality of life and reduce
> the level of fear in our neighborhoods.

The document states that the (police) department's 'ultimate goal':

> ... should be community empowerment. The Department
> will be most effective when it is able to create conditions
> under which communities can improve themselves up front,
> instead of always relying on the Department and other
> government agencies for after-the-fact responses.

Endorsement is provided at the start by Mayor Daley, who states in his foreword, that:

> As Mayor, I recognize that the police can't do it alone. If
> community policing means reinventing the way the Chicago
> Police Department works, it also means reinventing the way
> all City agencies, community members, and the police work
> with each other. Everyone must share the responsibility for
> the safety and well-being of our neighborhoods.

The implementation challenges of the move to community policing are recognised in the document laying out the strategy. The need for changes in management, organisation, performance measurement, training, recruitment, budgeting and technology, for example, are all acknowledged. Developing CAPS was known, in advance, to be a long and difficult haul.

Skogan *et al.*'s accounts of the long-term implementation of CAPS in practice is one of uneven development, Skogan notes that by 1999 it was 'languishing' (Skogan 2006: 87). But it was then reinvigorated, and given fresh impetus, with an 'implementation blitz' (Skogan 2006: 92). The main vehicle for community involvement was regular, generally monthly, openly-advertised beat meetings attended by the public and police and on occasion city service departments, school principals, business operators and so on. The intention of the meetings was to problem-solve in as systematic a way as possible: identifying priority community problems (be they serious crimes or other issues), analysing them in terms of location, victim and offender, developing strategies to address them based on their analysis (involving community members as and where possible), implementing the agreed strategies and then reviewing achievements. Police and community were trained in this problem-solving process, and were encouraged to think beyond conventional enforcement ways of responding to problems.

With regard to the problem-solving that lay at the heart of efforts to engage the community in the formulation of locally effective ways of dealing with problems, Skogan's verdict is one of disappointment. There was relatively little community-involvement in this, as called for in the theory, and that which did occur tended to happen more frequently when more college graduates attended meetings.

> Making problem-solving work was probably the most difficult challenge the department's new program presented, and CAPS got its lowest grade for it. (Skogan 2006: 75)

Skogan rightly adds, however:

> To be fair, every police department has trouble making problem-solving work: it requires a great deal of training, close supervision, strong analytic capacity, and organization-wide commitment. For all the rhetoric about gathering and analyzing data, thinking outside the box for solutions to problems, and involving tactics in addition to trying to make more arrests, a close examination of problem solving in practice can find it wanting. (Skogan 2006: 75)

In the case of Neighbourhood Watch in the UK we saw that it was easier to seed in low-crime neighbourhoods. Similar patterns had been identified in the US. In Chicago however, against some expectations it was found that beat meetings tended to attract a larger rate of attendance in higher rather than lower-crime neighbourhoods. The frequency, focus and promotion of the meetings in this sense appear to have achieved involvement where it was needed (Skogan 2006: 112–8). When, however, the attributes of attendees were examined, familiar biases were found: those already engaged in community organisations, homeowners, the elderly, long-term residents and the educated were more likely to come (Skogan 2006: 150–154). Attendees were not representative of the communities in which they lived. This is not to say, of course that they were incapable of representing the interests of a wider constituency of residents. Here Skogan, drawing on survey findings, reports that broadly comparable patterns of concern were expressed by meeting attendees and non-attendees on drug problems and physical decay, but that the relationship was weaker for crime, where attendees' views matched those of residents much less well.

Skogan highlights the problem in achieving neighbourhood involvement of the sort aimed for when he states that:

> While collective efficacy promises to be an important force for neighbourhood renewal, it remains unclear how areas where trust and reciprocity are low can develop or reclaim these features of community life. Neighbourhoods that need trust and reciprocity most by and large have the least. Collective efficacy is lowest in neighbourhoods of concentrated poverty and in racially or ethnically heterogeneous areas, and highest in stable home owning, predominantly white parts of town. (Skogan 2006: 173).

Skogan compares the recorded crime trends from 1991 to 2003 for homicide, robbery, burglary and auto theft in Chicago with those in the other nine cities in the US with populations of about a million or more. This is a bottom line measurement of crime prevention effectiveness. There is a common steady and substantial fall of roughly 50 per cent from 1991 to 2003 across cities and across crime types. Although there are some detailed differences by crime category, essentially Chicago does no better than the others.

Though the importance of working with the community has been stressed since the beginnings of professional policing in Britain, community policing has not quite reached the status bestowed on it in the US. It has tended instead to be a rather low-status specialism. Relatively recent moves to establish Neighbourhood Policing Teams throughout the country, in part inspired by the promising Chicago experience, represent a commitment to install a version of community policing throughout Britain. There are several differences from the Chicago model, of which the most important for our purposes is that in Britain there is not the same commitment to a comprehensive change in policing philosophy within which community policing is the core animating idea. Rather, Neighbourhood Policing takes its place, albeit an important one, alongside other forms of policing with which it coexists (Tilley 2008).

The government's commitment to Neighbourhood Police was laid out in *Building Communities, Beating Crime: A Better Police Service for the 21st Century* (Home Office 2004). This promised that Neighbourhood Policing Teams would cover all areas by 2008, with the appointment of 24,000 (subsequently reduced to 16,000) uniformed police community support officers (PCSOs)[1], to work alongside sworn officers in teams. As in Chicago, Sir Robert Peel is again invoked to add legitimacy to the plans for close working relationships between police and community. They would work in teams that would generally be led by a police sergeant. With roughly 140,000 police officers in Britain, it is unlikely that more than 5,000 would be dedicated to Neighbourhood Policing Teams, an important but not major fraction of the total.

The National Reassurance Policing Programme (NRPP) piloted efforts to install community policing in sixteen wards. As the name of the programme indicates a key aim was public reassurance, which is deemed an important issue where falling crime levels are not accompanied by corresponding increases in feelings of safety. Prevention as such was a concern, but a secondary one. The stated aims were: to reduce fear of crime and improve the sense of safety among residents; to reduce antisocial behaviour and hence the quality of life of residents; to increase public satisfaction with and confidence in the police, and to improve social capacity (i.e. increase collective efficacy).

The programme made use of the theory of 'signal crimes' (Innes 2004) according to which locally identified stimuli of crime fear can be dealt with to reassure without necessarily reducing underlying levels of crime. A suite of measures was put in place to attempt to achieve the aims of the programme: consistent visible patrol by dedicated neighbourhood policing teams; community engagement to identify concerns and devise action to deal with them; and joint problem-solving involving the police, community and local partners. The results were very promising in the sense that some reduction in crime, improved feelings of safety after dark (although not much reduction in fear of crime otherwise), and improved public confidence in the police (although not with police contact) followed the introduction of the scheme. There was, however, little evidence of impact on social capacity/collective efficacy (Tuffin et al. 2006).

NRPP provided a great deal of central support and control to create experimental conditions in the trial sites. The same impacts were not found in a follow-up study examining the results of neighbourhood policing as it has been rolled out more generally, though its implementation was found to be much less consistent and thorough in this case (Quinton and Morris 2008).

Notwithstanding the rhetoric surrounding community policing, dedicated community police officers have in practice been disparaged by many of their colleagues on both sides of the Atlantic, attracting such terms of opprobrium as 'hobby bobbies', 'empty holster guys', and 'teeny sweenies'. Implementing community policing has proven an enormous challenge. Even in Chicago, where consistent efforts were made for more than a decade to put community policing in place, progress was patchy.

As a form of direct social crime prevention triggering changes in the internal workings of communities to reduce crime levels, neighbourhood policing does not appear yet to have proved itself even where sustained and intense efforts have been made to implement it as fully as possible. There have been implementation problems. There have also been intrinsic difficulties in creating collective efficacy where its development is most needed. Collective efficacy seems to encourage community policing more than community policing produces collective efficacy. None of this is to suggest that community policing has been either unsuccessful or undesirable in many other ways. As a means of identifying community priorities on a regular basis, as a means of helping to decide what measures to put in place, as a site for understanding problems, as a vehicle for reassuring the public and as a site for improving the terms of engagement between police and public community policing may still have much to commend it.

Community engagement

Community engagement has come to be emphasised in Britain as an important end in itself as well as a means of addressing a range of social cohesion, renewal and regeneration issues including those related to crime and disorder (see for example www.homeoffice.gov.uk/comrace/civil/index.html and www.neighbourhood.gov.uk/).

In relation to crime prevention, the difference from community policing is that policing and the police are not necessarily the main players. Non-police led community engagement in crime prevention may thereby enjoy advantages. To the extent that community policing developed to address weaknesses in police–community relationships, it was premised on the assumption that there are a set of obstacles to community engagement to be overcome. These obstacles may exist not just because of mistrust of the police but also because of intimidation by offenders who want to discourage local people from reporting their activities. In either case police absence or police occupancy of a more minor role may provide more conducive conditions for community engagement.

Forrest *et al.* (2005: 2) summarise the implicit theory of and rationale for community engagement as follows:

- The community is critical for identifying and dealing with problems;

- The community is mostly understood in geographical terms, comprising those living or working within a particular area;

- Agencies are expected to be more sensitive and responsive to the wishes of community members;

- Community members are expected to play a larger part in the governance of their local areas;

- Communities of involved, trusting, interconnected members are thought to be better at dealing with problems as they emerge, and are less likely to face serious problems, than communities where members are uninvolved and mistrustful of one another.

Inclusive engagement has proven difficult with many sections of the population, including, for example: ethnic minority groups; gay and lesbian groups; children and young people especially the disaffected; disabled people; sex workers; homeless people; drug users; the mentally ill; single mothers; poor and acutely deprived people; illiterate people; non-English speakers; refugees; travellers; some faith communities; and transient populations (Forrest *et al.* 2005). Many of these are known to be at especially high risk of being victims of crime and of offending.

Mistry (2006, 2007) has looked in detail at one broad effort at community engagement in a large British city. Area-based 'Community Safety Groups' (CSGs) were established, within which both local residents and local agencies were expected to participate in identifying priority local problems and deciding what might be done about them. Consultants were appointed to try to maximise levels of community involvement. Mistry's findings were broadly consonant with those for Neighbourhood Watch and for community policing. Notwithstanding the fact that in this case the community-safety focused community engagement was not police led, the same class-related patterns of variation in participation were found. Engagement was easiest in lower-crime, better-off, high-social-capital neighbourhoods already showing some degree of social solidarity. There was little in higher-crime, more fractured communities. Here, community consultation, in particular, was only possible by making special efforts to canvass views by going to the neighbourhoods and speaking to people. Attendance at formal meetings as forums for engagement within these communities was poor. As Mistry says,

Some CSGs already had some form of local community involvement in the meetings. However, the types of people that were involved were described by service providers, consultants and stakeholders as the 'usual suspects', i.e. white, over-50, retired, and usually involved in other community activity. Most groups recognised that they needed to encourage a wider range of people from the local community to attend to make the group more representative. However, the evaluation observed and found in interviews with the consultants and service providers that they had found this difficult to achieve, and the consultants had not developed any effective methods to engage the 'hard to reach' groups, such as Black and Minority Ethnic (BME) communities. (Mistry 2006: 23)

The prospects for community crime prevention

The case in theory for community engagement in crime prevention and community safety has over a sustained period appeared to be compelling. This explains the persistent efforts to achieve it, for example through Neighbourhood Watch, community policing and community engagement. The practice, however, as we have seen has repeatedly been found to fall short of what is called for in areas of greatest need, and to have delivered limited outcome benefits. This has been the case even where there have been strong implementation efforts.

There are at least three possible responses to this. The first is to abandon community-based crime prevention efforts altogether. There are some weaknesses in the theory, which may be fatal. First, although this chapter has attempted to render a coherent account of the reasoning behind community-based crime prevention, it is difficult not to concur with Crawford's judgement that, 'much that passes for community-based crime prevention is untheorised, ill-considered and inconsistent' (Crawford 1998: 125). In this sense community crime prevention differs from other approaches discussed in earlier chapters of this book. Notions of 'community' are slippery (see Tilley 2003, 2008). It is at once descriptive and prescriptive. As description it normally refers to neighbourhood, but the nature, size and boundaries are poorly conceptualised in theory and in practice are often defined in administrative terms that may mean little to residents. As prescription community is attractive. It conjures up images of a consensual group with shared interests and a common purpose, attempting to achieve shared ends by working together. It is far from clear, however, that this is a realistic picture of how neighbourhoods in cities do operate or ever could operate. In this sense the aspirations may be utopian: mutual indifference, conflicts of interests and population transience seem to mark many areas. Insofar as there are collectives which can or do share interest and orientation, the 'communities' which they constitute may not be defined primarily in geographical terms. They may instead, for example, be defined more saliently in terms of occupation, faith, or ethnicity than shared neighbourhood residence. Second, as a vehicle for addressing root social causes of crime, the community may be the wrong focus. 'Root causes' of the sort described by Wilson may explain why there are community problems. The community may in this sense be too superficial a focus of intervention (largely the conclusion drawn from the much earlier Community Development Projects that ran from 1969–77[2]). The difficulty with this response is that community-related forms of crime prevention have achieved some preventive successes. Moreover, the community-level interventions have brought other benefits in terms of community reassurance and increased confidence in the police.

A second response would be to take a longer view and to persist in efforts to refine and improve efforts at delivering community-focused crime prevention and community safety. This is the view assumed in the British 'Together We Can' movement (HM Government 2006) which borrows its title slogan from the foundation document for Chicago's CAPS. This response acknowledges weaknesses but also notes the successes that have been achieved, for example in the NRPP, and attempts to build on these to deliver effective community involvement. Success depends, according to this, on persistence in working out and disseminating effective methods of community mobilisation.

A third response would also acknowledge some of the achievements of community level crime prevention, but attempt to match community involvement to variations between communities in terms of both objectives and methods (Forrest et al. 2005). In this it bears some comparison with the strategy proposed earlier for variations in Neighbourhood Watch according to community attribute. Forrest et al. propose a broad four-fold community typology:

1 Low crime, low fear of crime;
2 Low crime, high fear of crime;

3 High crime, low fear of crime;
4 High crime, high fear of crime.

Low crime, low fear of crime

Those living in neighbourhoods with these characteristics are relatively safe and feel relatively secure. There will generally already be established social networks of active citizens and formal agencies. The issue here is to keep crime and fear of crime down by dealing promptly and effectively with any potential threats to the status quo. This can be done by responsible organisations promptly removing potential 'signal crimes' such as graffiti or fly-tipping; voluntary groups reproducing social capital and identifying threats; and local shops and businesses watching over and helping to maintain order in public places.

Low crime, high fear of crime

In these areas, anxiety about crime is disproportionate to the low volume of serious crimes or incidents of disorderly behaviour. Some middle-class residential neighbourhoods, especially with significant elderly populations, will be found in this category. Here local residents, environmental agencies and groups of young people who inadvertently cause anxiety could help to identify and remove what are seen as signals of crime and disorder. In some cases residents will see the presence of ethnic minorities as a sign of disorder. Agencies would need to work with residents to combat this latent racism.

High crime, low fear of crime

These are high-crime areas where the victims and, in some cases, the offenders are not local residents. Examples include holiday resorts, towns with large numbers of foreign students, stations, motorway service areas, car parks, and dangerous inner-city areas unknown to visitors. Here the at-risk population is too ephemeral to involve them directly. Moreover, local residents may have little personal interest in the risks faced by the strangers. It may be possible here to engage managers of shops, stations, motorway service areas, and car parks in reducing crime risks, using situational measures of the sort discussed in Chapter 5.

High crime, high fear of crime

These include the most problematic high-crime, inner-city neighbourhoods where efforts at engagement are most difficult. Local residents may understand their problems well enough. They may also know who the offenders are. But, low collective efficacy, high levels of intimidation and low levels of trust in the police limit their ability to control or inhibit criminal and anti-social behaviour. If, however, agencies can persuade citizens to co-operate by providing them with information, they may be able to tackle crime and build confidence in the police. Such efforts are liable also to require complementary situational prevention efforts.

Forrest *et al.* also suggest, as shown in Figure 4.1, that external support will be needed to create conditions in which community engagement can be kick-started. This clearly resembles the crackdown and consolidation strategy already discussed in more detail in Chapter 2. Crackdown and consolidation has had promising results (see Farrell *et al.* 1998; Tilley and Webb 1994; Kennedy 2008). It is, though, untested specifically as a vehicle for triggering the development of collective efficacy and its expected community safety outcomes along the lines summarised in Figure 4.1.

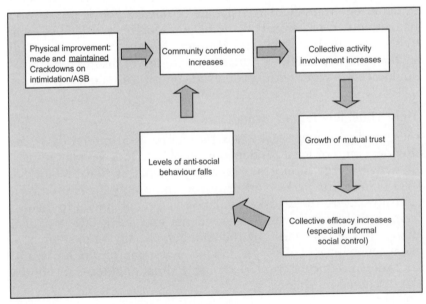

Figure 4.1 Circle of increasing social cohesion

Conclusion

The precise suggestions for a variegated, context-sensitive approach to community crime prevention sketched by Forrest *et al.* may be inoperable in practice or may still be too indiscriminate to produce crime reductions where they are most needed. This chapter has, however, found that across-the-board, standard community crime prevention approaches have produced disappointing results in crime prevention terms. Before internal community crime control mechanisms can be activated within the most difficult high-crime communities, it appears that other actions are required to create the necessary conditions. Whether these would be sufficient to lead to sustained falls maintained through community processes is uncertain. If there are deep-seated social and economic conditions of the sort described by William Julius Wilson in Chicago generating suites of problems, including crime and community instability, this would seem unlikely.

Exercises

1 In your neighbourhood what types of formal and informal social control operate in practice? Who is involved? How actively are they involved? How do local residents relate to the police collectively, if at all? Compare your experience with that of others in your group.

2 When is the last time you or your family had contact with the police? Who initiated the contact? What, if any, preventive element was involved? In what ways, realistically, might more crime prevention value have been added to the encounter? Compare your experience with that of others in your group.

3 Can understanding the social side of crime be used as a basis for formulating effective and equitable crime prevention public policy?

4 Think about the last time you broke the law (or some other formal rule) – for example: plagiarism or other forms of cheating, speeding, collusion with VAT fraud, misleading tax return, assault, drugs, driving having drunk excess alcohol, assault, vandalism, theft, fraudulent insurance claim, non-payment of bus or train fare, fly-tipping, inflated expenses claim, smuggling etc. Few, especially males, will have nothing to think about here. What would have stopped you going through with the offence at the time? Was anyone

around egging you on or permitting the offence? To whom would you be most reluctant to confess the offence? What would your excuse be for the offence? Anonymise and compare your answer to those of others. What are the implications for crime prevention?

Further reading

On Neighbourhood Watch see Laycock, G. and Tilley, N. (1995) *Policing and Neighbourhood Watch*. Crime Prevention and Detection Series Paper 60. London: Home Office.

On community policing see Skogan, W. (2004) *Community Policing: Can it Work*: Belmont, CA: Thomson Wadsworth.

On community conditions and the production of crime see Wilson, W. (1987) *The Truly Disadvantaged*. Chicago, IL: University of Chicago Press.

For differing general discussions of community crime prevention, see Hope, T. (1995) 'Community crime prevention', in M. Tonry and D. Farrington (eds) *Building a Safer Society*. Crime and Justice Volume 19. Chicago, IL: University of Chicago Press and Kelling, G. (2005) 'Community crime reduction: activating formal and informal control', in N. Tilley (ed.) *Handbook of Crime Prevention and Community Safety*. Cullompton: Willan Publishing.

Notes

1 PCSOs have far fewer powers and duties than sworn police officers, as laid out in the Police Reform Act 2002. Precisely what they are able to do varies by police service. What these were in May 2007 can be found at: http://police.homeoffice.gov.uk/publications/community-policing/PCSOs_Audit_Table_May_2007_1.pdf?view=Binary, accessed August 2008.
2 An outline of their experience and references to the quite extensive literature associated with them can be found at: http://www.wcml.org.uk/group/cdp.htm, accessed August 2008.

Chapter 5

Situational measures and mechanisms

Background

Some underlying sources of criminality are deemed to lie in social structure, genetic make-up, and unhappy childhood experience. Offenders are disposed to commit crime because they have had the misfortune to be born in disadvantaged social conditions, because they have suffered neglect, or because they exhibit an abnormal psychological make-up. Much of the preventive work described in Chapters 3 and 4 attempts to address these so-called 'root causes'. Situational crime prevention is very different. Its focus is on modifying the immediate conditions in which crimes are committed. It is not concerned much with criminality and its psycho-social origins. It is concerned rather with pre-empting crime events by removing or reducing opportunities for them. In so far as it is concerned with criminality and its sources, as we shall see, it highlights the ways in which opportunity for crime may foster criminality.

Most of us recognise that opportunity plays a large part in shaping behaviour. Smoking, over-eating, and borrowing large sums of money are all in part a function of opportunity and all can bring pathological consequences, respectively lung cancer, obesity and bankruptcy. A way of reducing the unwanted behaviour is to remove opportunities: creating fewer places where people can smoke, reducing the supply of fatty food in schools, and requiring more stringent credit-checks on those wishing to take out loans. In no case is the behaviour made impossible. In no case is the basic disposition changed. But in all cases opportunity-reduction is believed to change behaviour. Moreover, in all cases the prior provision of ready opportunity has also fostered the unwanted behaviour. Cheap and readily-available cigarettes, chocolate and credit encourage their use. Situational crime prevention attaches significance to opportunity in just the same way.

Clarke and Mayhew (1988) show how a specific change in opportunity produced a large and sustained fall in the number of suicides in Britain. They trace the number of suicides in Britain from 1958 to 1977 and the number committed using domestic gas. Figure 5.1 shows the results. They are striking. What happened over that period is that the composition of the gas supply changed. Highly toxic coal was replaced by non-toxic natural gas. Of course, this did not mean that suicide was no longer possible at all. There are plenty of alternative methods of taking one's own life. Only rarely will some specific individual, perhaps because of a disability, be incapable of taking their own life other than through using the domestic gas supply. The change in the gas supply, however, removed one especially convenient, painless and non-disfiguring means of doing so that many chose to use. The removal of this method was sufficient to lead to a substantial reduction in the total number of suicides. Although some may have switched methods the figures strongly suggest that many did not do so. A side-effect of changing the composition of the gas piped to homes for heating and cooking was a reduction in the opportunity for suicide and a real reduction in the number of suicides. Decisions to commit suicide are not taken lightly. Even here, however, the removal of one opportunity (of many others that are available) produced a substantial drop in overall numbers. Clarke and Mayhew suggest that the same will be true of crime, where it can be presumed that the actions reflect less deep-rooted motives.

In practice, most of us do adopt opportunity-reducing crime prevention measures in our everyday lives. We lock our houses and cars. We put our money in banks or building societies. We take care not to leave valuables on tables on trains or in cafes when we go to the lavatory. We walk on the better-lit side of the street. We avoid carrying large sums of cash. We take our more valuable jewellery off when out and about in public places. We give a wide berth to those

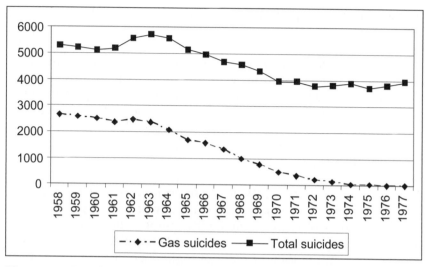

Figure 5.1 Trends in suicides in England and Wales 1958–77

who look threatening. We may remove our phone numbers from the telephone directory if we fear obscene calls. We avoid parts of town we believe to be especially dangerous. We walk or drive our children to school. We may travel in pairs at night. We may choose to sit on the lower deck of the bus. We take care to use secure payment arrangements when we buy goods over the internet, or we avoid such purchases altogether. Those believing themselves to be at higher risk take even more precautions. Smith (2004) has catalogued the very wide range of measures routinely taken by cab-drivers to reduce their risks of injury or financial loss. These include, for example, installation of safety shields, the screening of passengers, use of central door locks, avoiding pick-ups in dark places, asking for pre-payment of fares, limiting the amount of cash held in the cab, and use of an inside release for the boot/trunk.

Definition

Situational crime prevention attempts systematically to find ways of reducing crime problems by reducing or removing opportunities, in particular where existing efforts do not appear to be adequate. Ronald Clarke, the main architect of the situational approach to crime prevention, provides a formal definition, where he states that:

> Situational crime prevention comprises opportunity-reducing measures that (1) are directed at highly specific forms of crime; (2) involve the management, design or manipulation of the immediate environment in as systematic and permanent way as possible; (3) make crime more difficult and risky, or less rewarding and excusable as judged by a wide range of offenders. (Clarke 1997: 4)

Each of the elements mentioned is important. (1) Situational crime prevention promises no panacea. The measures are targeted at some specific sub-set of crimes. Thus, for example, rather than focusing on all crime, or all property crime, or all shop theft, for example, it might focus on the theft of racks of high-value fashion garments in clothes stores, the idea being to find some sub-set that is sufficiently homogenous to be amenable to manipulation of the immediate situation in ways that lessen opportunity. (2) The measures put in place relate to the immediate environment rather than to a distant or underlying cause and they are designed in ways that provide for sustained effects. Thus, for example, rather than attempting to detect and remove a particular offender or gang of offenders stealing the clothes, situational crime prevention would try to identify measures that would produce a sustained impact, such as die tags or use of hangers put on racks in alternate directions or the positioning of goods most likely to be stolen near to the pay station. (3) The main way the measures produce their effects is by increasing cost or effort in relation to the rewards. Armfuls of clothes are more difficult to remove quickly if hangers are hung on racks in alternate directions. Rewards from taking only one garment are reduced and the risks of being caught are greater if more time is taken to gather together several. If the removal of dye tags leads the clothes to be stained their value is reduced and likewise the rewards from taking them. Dye tags and placement of hangers in alternate directions would not make the theft of clothes impossible. Indeed, few situational measures make the crimes targeted impossible. Success is achieved if a wide range of offenders find the balance of effort, risk and reward sufficiently altered that they decide not to commit the offence.

Theory

The idea that focusing on reduction in opportunity could comprise a promising general approach to the prevention of crime was first laid out systematically in a Home Office Research Study, *Crime as Opportunity*, in 1976 (Mayhew *et al.* 1976). This drew together a range of previous research in which opportunity had been 'acknowledged in passing' (1986: 4), including a reference to research in Birmingham finding that incidents of self-gassing dropped from 87 in 1962 to twelve in 1970 as the toxic content of the gas supply fell, which explained almost entirely the reduction in overall rates of suicide in that city over the period. Mayhew *et al.* refer to the 'power of opportunity in determining behaviour' (1986: 6) and the variety of ways in which it may do so. They classify opportunities into those relating to people and those to objects. People's opportunities to commit crime vary by their age, sex and lifestyle. As potential victims, people generate variations in opportunity for offenders. People's opportunities for crime can, the authors say, also be affected by 'patterns of daily activity' that follow from 'forms of social organisation' (1976: 6). In regard to 'properties of objects' they refer to the 'abundance of goods', 'environmental opportunities' and 'physical security'. They also refer to 'surveillance and supervision'.

Crime as Opportunity gave a couple of worked examples: it provided an account of the effects of putting steering column locks in cars on car theft and of the effects of supervision on vandalism on buses.

Steering column locks were fitted to all new cars in England from January 1971. Mayhew *et al.* examined the change in numbers of thefts and unauthorised takings in the Metropolitan Police District in 1969 and 1973, as shown in Table 5.1. The data suggest no change overall but a substantial fall in the number and proportion of the new and a corresponding increase in the number of older vehicles taken. The authors conclude that the introduction of the steering column locks may have led to some displacement from newer to older vehicles.

With regard to vandalism on buses Mayhew *et al.* report a study in Manchester finding that it varied substantially by level of supervision. Upper decks had higher levels of vandalism than lower decks, and buses with conductors as well as drivers had lower levels of vandalism than buses operated by only one person. In regard to the top deck the rear seats of single-operated buses suffered

Table 5.1 Steering wheel locks and car thefts in London

	1969	1973
All cars taken	917	918
New cars taken	192	47
Old cars taken	725	871
% new cars	20.9	5.1

Note: Adapted from Mayhew *et al.* (1976) where a distinction is made between cars stolen and those taken without the owner's consent, a distinction that was hard to make in practice then and no longer made now. The figures have been combined in this table.

more than twenty times as much damage as the front seat of two-person operated buses. Similarly on one-person operated buses the upper deck had more than twenty times as many incidents as on the lower deck. This level of difference, the authors find, could not be explained by variations in passenger types using the upper and lower decks of buses.

Crime as Opportunity concludes with an argument that opportunity-reduction comprises a promising new approach to crime prevention but one that then required a stronger research basis. The authors say:

> Finally, it is hoped that this report has begun to illustrate that physical prevention is not simply a matter of intensive policing and crude security, but that it can, in imaginative and unobtrusive ways, utilise technological and architectural expertise to protect vulnerable property from theft and vandalism, curtail the means of committing crime (for instance by restricting the availability of dangerous weapons), and take advantage of the natural supervision of the environment by ordinary individuals. Hopefully, it has illustrated too that if physical prevention implies a different form of 'social engineering' from that of social prevention, it does not necessarily involve a greater degree of behavioural control. These are small beginnings, however . . . There is also a need to test the notion of 'general' displacement (i.e. the displacement of one type of criminal activity to disparate forms of crime), though this may prove . . . elusive . . . Thereafter perhaps, the most pressing need will be for

research which will allow the importance of opportunity relative to other factors in criminal behaviour, to be more precisely determined. Only then will it be clear whether opportunity merits as central a place in criminological explanation as it is given in the title of this report. (Mayhew *et al.* 1976: 30)

The thirty years since the publication of *Crime as Opportunity* have seen a substantial (and continuing) elaboration of the theory, a range of policy and practice drawn from it and a great deal of critical commentary all of which we come to in due course. This section gives an account of the theoretical developments building on the ideas floated in *Crime as Opportunity* as well as related ideas with which the general approach has subsequently been associated. The critical commentary is addressed towards the end of the chapter.

In practice situational crime prevention measures have a very long history indeed, even if the theory is quite recent, just as natural selection went on before Darwin! And the parallels are significant. Both human beings and other animal species have pretty much always used situational measures to try to avoid risks of predation, or what we humans now often define as crime. Think, for example, of hedgehogs' spines; squirrels' buried acorns; skunks' smelly squirts; squids' inky squirts; ptarmigans' seasonal plumage colour change; chastity belts and castle moats.

The mechanisms at work in situational crime prevention

This chapter has stressed that situational crime prevention focuses on the near causes of crime – the situation facing the prospective offender. Other approaches tend to stress the distant causes – the social and individual sources of criminality that dispose some to commit crime. But what is it about the immediate situation that leads the potential offender to commit or not to commit a crime? Another way of putting this is to ask, 'what are the underlying mechanisms through which situations (and changes in situations) affect levels of crime?'

In answer to this question Cornish and Clarke have articulated a theory of action underpinning crime commission choices (Cornish and Clarke 1986, 2003, 2008). This, in turn, has suggested a growing repertoire of techniques of opportunity reducing measures that might be put into place.

Clarke and Cornish's theory of action is a very weak version of rational choice. By 'weak' I do not mean that the theory is weak but that the rationality deemed to be used by offenders is very limited. It is emphatically not assumed that individuals weigh all options carefully in advance of each act before deciding what would be best for them. Equally it is not assumed that individuals value the maximisation of material utilities above all else in deciding what to do. Rather, rational choice as construed by Cornish and Clarke takes action to be purposive in relation to expected utilities and assumes that those contemplating crime take some account of risk, effort and potential reward in their criminal conduct. Cornish and Clarke also assume that those who make decisions as they commit crimes could have done otherwise. In other words, their behaviour is not mechanically driven by external factors. If these 'rational choice' assumptions are granted it follows that it may be possible to modify the conditions for choices in ways that will lead to changes in action among some who would otherwise choose to commit a particular offence. If we further assume for a moment that those who might come to commit a crime vary in the utility they attach to its potential yield then any change in the balance of risk, effort and reward will produce preventive benefits at the margin. That is, that fraction of potential offenders for whom the situation would previously just have led to expected benefits exceeding expected costs (in terms of risk and effort) will not commit the crime because of the reduced balance of expected benefits to costs.

The form of rational choice theory used by Cornish and Clarke says nothing about ends. They are a matter of taste, 'de gustibus non est disputandum.' Money, thrills, sex, or death, for example, may all be preferred ends. Patterns of choices will, however, change if the balance of cost, effort and reward is altered. In relation to suicide some evidently would prefer death over life in their circumstances. But even here it was found that changes in the balance of cost, effort and reward affected decisions about whether or not to proceed. The effort and risk of self-gassing at home is small and the immediate reward relative to expected pain high. The potential pain and disfigurement brought about by other forms of suicide is much higher, and more effort is required. It appears that removing opportunities for self-gassing as a method of suicide is enough to produce a substantial fall in the total number of people choosing to kill themselves.

In a few cases, of course, the changes wrought by situational measures may effectively make certain specific crimes no longer realistically possible. If safes can no longer be cracked then efforts to do so yield no potential utility and the crime stops, at least till someone figures out a new way to crack them. If football supporters of one team are effectively kept apart, however much they might wish to attack the supporters of an opposing team they will be unable to do so, again until they contrive some alternative way of encountering them face to face. For the most part, though, situational measures do not make crimes impossible. They change the expected balance of cost, effort and benefit at the margins.

Cornish and Clarke emphasise that the commission of crimes generally involves a series of actions, where decisions have to be taken at each point. Derek Cornish (1994) uses the term 'crime script' to capture the sequence of decision points involved as crime events unfold. Crimes may be inhibited if at any part of the sequence of stages in the script the risk, effort and reward balance tips such that the would-be offender decides not to proceed with the offence. Table 5.2 shows an example, given by Cornish (1994), relating to theft of motor vehicles for joy-riding, which offers the prospect of emotional utility. The scene/function categories – preparation, entry, pre-condition, instrumental pre-condition, instrumental initiation, instrumental actualisation, doing, post-condition, and exit – are quite generic. The script actions are specific to joy-riding. The failure explanations show how the potential offence may be disrupted.

Much of Cornish's example emphasises ways in which the potential for a crime event is thwarted by making it more or less impossible. If the car park closes, if no vehicle is available, if a particular vehicle is impregnable, and if the car park cannot be left then the specific crime can no longer occur. But scripts can also be disrupted if the action seems to be more risky, difficult or less rewarding: if the preferred car is not available the next best offers insufficient prospective reward; if drivers return then the perceived risk becomes too great; if the scaffold tube is not to hand it is too much effort to go back for it or find a substitute.

In early presentations of typologies of techniques of crime prevention, as shown in Table 5.3, Clarke (1992, 1995) referred to measures as if they had a direct effect on criminal behaviour. Even if they did not make the crime impossible they somehow acted directly on the potential offender by changing at the margin the cost-risk-benefit equation for that person. By 1997 there were changes both in examples and in major and minor headings (Clarke 1997: 18). Most importantly the three major headings: 'increasing

111

Table 5.2 Script for temporary use of stolen vehicle for driving fast for fun

Scene/function	Script action	Failure explanation
1 Preparation	Gather tools	Forget scaffold tube
2 Entry	Enter car park	Car park closed
3 Pre-condition	Loiter unobtrusively	Noticed by security
4 Instrumental pre-condition	Select vehicle	No Vauxhall Astra GTEs
5 Instrumental initiation	Approach vehicle	Driver returns
6. Instrumental actualisation	Break into vehicle	Vehicle impregnable
7. Doing	Take vehicle	Vehicle immobilised
8. Post-condition	Reverse out of bay	Crash into wall
9. Exit	Leave car park	Gates closed for night

Source: Cornish (1994: 164).

Table 5.3 Twelve techniques of situational crime prevention

Increasing the effort	Increasing the risk	Reducing the reward
1 Target hardening • Steering locks • Bandit screens • Slug rejector device	5 Entry/exit screening • Baggage screening • Automatic ticket gates • Merchandise tags	9 Target removal • Removable car radio • Exact change fares • Phonecard
2 Access control • Fenced yards • Entry phones • ID badges	6 Formal surveillance • Security guards • Burglar alarms • Speed cameras	10 Identifying property • Property marking • Vehicle licensing • Personal ID numbers for radios
3 Deflecting offenders • Tavern location • Street closures • Graffiti board	7 Surveillance by employees • Park attendants • Pay phone location • CCTV	11 Removing inducements • Graffiti cleaning • Rapid repair • 'Bum-proof' bench
4 Controlling facilitators • Gun controls • Credit card photo • Caller-ID	8 Natural surveillance • Street lighting • Defensible space • Neighbourhood watch	12 Rule setting • Customs declaration • Income tax returns • Hotel registration

Source: Clarke (1995: 109).

the effort', 'increasing the risk' and 'reducing the reward' were replaced respectively with 'increasing perceived effort', 'increasing perceived risks' and 'reducing anticipated rewards'[1]. In each case the amended heading highlights potential offender definitions of the situation. It is no longer that measures directly impact on potential offenders either by making it no longer possible for the event to occur (whatever the offender thinks) or by directly affecting the cost-benefit situation for offenders. Rather, the mechanism is one of changing prospective offenders' definitions of the situation, in terms of the likely reward, risk and effort that would be involved in committing the crime.

More recently, in addition to risk, effort and reward, two other types of situational cue have been identified. One of these relates to the removal of excuses and the other to the reduction in provocation. The former relates to the perceived moral status of an act at the point of its commission. Lights flashing speed limits are a case in point. These encourage the person tempted to speed to think twice about doing so, and many slow down. The latter refers to feelings that stimulate criminal acts, which are liable to be activated in some situations. Systems for dealing efficiently and fairly with customers waiting for taxis late at night, for example, are less likely to lead to feelings of frustration and consequent violence than a free-for-all contest to grab them as they become available. These types of situational cue may, with some effort, be incorporated into a rational choice framework. We may, thus, suffer painful cognitive dissonance (a form of emotional discomfiture where we are faced with contradictory impulses) if we behave in ways we know to be morally culpable and hence we are less likely to engage in those acts if reminded that they are inconsistent with our underlying moral principles. Also, if we are not provoked then the action that we would otherwise take will become relatively less rewarding as a release for our pent-up frustration. Indeed, Cornish and Clarke continue to emphasise rational choice as the basis for mechanisms underlying the ways in which situational measures change behaviour, incorporating into their schema provocation reduction and excuse removal. Others would take a different view. Though still accepting that the immediate situation is crucial to actions taken they would be inclined to argue that calculation of utilities, even in the weak sense described by Cornish and Clarke, does not capture all the ways in which actions are influenced. Moral and emotional matters, of the sort described by 'excuse removal' and 'provocation reduction' are real causal mechanisms *sui generis*, which operate alongside, but independently of, rational choice to influence behaviour (see Wortley 2001; Tilley 2004c).

Table 5.4 shows Cornish and Clarke's 25 techniques of crime prevention laid out under the five main headings, describing different ways in which situational measures may prevent crime: increase the effort, increase the risks, reduce the rewards, reduce provocations and remove excuses (Cornish and Clarke 2003).

Ekblom and Tilley (2000) have suggested that removing resources for crime comprises an important separate mechanism through which situational measures may prevent crime. Here the issue is not that of affecting offender choices, be they rational or otherwise, but of changing the offender's ability to commit particular crimes. Table 5.4 makes some reference to this, of course, in Box 5: 'Control tools/ weapons'. Ekblom and Tilley, however, argue that those minded to offend need to have the wherewithal to commit their intended crime at the point when the offence is contemplated, and that this offender-related situational attribute can usefully be distinguished from other types of situational attribute which are independent of offender capacities. The kinds of measures Ekblom and Tilley discuss include encouraging householders to keep ladders under lock and key to reduce their availability to burglars; clearing bottles from the street, to prevent their use as missiles; the use of biometric identifiers, to incapacitate the use of weapons by criminals; and the use of variations in crime prevention technique, to require offenders to carry more tools to overcome the obstacles they may encounter and to slow down the rate at which they can learn how to overcome predictable obstacles to crime.

Laycock (1985, 1997) has emphasised publicity related situational crime prevention mechanisms. In a study of property marking and domestic burglary in three South Wales villages, she argues that the effects were brought about by publicity rather than by property marking *per se*. A very high take-up rate was achieved amidst many efforts to promote the scheme, including door-to-door calls by police as well as carefully orchestrated media hype. Local offenders became convinced of the efficacy of the measures and were thereby persuaded not to commit burglaries in spite of the fact that real risks to them were not increased. This is partly reflected in Clarke's reference to *perceived* risk, effort and reward.

Felson and Clarke (1998) argue that opportunity can produce criminality in various ways. It is not just that the predisposed criminal may or may not find an opportunity, which they use if it is available. Rather, opportunity may itself stimulate criminality.

This suggests that it is mistaken to divide the population into offenders and non-offenders, the latter of whom may be thwarted with situational measures and mechanisms. Rather citizens with no special disposition to commit crime may be prompted to commit offences by virtue of the opportunity. Opportunity thus provides a temptation mechanism which may draw non-offenders into crime. By providing opportunities we may thereby create criminals. Felson and Clarke refer, among others, to a classic study, now 80 years old, in support of this view. Hartshorne and May (1928) had shown that schoolchildren given the opportunity to cheat in tests, to lie about the cheating and to steal from the puzzles used did so in large numbers. Few resisted the temptations. The children may have being acting rationally in that their utilities were maximised in the situation created by the experiment, which permitted rule-infraction. It may also be that their behaviour was reinforced by being rewarded. Behaviour that is found rewarding tends to be repeated. Felson and Clarke also refer to 'van Dyke chains', named after Jan van Dyke who described them. The idea is that one crime leads to another, where one repairs one's loss from a crime by committing another to replace the good stolen. Bicycles are an example. Trivially, the process can be observed in a restaurant where those sitting at a table with a missing item, say a glass or piece of cutlery, will often take a replacement from an adjacent table leaving a gap there which, in turn, is filled by taking the missing item from the next table and so on.

Side-effects

Crime as Opportunity had raised the issue of displacement. In the case of suicide it was found that a reduction in opportunities for using the gas supply were associated with a substantial overall fall in numbers of incidents. If there was displacement to other methods there was relatively little of it. In the case of steering column locks fitted to new cars there appeared to be displacement to the theft of older cars. Interest in displacement has continued but has been complemented by work on its more positive counterpart side-effect: diffusion of benefits. 'Diffusion of benefits' refers to the crime prevention effects that may be brought about beyond the operational range of crime prevention measures.

Six types of displacement have been identified: place, target, time, crime-type, technique or offender, or there may be any mix of these

Table 5.4 Twenty-five techniques of situational prevention

Increase the effort	Increase the risks	Reduce the rewards
1 Target harden • Steering column locks and immobilisers • Anti-robbery screens • Tamper-proof packaging	*6 Extend guardianship* • Taking routine precautions: go out in group at night, leave signs of occupancy, carry phone • 'Cocoon' neighbour-hood watch	*11 Conceal targets* • Off-street parking • Gender-neutral phone directories • Unmarked bullion trucks
2 Control access • Entry phones • Electronic card access • Baggage screening	*7 Assist natural surveillance* • Improve street lighting • Defensible space designs • Support whistleblowers	*12 Remove targets* • Removable car radio • Women's refuges • Pre-paid cards for pa phones
3 Screen exits • Ticket needed for exit • Export documents • Electronic merchandise tags	*8 Reduce anonymity* • Taxi driver IDs • 'How's my driving?' decals • School uniforms	*13 Identify property* • Property marking • Vehicle licensing and parts marking • Cattle branding
4 Deflect offenders • Street closures • Separate bathrooms for women • Disperse pubs	*9 Utilise place managers* • CCTV for double-deck buses • Two clerks for convenience stores • Reward vigilance	*14 Disrupt markets* • Monitor pawn shops • Controls on classifiec ads • License street vendoɪ
5 Control tools/ weapons • 'Smart' guns • Disabling stolen cell phones • Restrict spray paint sales for juveniles	*10 Strengthen formal surveillance* • Red light cameras • Burglar alarms • Security guards	*15 Deny benefits* • Ink merchandise tag: • Graffiti cleaning • Speed humps

Reduce provocations	Remove excuses
16 Reduce frustrations and stress • Efficient queues and polite service • Expanded seating • Soothing music/muted lights	*21 Set rules* • Rental agreements • Harassment codes • Hotel registration
17 Avoid disputes • Separate enclosures for rival fans • Reduce crowding in pubs • Fixed cab fares	*22 Post instructions* • 'No Parking' • 'Private Property' • 'Extinguish camp fires'
18 Reduce emotional arousal • Controls on violent pornography • Enforce good behaviour on soccer field • Prohibit racial slurs	*23 Alert conscience* • Roadside speed display boards • Signatures for customs declarations • 'Shoplifting is stealing'
19 Neutralise peer pressure • 'Idiots drink and drive' • 'It's OK to say No' • Disperse troublemakers at school	*24 Assist compliance* • Easy library checkout • Public lavatories • Litter bins
20 Discourage imitation • Rapid repair of vandalism • V-chips in TVs • Censor details of modus operandi	*25 Control drugs and alcohol* • Breathalysers in pubs • Server intervention • Alcohol-free events

(Reppetto 1976). That is, a thwarted crime of the same type may be committed elsewhere, or against another target, or using a different technique; or an entirely different type of offence may be committed by the same offender; or a different offender may commit the crime. Or there may be some mix of these, for example a different crime at a different place and time, using a different technique, may be committed. In practice there are complex measurement problems in capturing all forms of displacement that might occur. Detecting more distant displacement in terms of place and crime type as they spread across a wide area becomes more or less impossible. Most has been achieved in the measurement of more obvious forms of displacement, in terms of nearby places and similar crimes. These would appear to offer next-best choices for the offender. Empirical studies have generally concluded that fears of displacement have been exaggerated (Hesseling 1994). In some cases none has been detected, and complete displacement appears to be very rare within the limits of practical measurement. Clarke (2005) explains why displacement would seem unlikely in some cases. He refers to the use of slugs in the London underground in place of proper payment of fares. Slugs to replace 50 pence coins could be made easily by wrapping foil round 10 pence coins. When slugs also appeared for £1 coins local officials believed it was a function of displacement. Clarke suggests that this is unlikely. It is much more difficult to make a working slug for a £1 coin. To do so requires access to and use of metal working facilities. Moreover the underground stations where the two types of slug were found differed, suggesting different populations of offenders.

Diffusions of benefit have been quite widely found. An early example related to CCTV in car parks. Poyner (2002) found in a study at Surrey University that crimes were reduced not only at the three car parks that were covered but also at one nearby that was not covered. Since then many other examples have been found. Among the most interesting is referred to as an 'anticipatory benefit'. This is where crime drops occur before crime prevention measures become operational. Of course, this may sometimes be no more than a regression to the mean effect (the reversion in a local area to more normal rates following a spike, as explained Chapter 4). However Smith *et al.* (2002) find that it occurs frequently and may also result from publicity of the sort discussed by Laycock. News of a crime prevention initiative changes the perceptions offenders have of the risk and effort required and they adjust their behaviour accordingly. On quite a large scale Bowers and Johnson (2003b) found this looking across 21 domestic burglary prevention projects funded through the British Crime Reduction Programme.

Displacement and diffusion of benefits effects can, of course, both happen at the same time. The net effect of a situational crime prevention initiative comprises the direct preventive effects plus the diffusion of benefits effects minus the displacement effects. Suggestions for the measurement of this are found in Bowers and Johnson (2003a).

Over time, offenders are liable to adapt to new challenges presented by situational measures. This needs to be distinguished from displacement and diffusion of benefits which occur in relation to specific crime events at a particular place and time. Adaptation takes place over the longer term. Paul Ekblom has written about an evolutionary 'arms race' in which those trying to prevent crime and those with an interest in committing it are pitted against one another (Ekblom 1997). In relation to car theft, for example, new locks have led to adaptations by offenders to overcome the new obstacles to crime. Eventually points are reached where adaptation becomes much more difficult or expensive. The immobiliser has proven a more significant obstacle to theft of vehicles than many previous techniques (Brown 2004). Offenders adapted more easily in learning to overcome steering column locks.

Related theories of crime and crime prevention

There are important sister theories to situational crime prevention. These are concerned likewise to explain crime event patterns rather than criminality and they have been found useful in informing crime prevention, even though they were mostly not developed with crime prevention as the central focus quite as was the case with situational crime prevention. The following provides quite an extended account of routine activities theory which has a high level of generality and has also been highly influential in crime prevention practice. Other related approaches can be dealt with only briefly.

Routine activity theory

Routine activity theory was developed in the US by Laurence Cohen and Marcus Felson and presented in a major, much-cited article on American crime trends in 1979 (Cohen and Felson 1979). The theory has since been substantially elaborated and applied further by Felson (2002). It has had a major impact on criminological thinking as well as informing crime prevention initiatives. Though emerging at much the same time as *Crime as Opportunity*, the origins of routine activity theory were independent of the British work. There were no cross references in the 1970s between the work on either side of the Atlantic.

According to routine activity theory, as it was originally formulated, for a direct contact predatory offence to take place three conditions must converge in space and time:

- A likely offender – someone liable to commit a crime;

- A suitable target – a person or thing that the likely offender will focus on; and

- Absence of a capable guardian – someone who is able to protect the target.

Put this way the theory might seem to suggest, implausibly, that classes of likely offender, suitable target and capable guardian can be clearly marked out from one another. In fact, of course there are more and less likely offenders, more and less suitable targets and more or less capable guardians. Moreover, *guardian capability* may be less important than *guardianship credibility*. A conscientious, fit, trained, and intelligent body-guard, for example, may provide pretty capable guardianship and make some crimes in practice very hard to commit. However, at least at some points in time and in some places, poorly functioning and dummy closed-circuit television appears to have had sufficient credibility, while no real capability, to provide adequate guardianship so far as many potential offenders go.

Less elegantly, but more accurately, routine activity theory may be restated in the following way: direct contact predatory crime requires the convergence in space and time of:

- A sufficiently likely offender;

- A suitable enough target; and

- Absence of sufficiently credible guardianship.

Later refinements to routine activity theory have added presence or absence of an 'intimate handler' to the conditions relevant to criminal acts (Felson 1986). An intimate handler is some significant other in front of whom a likely offender will be reluctant to commit a crime. A disapproving mother, for example, may comprise an intimate handler whose presence in conditions otherwise conducive to a criminal act will avert its commission because of her influence on the likely offender. The mother's role is different from that of the credible guardian in that she does not prevent the crime by protecting the suitable target but rather by disapproving the behaviour of the potential offender who is concerned with her good opinion. Intimate handlers may, of course, also provoke criminal action where undertaking it is deemed by the offender to increase the regard in which they are held. Peer groups members are liable to play this role where they egg on one of their number to behave criminally.

At first sight routine activity theory can seem banal, even tautologous. Is it not obvious, almost as a matter of definition, that the three conditions are needed for most predatory crimes to take place, and that intimate handlers may also be significant? Perhaps, but the real payoff comes when the implications are spun out for explaining crime patterns. Many of the post-war crime patterns in western countries can be understood quite simply in terms of changes in supply, distribution and movement of relatively suitable targets, relatively likely offenders and relatively plausible guardians. For example, the mass production and consumption of easily transportable, desirable consumer durables has provided an ample, continuously replenished, supply and wide availability of crime targets for which there is a ready stolen goods market. The increased participation of women in the paid labour market, as well as reductions in the size of families, have reduced the level of credible guardianship in many homes. Decreases in domestic chores for young people and reductions in levels of shared family activity have freed young people, who are those most likely to commit and be targets of criminal activity, to spend time together away from the guardianship and intimate handling that are furnished by parents in and around the home.

There is an old Slovenian proverb that has it that 'even the bishop is tempted by the open strongbox'. Rightly or wrongly, this suggests that few if any pass a point in the scale of offender likelihood where no crime would ever be contemplated. Gabor (1994) provides a host of evidence to substantiate the spirit of the Slovenian proverb. This rather general potentiality for involvement in criminal acts may explain why proponents of routine activities theory have tended to concentrate on target suitability and guardianship in their discussions of prevention. And it is the supply, distribution and movement of suitable targets and credible guardianship that provides patterns of opportunity for crime.

There is, though, a further refinement to routine activity theory that is relevant to opportunity, which helps us get a little further in understanding what makes for a likely offender. This relates to the capabilities of the potential offender, which were mentioned earlier in this chapter (Ekblom and Tilley 2000). Some crimes require little or nothing by way of specific capability. The bishop faced by the open strongbox, requires no special tools or abilities. Some container to carry or to conceal the swag is all that might be needed. But other actions require capabilities of one sort or another, in order that the offender disposed to commit a crime is able to do so. One of the main reasons homicide rates are so much higher in the US than in England and Wales has to do with the much readier availability of firearms in the US, which substantially increases the capability for one person to murder another. It was the piping of toxic domestic gas to households that had supplied potentially suicidal folk in England and Wales with the ready wherewithal to take their own lives. The motor car provides both a target for and a useful resource improving the capability to commit many offences. Thus, to sufficiently likely offenders, suitable enough targets, absence of sufficiently credible guardian and absence of sufficiently significant and censorious handler, we need to add adequate capabilities as conditions enabling a predatory crime to take place. Moreover the supply, distribution and movement of all five will determine the patterns of convergence across space and time and hence the crime patterns generated. Furthermore, except for the disposition of the potential offender (what they would like to do or to get) they are all matters of contingent opportunity. At least in principle, policies and practices orientated to modifying these are possible and this is the point at which the theory meets situational crime prevention.

Spatial and environmental theories of crime

C. Ray Jeffery (1971) believed that the environment determines behaviour, including that which is criminal. Influenced by the behavioural psychology of B.F. Skinner, Jeffery took the view that the consequences of actions cause their repetition or non-repetition. If the environment were to be designed in ways that pre-empted (or were less conducive to) criminal actions that would be reinforced when successful, then there would be fewer crimes. Instead of weak rational choice as the major mechanisms lying behind choices to commit crime, Jeffery stressed the reinforcement of behaviour as the key determinant of crime. The environment offers opportunities and reinforcements that could be modified to reduce crime. It is to C. Ray Jeffery that we owe the term Crime Prevention through Environmental Design (CPTED). In practice that term is now used more widely to describe efforts to design and redesign buildings and neighbourhoods in ways that will reduce opportunity without necessarily embracing Jeffery's underlying psychological theory. Some of the the police specialists in crime prevention mentioned in Chapter 2, notably Crime Prevention Design Advisers, deliver advice rooted in CPTED.

It was Oscar Newman (1972) who coined the CPTED-related and popularly used phrase 'defensible space'. Fostering defensible space comprises a means of controlling crime. Increasing defensible space involves improving territoriality (the ways in which building design may encourage a proprietary and hence protective orientation to areas which residents identify as theirs); surveillance (the scope buildings offer for watching over the relevant areas); image (the avoidance of stigma being attached to the development); and environment (safe nearby areas). Alice Coleman (1990) followed this up with a 'design disadvantage index' which provided a metric for features of the design of housing that would encourage crime. The creation of defensible space comprises a means of increasing difficulty and risk for prospective offenders.

Crime pattern theory is most associated with the work of Paul and Patricia Brantingham (1981, 1984, 2008). It describes and explains the geographical distribution of crime. It does so by looking at routine activities and at the 'awareness spaces' that prospective offenders have. Crimes will be distributed according to the supply of suitable targets within the awareness spaces of those minded to offend. Routine movements take people between their main zones of activity, typically home, school, work and recreation ('nodes'). Their awareness spaces will relate to the routes between these and the surrounding areas ('paths'). These awareness spaces will include some places that provide suitable targets for crime. Known 'edges' lying at the fringes of particular land uses will tend to suffer high rates of crime, in offering spaces where strangers are not recognised. The routines of prospective offenders will provide some likely times for crime, as well as locations for it. Crime will, thus, tend to be concentrated in times and places that lie within offender awareness spaces, where there are ample targets for crime. In addition, offenders will tend, they suggest, to avoid committing crimes in places close to home where they risk being recognised.

The Brantinghams also suggest that some places may act as crime attractors, some as crime generators and some as both (Brantingham and Brantingham 1995). Crime generators are those places with opportunities for crime that many, including some who happen to be offenders, will encounter. Crime attractors are those places with known suitable targets for crime which are visited by offenders with crime in mind. Shopping malls act as generators and attractors. Hodgkinson and Tilley (2007) suggest that places with a large supply of victims unaware of potential risk, such as major transport hubs, act as attractors for personal crime. The affinities between crime pattern theory and routine activity theory are obvious. Crime pattern theory has been used not only to inform the targeting of preventive efforts but has also been developed for the geographical profiling of prolific offenders whose likely routine activities can be gauged from the distribution of their offences.

Broken windows

'Broken windows' theory, as formulated by Wilson and Kelling (1982), has enjoyed a great deal of press coverage. Much policy and practice has been put in place in its name, though not always quite as intended by its authors. Broken windows is avowedly not a manifesto for 'zero-tolerance' policing as has sometimes been assumed, although it is not difficult to see how and why it has come to be interpreted that way where there have been calls for get tough policing policies. The key tenet of broken windows is that if small signs of disorder are allowed to build up, a permissive environment for antisocial behaviour may seem to develop. A point may be reached at which crime may spiral out of control, when no-one seems to care about it and where marginal increases are no longer noticed. It then becomes very difficult to recover the situation. Lessening obvious signs of disorder is one step in recovering a sense of order. The rapid removal of graffiti was pioneered in the New York subway system. Those producing it were deprived of the pleasure that came from seeing their work on display: carriages were removed as soon as graffiti reappeared on those that had been cleaned. Eventually the whole stock was clean and the appearance of new graffiti tailed off. The mechanism was the situational one of *reduced reward*. This, though, formed part of a strategy to remove those general signs of disorder that were deemed, according to broken windows theory, to foster high levels of crime in some places.

Links to other crime prevention approaches

There are points at which situational crime prevention meets those approaches discussed in previous chapters, albeit that its distinctive focus is on crime events and the immediate precursors to them. One example relates to incapacitation. It clearly works by making crime outside prison more difficult for those who are incarcerated. But there are other examples too.

Tillyer and Kennedy (2008) have argued that 'focused deterrence' complements situational crime prevention by embedding various situational crime prevention mechanisms, albeit that it is offender-based. Focused deterrence was the approach adopted in the Boston Gun Project discussed in Chapter 2, which was concerned with serious gang-related youth violence. Focused deterrence involves identifying the key individuals generating a specific crime problem so that they could be targeted by criminal justice agencies on the basis of what is known about their general criminal conduct. That they are then open to targeting on the basis of what is known of their behaviour is then advertised directly to them, stressing the real increased chances of sanction they face if they or their associates misbehave in the ways specified. *Real and perceived risk* is thereby increased. Then, the rationales that offenders characteristically give for the criminal behaviour in question are undermined by challenging face-to-face the 'narratives' they use to justify their acts in the company of significant others from the community, as well as formal agency members. Offenders are thereby confronted with the implausibility of their rationalisations for what they do, and with the disapproval of those about whose opinions they care deeply. This comprises *excuse removal*. The key individuals who go through this process have an interest in discouraging the targeted behaviour of their associates, as they will not want to draw attention from the police, who they know to have evidence that could convict them. This comprises *reward and provocation reduction. Effort is increased* to the extent to which the conditions created make it more difficult to recruit co-offenders to commit the specified crimes because of the increased risk that they know they face. The meetings also include offers of help in exiting the criminal lifestyle in which offenders are immersed, by *offering resources* and also *removing excuses* for committing crime for lack of alternative opportunities.

Crime prevention that focuses on trajectories and turning points may also complement situational crime prevention. It is less concerned with root causes than the emergence of situations in individuals' biographies where the opportunities for crime may widen. Changing schools, moving house, family breakdown, entering or leaving local authority care facilities, and forming or leaving a partnership, for example, all affect the risk, effort, reward, provocation and availability of excuses and resources for committing crime. New places, new peer groups, new family members, and new routines create changed opportunity structures that may take some people away from crime careers and steer others towards them. Preventive interventions by schools, social services and probation services which target these points in individuals' lives are not necessarily addressing 'root causes' of criminality, if by this we mean individual and social pathologies. Rather, they may produce their positive effects to the extent to which they reduce or remove what might otherwise furnish new opportunities for crime for those whose circumstances change.

Methodology/practice

The standard methodology for responsive situational crime prevention is action research. Clarke (2005) describes five stages:

- Collection of data about the nature of the specific crime problem;
- Analysis of the situational conditions permitting or facilitating the commission of the crimes;
- Systematic study of possible means to block opportunities, including their costs;
- Implementation of the most promising in terms of feasibility and costs;
- Monitoring results and dissemination of experience.

This action research approach is embraced in problem-oriented policing (POP) (Goldstein 1979, 1990), which often uses a SARA process to describe what is undertaken (Eck and Spelman 1987). SARA refers to Scanning, Analysis, Response, and Assessment, the first three of which clearly have affinities with Clarke's first three bullet points and the last of which combines Clarke's final two points. Ekblom (1988) provides a neat diagram (Figure 5.2) which has the benefit of showing feedback, a process which often occurs throughout the course of action research problem-solving.

POP[2] has provided an important vehicle for delivering situational crime prevention. This has included collaboration between the major figures developing each of them: Ronald Clarke and Herman Goldstein (Clarke and Goldstein 2003a, 2003b). POP stresses the importance of identifying recurrent problems, critiquing existing responses and working out what might otherwise be done to address them, assessing effectiveness rigorously, and then disseminating lessons learned. In principle POP allows for any ethical approach to reducing crime, but it has particular affinities with situational crime prevention. This is in part because of the similar action research methodology and in part because situational crime prevention has provided a suite of practical mechanisms that can be activated when

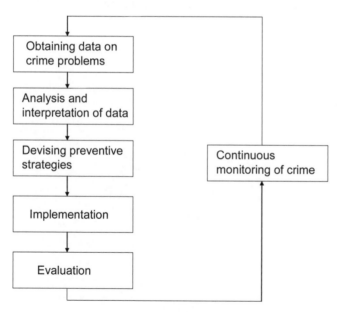

Figure 5.2 Ekblom's preventive process

the police are faced with persistent crime problems which have been found unresponsive to conventional police patrol and enforcement strategies.

POP has made extensive use of the 'problem analysis triangle' as a means of analysing problems and working out options to address them (see Clarke and Eck 2003). In practice, as Figure 5.3 shows, two triangles have come to be used, the one embedded in the other. The inner triangle is used to identify conditions generating problems and the outer what might be done to remove or counteract them. The affinities with routine activity theory are obvious. The offender equates to the motivated offender, the place to the absence of capable guardianship, and the target/victim to the suitable target. The presence of suitable handling may act as a disincentive to the offender, the introduction of a place manager provides for surveillance increasing risk, and guardianship provides for reduced availability of the suitable target.

In addition to action research and its expression in problem-oriented policing, situational crime prevention is also used in efforts to design out crime before problems surface. Ken Pease has pointed out that it has often been necessary to 'retrofit' solutions to problems that could have been pre-empted with more effort at the design stage (Pease 1997).

Figure 5.3   The problem analysis triangle (PAT)

Three broad areas of design have been identified: design of places, design of products and design of systems. Each may inadvertently create crime opportunities. Each can be configured to minimise them. Places vulnerable to crime where designs could reduce levels may include, for example, housing estates, city centres, shops, universities, schools or bars. Hot products, which could be designed to lessen the crime that would otherwise be expected, may include, for example, mobile phones, bicycles, credit cards, coins, bank notes, televisions or satellite navigation devices. Systems where crime may otherwise be produced may relate, for example, to returned goods in shops, queues for taxis, staff selection and deployment, and financial auditing. In all cases patterns of risk, effort, reward, excusability and provocation will be produced that will either foster or inhibit crime.

Barry Webb (2005) has shown how all three design domains have been relevant to vehicle crime. He shows that design of cars can reduce theft. Those with more security are stolen less. But people often neglect to activate the preventive measures, clearly reducing their impact. Where their operation is automatic, as with immobilisers activated when the ignition key is removed or with centralised locking, the effect increases substantially. Car parking design is also found to affect rates of vehicle crime. For example, unmanned car parks with pay and display, especially surface (non multi-storey) ones used by commuters, are most risky. Exit barriers control theft of but not theft from vehicles. CCTV has been retro-fitted in many cases where car parks suffer high rates of crime but the effects appear to be short-lived where they depend on the impression, but not the reality, of increased risk to the offender. Webb also shows how the design of provisions for parking at home is strongly related to the risk of car theft. Those parking in communal bays compared to those parking on private driveways, in otherwise similar housing estates, had been found to suffer five times the rate of theft of cars (40 vs 8 per 1,000 households) and two and a half times the rate of theft from vehicles (39 vs 16 per 1,000 households). Housing estates can be better or worse designed to prevent vehicle crime. Webb finally shows how the vehicle registration and licensing system can be designed in ways that may either foster or inhibit theft of vehicles as well as other vehicle-related crimes. Alongside Smith and Laycock (Webb et al. 2004), he lists a range of system design modifications for Britain and the mechanisms through which these could reduce vehicle crime (Table 5.5). Webb et al. also note that the more robust registration

129

Table 5.5   System redesign and vehicle crime

Measure	Mechanism	Expected outcome
Requirement for vehicle registration document to re-license	Increases difficulty in selling stolen vehicles	Reduced theft for financial gain
Keeper liability for vehicle until scapped or registered by another	Increases difficulty in stealing and re-use vehicle identities	Reduced theft for financial gain
Harmonisation across EU	Helps identify stolen imported/exported vehicles, increasing risk	Reduced theft for financial gain
Increased enforcement through ANPR (automated number plate recognition)	Increases risk when driving stolen vehicle	Reduced theft for financial gain and temporary use
Real time linkage of various motor vehicle databases	Increases difficulty in stealing identity of scrapped vehicles	Reduced theft for financial gain
'Chips' in vehicles with roadside readers for checking	Increases risk when driving stolen vehicle	Reduced theft for financial gain and temporary use

Note: Adapted from Webb *et al*. (2004: 72).

arrangements in Germany are associated with a much lower rate of vehicle crime than in Britain.

Design-developments, in response to anticipated crime harvests that could be expected in the absence of forethought, clearly requires something other than the action research methodology used in problem-oriented policing, which is largely responsive to issues that have arisen. To be generalised such an approach would require a 'greening' of crime prevention, whereby it becomes a routine consideration when new developments are contemplated, be they to do with products, places or systems. Continuous scanning of developments is required where their potential to produce crime consequences is routine, with attendant thought about ways in which preventive designs can be built in, maximising legitimate consumer use while thwarting would-be offenders and meeting other design desiderata (see Ekblom 2005).

Assessment

Situational crime prevention came to be advocated as policy in the mid to late 1970s in response to the apparent failures – of the welfare state, of standard policing activities and of efforts at rehabilitation – to stem the then steadily increasing crime rates (Tilley 1993a). The environment was ripe for fresh thinking. The Home Office Research Unit was ideally placed to provide it. Opportunity theory promised a new means of addressing crime problems and the results of situational crime prevention initiatives suggested that it could be effective. The Home Office set up a Crime Prevention Unit in 1983 which was largely (though not exclusively) concerned to find opportunities to put in place situational measures to prevent crime. A series of initiatives followed alongside a programme of follow-on research within the Home Office, but elsewhere also, some of which has been discussed in this chapter. By now there is a very substantial number of studies showing that situational crime prevention can prevent crime. The most recent count identified more than 200 of them (Guerette 2008).

This has not meant that other approaches to the prevention of crime have been abandoned. Situational crime prevention has also been widely criticised on the following grounds:

- It merely displaces crime;
- It fails to address root causes of crime;
- It is guilty of victim-blaming;
- It leads to a fortress society;
- It is socially divisive;
- It threatens civil liberties.

These are important objections that deserve to be taken seriously, but for the most part relate less to situational crime prevention *per se* than to particular applications of it. Let us look briefly at each in turn.

Situational crime prevention merely displaces crime. The evidence suggests that this is not the case. To the extent to which displacement processes take place as a matter of course, as offenders choose crimes, locations, methods for their offending, everyday situational crime prevention practices will of course affect the distribution of crime. This means that those better placed to use such measures as part of their everyday life may be diverting crimes towards those less able to do so. With regard to public policy, situational measures aimed at high-rate targets and places can be expected to produce a net reduction in crime but also will tend to redress a balance of displacement effects that have tended to advantage those most able and most likely to try reduce their own risks. In regard to property crime this latter group will include the better off who have both more to steal and more resources for self-protection. If their efforts produce displacement it may be to the worse off, who have less to steal but who also have fewer resources to devote to improvements in security. Public policies targeting the relatively poor suffering relatively high levels of crime could, however, be expected, insofar as they produce a displacement side-effect, to divert crime back towards the better off. In this way situational measures would become a vehicle for distributive justice. Displacement clearly matters, but its risks have been overstated. Diffusion of benefits appears to be a more common side-effect. Moreover, not all displacement is malign, although some of it, of course, can be. Public policies that may displace from less to more serious crimes and from the less vulnerable to the more vulnerable are clearly to be avoided, but this is not an argument against situational crime prevention, only against particular ways in which it might be applied.

Situational crime prevention fails to address root causes of crime. There are strong arguments that opportunity is one root cause of crime. Even if situational crime prevention does not deal with all root causes of crime, there is compelling evidence that crimes can be prevented without removing them. As previous chapters have shown it is very difficult to remove root individual and social causes of criminality. Moreover success tends to be achieved only in the long term and in the short term situational measures can reduce crime relatively quickly. This is not an argument against other forms of crime prevention, only that situational measures have an important part to play.

Situational crime prevention is guilty of victim-blaming. Ultimately, of course, we assume that offenders are to be held to account (and hence 'blamed') for the crimes they commit. That said, it may be reasonable to expect others to accept some responsibility where their designs of place, product or system predictably put them (and third parties) at unnecessarily high risk. It may, thus, be that some victims do share responsibility for the crimes they suffer. If shops sell goods in ways that facilitate shop theft then it is far from clear that they are free from blame. The rest of us bear the costs of processing the offenders through the criminal justice system. Moreover if the easy crimes committed in supermarkets inculcate criminality there are further social costs for which the shops might reasonably be expected to take some responsibility. Much situational crime prevention, however, does not involve any blaming at all. Caller-ID systems to deal with obscene phone calls, for example, do not allocate blame to the victim, nor do queuing arrangements designed to reduce anger and provocation. There is a risk, of course, that victims may feel that they are blamed when this is unjustified. The example often raised is that of young women wearing short skirts being blamed for the sexual harassment they experience. This does not invalidate situational crime prevention as a process, even if it suggests that some applications are mis-directed or that the measures which might be suggested would involve sacrificing more important principles such as the right to walk unmolested while being free to wear whatever clothes one wants. Issues of responsibility and competency in crime prevention are discussed further in the next chapter.

Situational crime prevention leads to a fortress society. Some physical security measures are ugly, but not all of them are visible, for example bank vaults. Many of those that are visible are innocuous, for example locked doors, and some that are visible and sometimes ugly can also be made attractive, for example decorative shutters. Not all situational measures involve security measures, for example the rapid removal of freshly applied graffiti. The selection of situational measures involves more than their technical efficacy. Aesthetic issues, among others, have also to be considered. That this is the case does not invalidate the situational approach to crime prevention.

Situational crime prevention is socially divisive in promoting selfishness and mistrust. Although in practice children are at greatest risk from those they already know, 'stranger danger' attempts to protect children by reducing their availability to predatory adults. It does so by inculcating mistrust. For many parents the reduction in risk to their own children justifies the creation of mistrust, even though well-meaning individuals will be treated as if they were untrustworthy. The downside, in terms of situational crime prevention, is that adults come to fear that they could be defined as paedophiles if they speak to children they do not know: their potential as capable guardians of distressed children is, thus, weakened (Furedi and Bristow 2008). That sub-set of children in whom mistrust is not successfully inculcated face especially increased risk from predatory strangers if they are deprived of everyday strangers' solicitude. Concern for the welfare of strangers, be they children or adults, will clearly include their vulnerability to crime. One characteristic of a good society would seem, to many of us, to be that strangers intervene when others appear to be in difficulty. Offenders' expectations that passers-by will intervene, if they try to commit a crime, comprises a situational crime prevention measure that is compromised where safety and security are deemed purely private matters. In this way trust and social solidarity are required for some spontaneous situational crime prevention mechanisms to operate. If, for whatever reason, that trust in others which is needed for these mechanisms to operate is undermined, private means of protection may understandably be chosen. But this is not intrinsic to situational crime prevention. It may, though, be that mistrust (from whatever source) begets divisive forms of situational crime prevention. Moreover, once divisive situational crime prevention methods are in place mutual mistrust is reinforced as the social and physical distance between individuals and communities grows.

Situational crime prevention threatens civil liberties. The main recent source of this concern has been the proliferation of closed circuit television (CCTV) cameras in Britain. Substantial government funding has been made available for public space CCTV systems since the early 1990s. There have been technical improvements in the images captured, in their storage and in their retrieval. The collection of this material may certainly jeopardise rights to privacy. The concerns for privacy raised by CCTV extend to the use of biometrics more generally as a method of making people more identifiable and thereby making risks to them increase if they behave criminally. Earlier concerns with privacy were expressed when tachographs were fitted in the cabs of lorries to check that drivers were not speeding or driving for such long periods that they became dangerously tired. Potential threats to privacy grow with increasingly powerful surveillance technologies (Royal Academy of Engineering 2007). In particular circumstances some sacrifice in privacy may be warranted, as argued by Newburn and Hayman (2002) in relation to CCTV in police custody suites. There are clearly trade-offs where crime risks are reduced but at the expense of civil liberties. This neither means that those technologies may never be justified nor, of course does it comprise a general argument against situational crime prevention, much of which does not involve threats to civil liberties at all. For example the provision of separate lavatories for men and women increases, rather than decreases, privacy.

Conclusion

It is clear that situational crime prevention can produce falls in crime. It is equally clear that it does not do so by providing a few silver bullets that will cut all crime at a stroke. Situational crime prevention requires tailored identification of measures that are relevant to particular subsets of offences that are sufficiently alike. With regard to existing crime problems, therefore, situational crime prevention offers a painstaking piecemeal approach. With regard to the pre-emption of future crime problems, situational crime prevention provides a set of principles that could help prevent crime problems surfacing and the need then to look for retrofit solutions. The range of measures and mechanisms included within situational crime prevention is wide. All relate to the immediate conditions that face the prospective offender, but these conditions are diverse and may be altered in ways relevant to crime commission in many different ways. The choice of situational measure is partly a matter of cost and efficacy, of course, but normative considerations are also important.

Situational crime prevention lacks the ideological pull of other approaches. It lacks the punitiveness that is called for in much common-sense criminology. It also lacks the sympathy called for in other criminologies, which see offenders as victims of their biology or the disadvantaged social conditions they have endured. Situational crime prevention sees us all as potential offenders, even if the levels of our disposition vary. It also tends to explain a great deal of crime by reference to developments we generally welcome (such as increasing wealth and technological progress), rather than by invoking underlying social pathologies. This is a counterintuitive position. It does not endear the approach to politicians, the public or to many conventional criminologists. It does not, however, stop all from making routine use of situational crime prevention in their personal or political lives!

What situational crime prevention offers, which is rare indeed in the social sciences, is a cumulative research and practice programme that has been sustained for over 30 years.

Exercises

1 List all the situational crime prevention measures you encounter one day when you go into town.

2 List all the situational (opportunity reducing) measures you take in a day to reduce your own crime risk or that of your family.

3 Using the lists of what you notice and what you do, which raise problems of civil liberties and which do not do so? Explain your answers.

4 Assuming that nothing you noticed was in place and that you (and others) took none of the precautions you listed, what do you think would happen to crime levels and patterns, and why?

5 Pretend you are a generalist criminal interested in acquisitive crime. List all the opportunities you notice. Which would you prioritise and why? What would need to have been different to put you off going through with the crime? Compare your findings with those of others.

6 Under what circumstances is situational crime prevention inequitable? What would make it more equitable?

Further reading

Brief and accessible accounts of opportunity reducing approaches, by some of the leading authorities in the field, can be found in Wortley, R. and Mazerolle, L. (2008) *Environmental Criminology and Crime Analysis*. Cullompton: Willan Publishing.

A step by step guide to working out what is needed and how to do and evaluate opportunity reducing approaches in the context of problem-oriented policing and partnership is Clarke, R. and Eck, J. (2003) *Become a Problem-Solving Crime Analyst: In 55 Small Steps*. London: Jill Dando Institute of Crime Science.

The Crime Prevention Studies series includes a large number of papers about theory, practice and policy in situational crime prevention. Early volumes can be accessed at www.popcenter.org.

Notes

1 *Crime as Opportunity* had recognised the need to sort out perceived and actual opportunity, saying, 'reconciling the objectively important component of opportunity with the subjectivist claim that, in the last resort, opportunities are only perceived opportunities, is a problem that remains to be tackled.' (Mayhew *et al.* 1976: 7). This continues to be a problem.
2 The term problem-oriented partnership is used more often now in Britain to reflect the significance and statutory basis of crime reduction partnerships (see Bullock *et al.* 2006). The methodology used is identical.

Chapter 6

Implementation

Crime prevention initiatives can sometimes fail because of weaknesses in the underlying theory: the problem was not what it was thought to be; the measures were incapable of producing the effects that were hoped for; or the conditions were not of a kind favourable to the measures producing the initiative's objectives. Crime prevention initiatives can also sometimes fail because they were not implemented properly: no measures were put in place; the planned measures were not put in place; or the planned measures were put in place so poorly that they could not have an impact on the problem. Of course crime prevention initiatives can sometimes fail finally because of weaknesses both in theory and in their execution: here, they are doubly flawed. Success depends on a good enough theory and strong enough implementation.

The previous four chapters focused on theory. This one focuses on implementation: the messy business of translating theory into practice. Successive studies have highlighted problems in getting measures put in place (Hope and Murphy 1983; Laycock and Tilley 1995b; Bullock and Tilley 2003b; Homel *et al.* 2004; Bullock 2007). It has become clear that effective crime prevention depends on understanding and being able to overcome a range of implementation hurdles. Failures to appreciate difficulties in implementation lie at the heart of some major crime prevention programme disasters, and failures to work out methods of overcoming fully-appreciated difficulties lie at the heart of decisions leading to weak and short-term crime reduction strategies.

Two main sections follow, each of which deals with a different major implementation problem. The first concerns competency and responsibility. How can those individuals, agencies and organisations that are *competent* to take effective crime prevention action be persuaded that they should accept *responsibility* for doing so? And what are the limits of their responsibilities? The second concerns delivery. By what means is it possible to ensure that the measures planned for a crime prevention strategy are put in place as intended?

Competency and responsibility

A useful distinction can be made between responsibility and competency in crime prevention (Engstad and Evans 1980; Laycock 2004; Laycock and Webb 2000). Competency refers to the scope to act in ways that may lessen (or increase) the chances that crimes will take place. Responsibility refers to the expectations formally or informally bestowed on and accepted for controlling crime. Table 6.1 shows the main approaches to crime prevention discussed earlier and an indication of who seems to be held responsible in each case and also who has competency in principle. It is clear that those ordinarily bestowed principal responsibility represent only a small sub-set of those who are competent to prevent crime.

What some have termed a process of 'responsibilisation' has occurred over the past couple of decades (Garland 2001). The presumption that the police, in conjunction with the criminal justice system more generally, could sensibly be bestowed major responsibility for controlling crime has lost plausibility in the eyes of all but the most naïve. The term responsibilisation is rather uglier than the phenomenon, and the process less new than it may at first appear. In the case of citizens, 're-responsibilisation' might be a better if even uglier term. The assumption that the professional police can and should be held accountable for our safety through the exercise of their enforcement powers is a distinctly modern one. The Statute of Winchester 1285, for example, formalised and strengthened historic citizen obligations to intervene and help in the event of crime, obligations that persisted for several more centuries (Rawlings 2003). In future 'responsibilising' the police at the expense of others may be looked back on as a quaint conceit that took hold for a while, encouraged perhaps by a new organisation with an interest in promoting its status and power.

139

Table 6.1 Major patterns of responsibility and competency for crime prevention

Main approaches	Major responsibility	Competency
Criminal justice	Police Prosecutor Courts Probation Prison	Victim Witness Police Prosecutor Courts Probation Prison
Individual	Individual Family	Individual Family School Peer group Health and social services Employers
Social	Local authority Government	Church Local authority Housing department Voluntary organisations Citizens
Situational	Police Local authority	Shops Manufacturers Distributors Developers Planners Banks Transport providers Government Individuals Households Parks Schools Trading standards Health and Social Services

Of course competencies will vary by crime type. Take theft of motor vehicles as an example.

- As individuals we may or may not steal cars; we may or may not be open to purchasing a car or car part known to be stolen; we may or may not lock our cars; we may or may not inform on a known car thief; we may or may not leave our keys available for anyone to pick up if they break into our house; we may or may not look for safe places to park our car; we may or may not report suspicious behaviour where a car theft may be taking place; we may or may not intervene if we see an offence in progress; we may or may not agree to make a statement or appear in court as a witness.

- As car park owners, we may provide few or many entry and exit points; we may or may not design the car park to enable surveillance from passers-by or nearby residents or businesses operating in or near the car park; we may have staffed exits or automatic exits; we may provide pay and display or barrier exits; we may provide strong or weak lighting; we may or may not install CCTV; and we may maintain and actively operate CCTV or we may not do so.

- As planners, we may provide for or require safe parking for residents' cars, for example in garages or drives, or we may fail to provide for parking or provide it in insecure locations with no natural surveillance; we may also provide more or fewer secure parking spots in city centres.

- As motor vehicle manufacturers, we may install more or fewer, better or worse security devices.

- As government or government agencies, we may or may not provide for and maintain registration arrangements that facilitate or inhibit the theft, movement, disappearance and reappearance of stolen vehicles with new identities.

- As criminal justice policy-makers and practitioners, we may or may not prioritise theft of vehicles; we may or may not examine stolen vehicles for physical evidence; we may or may not follow up suspects; we may or may not prosecute suspects; we may give heavier or more lenient sentences; we may or may not provide services aimed at rehabilitation.

- As insurance companies we may provide greater or fewer incentives and disincentives for drivers to maximise the security of their vehicles or to contrive the appearance of vehicle theft in pursuit of fraudulent insurance claims.

The range of people, agencies and organisations with some competence to prevent theft of motor vehicles is very wide. A key question for those trying to reduce crime is that of persuading those who are competent to contribute to crime prevention that they should do so.

'Sticks, carrots and sermons' comprise one way of classifying policy instruments that are used by authorities to persuade third parties to act differently (Bemelmans-Videc *et al.* 1998):

Sermons comprise a non-coercive means of persuading those who have competency to act to prevent crime. They involve exhortation of some kind. Sermons might include raising awareness of a problem by providing information about it (say the number of car thefts in a given car park over a given period), advice (say on methods of making the car park less vulnerable to car thefts), formal or informal requests (asking the owner of the car park to improve the security of the car park), moral pressure (for example arguing that the car park owner has some responsibility to operate their car park so that those using it are at reduced risk of having their cars stolen), suggestions that the changes may be in the interests of the targeted person or organisation (for example arguing that a more secure car park will attract more customers), or public shaming (for example publicly naming the car park as one where those using it are at especially high risk of having their car stolen). The advantage of sermons as a means of generating preventative action is that they are relatively cheap and do not require any legislative mandate. The disadvantage is that the audience for the sermon is free to ignore it. Asking people to change their behaviour in ways that will heighten cost, inconvenience or risk to them may, if there is little or no compensating benefit, receive a rather dusty or evasive response. In particular, many private sector businesses may be reluctant (or even unable) to incur the costs of changes that bring them no benefits, even if they provide greater protection to customers.

Carrots comprise rewards for making changes, most commonly in the form of economic incentives. Some patterns of crime prevention activity are largely a function of the supply of carrots. The very large number of closed-circuit television cameras in public places in Britain is largely the result of central government funding programmes, the most recent of which was £150 million as part of the 1999–2002 Crime Reduction Programme. This compares with an additional £250 million which was provided for the remainder of the programme, to incentivise other police and partnership crime reduction efforts (Homel 2005). In the US the 1994 Crime Bill provided resources for 100,000 additional or redeployed community police officers over five years. Other financial carrots include performance-bonuses that are provided for individuals whose behaviour and achievements accord with stated crime prevention priorities. The advantage of economic incentives is that they have benefits for those enacting the measure and tend therefore to be more effective in galvanising action. The disadvantages, of course, are their cost, the fact that for those measures that call for revenue expenditure the effect lasts only so long as the funds are provided, that they are open to artful exploitation by those aiming to make use of funding but not necessarily for the purposes intended, and that they pay for activities that would have occurred even without provision of the extra resource. Moreover, most importantly ill-directed incentives may lead to activity that is ineffective or addresses relatively minor problems simply because the funding or rewards are made available for it. This is almost certainly the case with the monies made available for installing CCTV in public places.

Non-economic incentives such as prizes or kite marks represent alternative carrots. The Goldstein and Tilley Awards, respectively in the US and UK are designed to recognise and encourage strong problem-solving activities by police and partnerships (see www.popcenter.org where entries can be downloaded). The principal benefit for the winner in both cases is recognition rather than the relatively small material rewards. In relation to car crime the Safer Car Parks scheme, operated under the auspices of ACPO Crime Prevention Initiative, provides a kite-mark for car parks that meet required security standards in Britain: the Park Mark Safer Parking Award.

Carrots can also be used as a disincentive: the withholding of benefits, or the provision of negative publicity where crime prevention behaviour fails to accord with that which is wanted. Funding may be kept back if and where preventive standards are inadequate. League tables provide both positive and negative incentives. Those at the top are rewarded through recognition of their achievements and those at the bottom may be shamed into attempting improvements. The Car Theft Index comprises a powerful example of a league table that seems to have prompted improvements in the security of vehicles (Laycock 2004). Makes and models have been listed in order of their theft rate. In this case being at the top was a sign of failure. Publication of the first Car Theft Index in 1992 (Houghton 1992) was followed by a rapid improvement in the levels of security built into new cars and has been associated with a steady decline in the rate of car theft since. Moreover repeated publication of the Car Theft Index has helped maintain attention to vehicle security (Laycock 2004). The Car Theft Index was technically quite difficult to calculate and launch but has been overall an inexpensive way of leveraging attention to theft-risks by that constituency (the manufacturers) most competent to reduce car theft but hitherto not held responsible.

It might seem that the discussion has strayed into *sticks* in referring to negative incentives. The term 'sticks', however, is reserved for compulsion by way of statute. It refers to legal requirements that individuals, agencies or organisations act in particular ways. The European requirement that new cars be fitted with immobilisers from 1998 (mandate by EU directive 95/56/EU in 1995) is a case in point (see Brown 2004). Legislative requirements leading to the installation of steering wheel locks in all cars in Germany from 1963 and to new cars in Britain from 1971, are earlier examples of sticks used on vehicle manufacturers obliging them to design that security measure into vehicles. The Crime and Disorder Act (1998, as amended by s.97 and s.98 of the Police Reform Act 2002 and s.1, Clean Neighbourhoods and Environment Act 2005) imposes statutory duties in England and Wales on police, police authorities, local authorities, fire and rescue authorities, local health boards and primary care trusts to address local crime and disorder issues in partnership.

Some sticks bestowing crime prevention responsibilities are clearly more effective than others. Section 17 of the Crime and Disorder Act 1998 imposes responsibilities on a range of authorities to take account of crime in their decision making and activities. It describes an effort to mobilise routine attention to the potential crime consequences of policies and practices that ostensibly are unrelated to crime and hence addresses the ways in which crime may be generated unintentionally (Bullock *et al.* 2000). It is, though, quite a loose requirement that has in practice lacked teeth, and of course, relates only to a limited range of public bodies that might be competent to reduce or pre-empt crime. While often referred to there are few examples of its application.

Local partnerships have sometimes made imaginative use of sticks at their disposal, to put pressure on organisations that are competent to act to reduce crime but may otherwise be reluctant to do so. One case in point in Salford was to draw on the Health and Safety at Work Act 1974. This assigns a duty to employers to ensure the health, safety and welfare at work of all employees, including attention to the risk of violence. The Act also bestows powers of entry to premises, used by local authority Environmental Health Officers, to check that responsibilities are adhered to. The legislation is being used to persuade those running businesses, where there is a high risk of commercial robbery as revealed by local crime statistics, to operate their businesses and install security measures aimed at reducing the chances that staff will become victims or, in the case of premises already victimised, repeat victims of what is a violent offence.

The clear advantage of sticks is that they provide a means of coercing action from those who would otherwise be inclined to refuse to take it. The downside is that it can take a great deal of time and effort to pass legislation, that drafting is difficult and the final product can often lack effective teeth, that pursuing prosecutions is generally costly, and that it can elicit resistance and resentment from those who believe that unreasonable burdens are being placed on them.

Herman Goldstein has produced a hierarchy of types of lever that can be used to try to persuade third parties to act differently where needed in the interests of reducing local crime and disorder problems (see Scott and Goldstein 2005). These very roughly go from sermons to carrots to sticks as described here:

1 Education;
2 Informal requests;
3 Confrontational requests;
4 Engaging another existing organisation;
5 Pressing for the creation of a new organisation;
6 Shaming a delinquent body
7 Withdrawing services;
8 Charging fees for services;
9 Pressing for legislation mandating others to take measures;
10 Bringing a civil action.

Goldstein's advice is to use the least coercive measures possible. They will tend to be cheaper, quicker, more practicable and less likely to elicit resistance and hostility.

Delivery

Implementation weaknesses have dogged crime prevention work. It has proven remarkably difficult to deliver crime prevention initiatives effectively. Implementation has received rather less attention in academic research than the formulation of methods of reducing crime (Bullock 2007). Yet more or less serious shortcomings are characteristically found. The following comprise five styles of delivery which characterise the scale and scope of crime prevention work. In each case substantial implementation weaknesses are found.

- Large-scale programme;
- Project;
- Replication;
- Mainstreaming;
- Style of working.

One example is given for each type of implementation situation. It needs to be emphasised that what are described are entirely typical difficulties. These are not exceptional cases where the problems described arose only because abnormal circumstances prevailed or because especially stupid or obtuse groups of people were involved.

Large-scale programme

The Crime Reduction Programme, which was briefly mentioned earlier in this chapter, ran from 1999–2002 though originally it had been hoped that it would be extended to 2009. Except for the funding for CCTV for which there was no real evidential support at the time, money was made available by the Treasury on the basis of a Home Office review of research findings about what was and might be effective in reducing crime (Goldblatt and Lewis 1998). The programme was intended to capitalise and build on the existing evidence base to prevent crime. In addition to CCTV there were individual streams relating, for example, to offender treatment, domestic burglary, school management, drugs, youth inclusion, locks for pensioners, and domestic burglary. It is, thus, clear that this was a very broadly based programme. Most of the funds were allocated through competitive bidding. The programme was widely welcomed by the practitioner, policy and academic communities concerned with reducing crime.

Yet it was a fairly unequivocal implementation flop and the funding was cut short (Maguire 2004; Laycock and Webb 2003; Tilley 2004a; Homel *et al.* 2004). At the level of overall programme administration, previous experience of running crime reduction programmes, notably Safer Cities, was not drawn on. There were early underspends of grant funding, which concerned ministers who were impatient to see action on the ground. There were tensions between the central research and policy interests in the programme and its administration. In practice little use was made of the evidence base for crime prevention in funding bids, both in the sense that the existing literature was little drawn on and in that local problems were rarely analysed in any depth. There was little innovation from which new methods of reducing crime could be learned. In a large number of projects what had been planned was not implemented. Systems of monitoring what was being delivered were weak. The research community was too small to produce high quality evaluations on the scale called for. The evaluation findings proved in some cases contentious, with accusations that they were being misused. External events conspired to change the direction in which the programme was taken, notably increases in crime rates that led to new priorities. Locally the funding made available through the Crime Reduction Programme was insufficient to compete for sustained and serious local attention in comparison with other central funding streams for which local partnerships were bidding. Local co-ordination and leadership of funded programmes was weakened by staff turnover and by lack of experience in initiating new or changed patterns of activity. Few projects were implemented as originally conceived.

Overall assumptions about what could be achieved were wildly over-optimistic and the sense of disappointment and failure was enormous in light of the failures.

Individual project

The Manchester gangs and guns project was funded through the Crime Reduction Programme (Bullock and Tilley 2002, 2003a, 2008).

It exemplifies implementation difficulty at the level of the individual project.

South Manchester was notorious for gangs and shootings. Manchester was suffering from the soubriquet 'Gunchester' as a consequence. A project costing £500,000 was agreed to try to address the problem. Initial analysis of youth gangs and firearms offences was undertaken by Home Office researchers in conjunction with locally based Greater Manchester Police civilian employees who helped extract and collect the data used. On the basis of the findings a strategy was universally agreed by a multi-agency group comprising police, probation, various departments of the local authority, and the Youth Offending Team. This strategy involved highly publicised, co-ordinated, multi-agency crackdowns on gangs-as-a-whole in the event of a gun-related crime or serious assault by any member. It was hoped that a 'firebreak' in the reciprocal inter-gang patterns of shootings would thereby be created, as the gang members developed an interest in controlling one another's behaviour. This firebreak would in turn provide conditions in which a variety of other measures could be put in place and operate effectively, to divert youngsters from joining gangs and to facilitate their exit from them. The plan also included provision for community engagement to elicit ownership and support for the strategy, whose main aim, the reduction in numbers of youngsters shot, was thought likely to win widespread endorsement. The project plan was loosely based on the Boston gun project, which is discussed in earlier chapters of this book. A project team headed by a police inspector was appointed. It included representatives from housing, probation, the Youth Offending Team, and social services as well as the original civilian police employees who had helped with data collection for the original analysis, and two ex-gang member youth outreach workers.

In the event what was delivered bore little resemblance to the original strategy. Soon, over 100 potential interventions were recommended. This was whittled down to just 31 that were agreed. In the event only half of these were acted on. No gang-related crackdowns were put in place, let alone multi-agency co-ordinated ones. Many of those who were appointed to work on the project were uncomfortable in practice with adopting enforcement responses, although initially they had expressed support for the original strategy. They conflicted with those others appointed to the project who did support enforcement. The project's main focus turned to individuals who were members of gangs, on the fringes of gangs or deemed at risk of joining gangs. Enforcement continued to feature as a possibility in the project but as a threat to those who would not co-operate with the services provided to them. It was very rarely used. A large number of potential recipients of help were identified (some 800), but only a small fraction could be focused on (around 80–100). This created the need for selectivity and was again a source of contention within the team. In addition to the focus on individuals there were efforts at developing a Gang Resistance Education Programme though this had not been launched when funding ran out, at highlighting the significance of gangs and guns within local agencies, and at engaging with the local community.

What was delivered in Manchester was not necessarily inappropriate. However what was originally envisaged and agreed certainly was not what was put in place. Moreover much that was then planned was not delivered. And what action was taken was often in the context of serious fractiousness within the project team.

Replication

Small-scale demonstration projects are quite commonly used in crime prevention. They are designed to yield lessons that others can follow with better prospects of being effective. The Kirkholt Burglary Prevention Project has probably been the most influential crime prevention demonstration project conducted to date in the UK. It seemed to produce a very substantial fall in domestic burglary in a high crime housing estate in Rochdale (from 25 burglaries per 100 households to six per 100 over a three year period). Because of its apparent effectiveness others were encouraged to emulate it. The Safer Cities Programme had recently been initiated at the time the reports of the Kirkholt project were publicised (Tilley 1993b; 1996). Domestic burglary rates were high nationally at that time, accounting in 1990 for some 12 per cent of all recorded crime[1]. Because of this and because domestic burglary tends to be particularly distressing to victims it was a policy priority.

The problem for those attempting replications was to determine what needed to be taken from the Kirkholt scheme to replicate it, and how much and what kind of similarity was required among those attributes deemed to be crucial. There could be no question of duplicating Kirkholt exactly: the estate, the offending patterns, the individuals delivering the programme, and the levels of funding were perforce going to differ to greater or lesser extents. Moreover the details of exactly what was done and how it was delivered could never be described in all its complexity. Some interpretation and some selectivity in deciding what to do was inevitable, even if this took place only unconsciously. In the event different replication projects selected rather different attributes from Kirkholt as their focus of attention. Table 6.2 shows some comparisons between the Kirkholt project and a sample of its intended replications. It is clear that conditions, resources and measures varied. The changes in crime pattern associated with the projects also varied widely. This is unsurprising!

What would count as successful implementation was not clear and could not be clear to those attempting replications. The 'failure', if that is the right term, was in this case inevitable, given that duplication, as already indicated, is impossible and that there was no unequivocally correct way for those undertaking the replications to determine what comprised the crucial ingredients they needed to include.

Mainstreaming

Mainstreaming has some similarities to replication but is not quite the same. Mainstreaming describes the rolling out or normalising of a service or intervention that has been put in place temporarily or in only one location, where it seems to have been effective. The dilemmas that are inevitably present in replication are largely removed. The established practices are simply extended and made routine.

The Killingbeck domestic violence initiative was a demonstration project in one part of Leeds in West Yorkshire (Hanmer *et al.* 1999). Domestic violence is an archetypal, serious repeat victimisation offence. The logic of the preventive model pioneered in Killingbeck was to apply a graded response, with increasing intensity in intervention following repeat incidents coming to the attention of the police. The results were impressive. A sharp fall in the proportion of repeat calls was achieved: one-off attendances increased from 66 per cent to 85 per cent; moreover it was taking longer for repeat incidents to take place when they did occur.

The mainstreaming plan was to apply the model throughout West Yorkshire and also to apply it to racist and homophobic incidents (Hanmer 2003).

Table 6.3 shows the graded response model that was planned, levels and types of intervention changing as and when repeat

Table 6.2 Kirkholt and its intended replications

Attribute	Kirkholt	Replication 1	Replication 2	Replication 3
Status and funding	Demonstration project: £300,000	Safer Cities Scheme: £95,000	Safer Cities Scheme: £55,000	Safer Cities Scheme: £51,150
Area size	2,280 households	8,000 households	835 households	3,936 households
Initial burglary rate	25 per 100 per annum	6 per 100 per annum	9 per 100 per annum	5 per 100 per annum
Interventions	Cocoons for victims (mini homewatch); Removal of prepayment meters; Security upgrades	Neighbourhood Concern Groups in hotspots; Security upgrades	Security upgrades	Security upgrades
Targeting	Victims	Council tenant victims; Housing association tenant victims; Other vulnerable tenants	All estate residents	Victims; At risk households
Approach	Initial and continuing local research informing repeat victimisation focus and use of locally relevant measures	Local research throughout; Selective repeat victimisation plus vulnerable tenant focus	Target hardening plus universal focus	Initial crime mapping and then repeat victimisation plus at risk focus

Table 6.3 West Yorkshire Killingbeck mainstreaming model

Intervention Level	Victim	Perpetrator Common law offences*	Perpetrator Criminal offences
Level 1	• Gather information • Information letter 1 • Police Watch	• Reiterate Force policy • First official warning • Information letter 1	• Magistrates – conditional bail/checks • Police Watch • Information letter 1
Level 2	• Information letter 2 • Community constable visit • Cocoon** and Police Watches • Target hardening property	• Reiterate Force policy • Second official warning • Police Watch • Information letter 2	• Magistrates – bail opposed/checks • Police Watch increased • Information letter 2 • Crown Prosecution Service (CPS) file jacket and domestic violence (DV) history
Level 3	• Information letter 3 • Police Watch • Domestic Violence Officer visit • Agency meeting • Panic button/ Vodaphone	• Reiterate Force policy • Third official warning • Police Watch • Information letter 3	• Magistrates – bail opposed/checks • Police Watch increased • Information letter 3 • CPS file jacket and DV history and contact CPS
Emergency Intervention	Implement – log reasons for action	Not applicable	Implement and log level of action undertaken

*Common law offences are primarily breach of peace.
**Cocoon Watch requests the help and support of neighbours, family and relevant agencies in further protecting the victim by contacting the police immediately if further incidents occur. A Cocoon Watch is only implemented with the informed consent of the victim, and the perpetrator is made aware of the action.
Source: Hanmer (2003).

incidents take place, providing increasing protection and support for victims and stronger enforcement responses to perpetrators.

What was originally intended as a standard, consistent well-grounded strategy for dealing with repeat incidents was in practice implemented in inconsistent ways which lacked fidelity to the original model. Variations in priority, uneven and inconsistent training, efforts to align the model with existing local practices, and use of officer discretion led to drift from what had been intended. Rather than consistently increasing intensity of intervention it was on occasion decreased in intensity with repeat incidents, according to officers' opinions of the seriousness of the incident attended. Moreover there were failures in the accurate record-keeping that was essential to tracking cases and providing for stepped responses. Poor record keeping and officer discretion meant a radical departure from the strict intervention-intensity-increase model that had previously delivered the measured benefits.

Style of working

'Problem-oriented policing' is an approach to policing conceived by Herman Goldstein (1990). The basic idea is very simple: police should focus on resolving or reducing police-related problems that concern the public, rather than simply reacting to the incidents to which they are called. Moreover they should formulate responses on the basis of their likely effectiveness. This will often involve departure from traditional police enforcement and patrol practices. It will also often require the involvement of third parties, where the police are unable directly to apply measures that may be needed to address the problem most effectively. Problem-oriented policing is sometimes given different labels, such as partnership problem solving or problem-solving policing, but the core idea remains the same.

As we saw in the previous chapter, a short mnemonic, SARA (referring to Scanning, Analysis, Response, and Assessment), is generally used to capture what is supposed routinely to take place in problem-oriented policing. The idea is that the police (or police and their partners) systematically identify problems for prioritisation. These problems are carefully analysed to identify 'pinch-points', that is the most readily available site for measures that will reduce or eliminate the problem. On the basis of that analysis they then formulate a set of responses that are likely to involve co-operating with community members or third-party agencies. The results of the efforts to deal with the problem are then assessed and lessons learned for future work. In practice the simple four-stage model requires a good deal of iteration as scanning and analysis feed back and forth and experience of responses seems to call for fresh analysis and revised strategies.

It is easy to understand the appeal of problem-oriented policing.

It looks like straightforward common-sense. It promises to lead to effective ways of dealing with problems that concern the community. It provides a basic and pragmatic methodology for addressing problems at any level: from the local patch to the local authority, force or country depending on the nature of the issue and the availability of pinch-points. Who could object to it? Yet efforts at implementation have encountered multiple problems and no British police service has succeeded fully in putting it in place, despite widespread and in some places consistent efforts over more than a decade. The same goes more generally for efforts in other jurisdictions (Knutsson 2004; Scott 2000).

A series of implementation weaknesses were identified in one national study of efforts to introduce problem-oriented ways of working (Read and Tilley 2000):

- Poor analysis of problems, lack of analysts, and failures of analysts to focus on identifying and working out what to do to reduce crime;

- Restrictions on data sharing across agencies and shortcomings in data quality;

- Failures to draw on crime reduction experts and specialists to devise evidence-based responses;

- Inadequate time to develop and put in place problem-solving strategies;

- Exclusive focus on local low-level problems and neglect of problem-solving at the level of the local authority, force, region or country;

- Crudely operated performance management arrangements that shaped the focus of effort rather than local issues of concern to the public;

- Inattention to and, when undertaken, serious technical flaws in the outcome-evaluation of problem-solving efforts;

- Inadequate involvement of partnerships in problem-solving.

A recent study of problem-oriented policing in Britain included a detailed examination of the way it was working in two forces where it had been consistently promoted over several years. This found that significant implementation weaknesses remained despite sustained efforts to address them (Bullock *et al.* 2006).

Why are implementation weaknesses the norm?

It should not be thought that implementation weaknesses are confined to efforts at crime reduction (see, for example, the classic Pressman and Wildavsky 1973, and the more recent Peck and 6 2006). They are widely experienced in other areas of policy and practice. The surprise is not that implementation failure is found. Rather, the surprise is that it is found surprising by so many, who are apt to attribute it to individual shortcomings in the persons or organisations involved. Those who laughingly refer to 'SNAFU'[2] when talking about implementation are closer to the mark, though the consequences are no joke.

Various processes conspire recurrently to compromise smooth implementation:

- *Routine disruption* – In crime prevention, issues of implementation arise when change or novelty in policy, practice or service delivery is called for. These changes require some disruption in existing routines. It is ordinarily the case that existing routines serve the interests of individuals or organisations with an investment in them.

- *Threatened interests* – Existing, taken-for-granted and culturally approved practices, relationships, rewards, assumptions and ways of working provide a source of both ontological and material security for many implicated in their everyday reproduction. The planned innovation or change required by new crime prevention policies and practices actually or potentially threatens those interests, or at any rate they are perceived to do so. Suspicion and resistance are therefore to be expected.

- *Exercise of discretion* – Front-line, street-level bureaucrats (Lipsky 1980) have the autonomy to exercise their discretion in the delivery of the new measures. They are in a strong position to subvert them if they so choose and are liable to exert that discretion if they anticipate losses from their introduction.

- *Autonomy and reciprocity* – The sociologist Alvin Gouldner (1959, 1960) described the efforts made by member parts of organisations to achieve and maintain their autonomy, the efforts of the centre to retain control over these parts, and the characteristic tension between the two. Crime prevention both within agencies and between agencies purporting to work in partnership reveals this

155

tension. It is unrealistic to expect autonomy to be willingly ceded in the interests of pursuing a collective goal.

- *Open systems* – Crime prevention programmes and practices take place in 'open-system' conditions where external events and fresh imperatives are liable to produce new and changing priorities that recurrently threaten to disrupt embryonic new ways of working before they have become embedded.

- *Infrastructure* – New programmes generally require infrastructural supports of various kinds: for example, staff, equipment, data, vehicles, office-space, training, and administrative procedures. It takes time to acquire these and their absence undermines the capacity to deliver new activity. Programmes are sometimes deemed failures before the conditions for their successful implementation have been put in place.

- *Theory translation* – Crime prevention programmes and activities are theories incarnate (Pawson and Tilley 2005). They comprise the practical operationalisation of expected crime-control causal processes. It may, of course, be that these theories are not believed or understood by those charged with delivering action on the ground. Staff changes, existing agency folklore, and simple differences of opinion can produce mismatches between what the theory requires and what is delivered in practice. The more complex the programme theory, and the more agencies or parts of agencies that are therefore involved, the greater the chance that variations in forms of understanding will lead to departures from the delivery of theoretically-relevant practices on the ground. Partnership work in crime prevention opens the scope for this source of implementation failure.

It is clear that programmes requiring new patterns of activity are, for a variety of reasons, fragile affairs. They can be and often are easily thrown off course. Just as importantly preventive interventions will almost always require fine tuning. Unexpected contingencies will call for some initial flexibility, so that mechanical adherence to detailed programme prescriptions is undesirable and likely to lead to implementation failure. Some degrees of informed and programme-sympathetic implementation drift are therefore desirable for implementation success, although the more major mismatches between the programme ideas and actions on the ground, that are generally seen, are clearly marks of implementation failure.

Table 6.4 shows how these sources of routine implementation failure relate to the five examples outlined earlier.

Table 6.4 Systematic sources of recurrent implementation failure

	Large scale: Crime Reduction Programme	Project: Manchester Gangs and Guns	Replication: Kirkholt Burglary Reduction	Mainstreaming: Killingbeck Domestic Violence	Work style: Problem-Priented Policing
Routine disruption	Most constituent projects need to change and adapt	Local authority departments and probation change in priority and operating practices	?	Existing police practices	Change from established response policing methods
Threatened interests	Police	Agency groups defending turf	?	Local police units	Specialists in traditional policing methods
Exercise of discretion	Local partnerships decision-making	Probation and YOT client responsibilities	?	Local police BCUs	Scope to neglect problem-solving at all levels
Autonomy and reciprocity	Police and Home Office tension	Probation and project staff tension with leadership and each other	?	Front line officer discretion	Partner neglect and frustration
Open systems	Ministers and crime levels	Concurrent court case preventing required publicity	?	Competing priorities	Performance indicator priorities
Infra-structure	Bidding partners and Home Office capacity	Project leadership inexperience and tensions	?	Training; Central direction; Database	Data quality, availability, and analysis; Training
Theory translation	Bidding partners lack of understanding of crime prevention	Project staff group lack of understanding or commitment	All projects varied and uncertain understanding of Kirkholt	Non-specialist staff lack of understanding	Problem-solving not grasped above local beat level

Note: '?' appears where no evidence was available from the sources consulted.

Conclusion

A necessary condition for success in crime prevention is clearly that measures are implemented. A necessary condition for learning whether measures are effective is also that they are implemented properly. Yet implementation is rather a dull topic, for worthy rather than imaginative or creative individuals. Reputations are built on innovation rather than on solving the day to day headaches of making sure that measures are put in place and operated as intended. Of course even though implementation failure is normal it is by no means inevitable. Ironically, success for any but the simplest of measures seems to require the involvement of individuals of quite exceptional ability. So much so that their names readily spring to mind: David Forrester, Sylvia Chenery, Stuart Kirby, Mike Barton, and Max McLean are British examples. There may, on this basis, be good grounds for preferring simple over complex crime prevention measures, where at all possible.

As a rough practical guide implementation failure becomes more likely in proportion to:

- The naïve optimism of policy/project or scheme architects;
- The number of interventions;
- The number of independent agencies/parts of agencies involved;
- The number of separate lines of accountability;
- The space for unfettered practitioner discretion;
- The number of changes to the personnel, especially leaders;
- The indifference of leaders at all levels;
- The changeability of the context for the initiative.

Those interested in having crime prevention measures implemented successfully would be well-advised to avoid, so far as they can, these conditions and to find someone with outstanding ability to take responsibility for the delivery of the programme in its early stages.

Exercises

1 Who is responsible for and who is competent to reduce fly-tipping? How would you persuade those who are competent that they should assume responsibility?

2 Who is responsible for and who is competent to reduce shop theft? How would you persuade those who are competent that they should assume responsibility?

3 Take any recently announced crime reduction initiative and try to anticipate the implementation problems that can be expected. How might the problems most effectively be addressed?

4 Is implementation failure inevitable in crime prevention programmes?

Further reading

On leverage of third parties capable of reducing crime see Scott, M. (2005) 'Shifting and sharing police responsibility to address public safety issues', in N. Tilley (ed.) *Handbook of Crime Prevention and Community Safety*. Cullompton: Willan Publishing.

A classic study of implementation is Hope, T. and Murphy, J. (1983) 'Problems of Implementing Crime Prevention', *The Howard Journal*, 23: 38–50.

For a series of essays discussing various implementation problems, see the collection by Bullock, K. and Tilley, N. (2003) *Crime Reduction and Problem-Oriented Policing*. Cullompton: Willan Publishing.

Notes

1 This had fallen to six per cent by 2004–5.
2 Situation Normal All Fucked Up, according to Wikipedia originating in the US army in the Second World War.

Chapter 7

Evaluation

Unless useful lessons for future action are learned from evaluation there is little point in investing heavily in it. Useful lessons will only be learned if the evaluation is technically adequate, honestly published, and properly read. Much crime prevention evaluation that has been undertaken in the past falls short of even basic technical adequacy. Two skilled and experienced evaluators note 'a great deal of self-serving unpublished and semipublished work that does not meet even the most elementary criteria of evaluative probity' (Ekblom and Pease 1995; see also Sherman *et al.* 1997). At best this has involved wasting resources that could have been better put to other uses. Worse, shortcomings in the evaluation have been overlooked, misleading conclusions drawn and effective practice abandoned, or ineffective practice spread. Worst of all, well-intentioned but harmful interventions have been encouraged.

It is easy to understand how and why many inadequate or misleading evaluations have been produced and published (see Tilley 2000b). It has been a routine requirement of funding bodies that 'an evaluation' be produced. There are often few resources to undertake it: spending on evaluation is deemed to divert attention from the more important business of service delivery. Evaluations are often begun only as projects draw to a close, when key data can not be recovered. Those assigned to undertake evaluations often lack the skills and experience to avoid basic errors in measurement and method. There are frequently strong pressures to produce a success story to please funding bodies or bosses who have a vested interest in being seen to have triumphed, and evaluations are often undertaken by those who are relatively junior or in other ways dependent on those looking for 'good news'. There can be a great deal of wishful thinking in interpreting findings, accentuating the positive or qualifying the negative according to the tastes of the authors or of those clearing the evaluation report for publication. Once an evaluation report enters the public domain its reading and use is likely likewise to be shaped, consciously or otherwise, by interest, ideology and varying levels of ability to understand what is and can be concluded from it.

The problems of evaluation are magnified for the newcomer by the fact that even among those with some technical expertise in evaluation, who would broadly share the judgements expressed here about the prevailing patterns of production and use of evaluation studies, there are quite fundamental debates over methodology (Pawson and Tilley 1997).

General problems in evaluation

Data quality

Police recorded crime data have well-known limitations (Burrows *et al.* 2000; Povey 2000) although basic classificatory practices in Britain have improved (Audit Commission 2007). Not all crime is reported and not all of that which is reported is recorded. The fraction of offences cleared up is small for many crime types and the attributes of offenders therefore unknown with any certainty. The records of victims, incidents and offenders are apt to contain errors and ambiguities, for example in relation to names, addresses, ages, weapon types used, modus operandi and ethnicity. The format in which records are kept can render them very difficult to analyse, for example where goods stolen are simply listed, categories used are neither mutually exclusive nor exhaustive, or classes fail to correspond to those used in national statistics, for instance ethnic groupings. The conscientiousness of data collection, the conditions for reporting crime and the categories used in crime records are all apt to change making it impossible to assume that shortcomings in the data can be averaged out or treated as constants over time.

Survey data are sometimes collected instead. There are periodic international victimisation surveys (see, for example, van Dijk *et al.* 2007) and many countries operate their own national victimisation surveys. In England and Wales, for example, from the first relatively modest British Crime Survey of 1982, there is now a rolling survey involving some 40,000 respondents per annum (Hough and Maxfield 2007). Crime surveys avoid many of the difficulties in recorded data but are not without their own limitations. Conducting strong social surveys requires a range of technical skills if the data collected are to be of any real value. The framing and ordering of questions can strongly influence findings and slight changes in these from sweep to sweep can influence patterns of response. Respondents have fallible memories and when asked about past events can mistake their timing or their attributes. Identifying suitable sampling frames (the population from which the sample is selected) can be very difficult – suitable lists covering the relevant respondent groups and no others are often unavailable. There are always problems of non-response, with uncertainties about whether the non-respondents differ in significant ways from the respondents. For most of the population crime is quite a rare event and samples need to be very large to find sufficient numbers of victims to make before and after comparisons of crime levels using survey data. This makes collection of survey data very expensive.

Monitoring

Evaluations are undertaken in relation to sets of interventions. Unless records are kept of what was done, where, when, how and to whom it will not be possible to know what measures were put in place and therefore what is being evaluated. As set out in the previous chapter, planned interventions are rarely implemented exactly as expected and in any case plans are often rather imprecise. Record-keeping is, however, characteristically poor. Those involved in running initiatives are rarely keen to keep track of what they have done. Where records are kept they are inevitably selective and therefore partial. Detailed records will also need to be kept, of course, of changes other than those brought about by the intervention that may have affected the crime patterns of interest. This rarely happens.

Internal and external validity

There are substantial challenges in achieving both internal and external validity for findings of evaluations (Shadish *et al.* 2002; Eck 2002). Internal validity relates to the association of the measure with its supposed effects. Given that a change occurred, was it the intervention itself that brought it about or something else? External validity relates to the generalisability of the finding. Can we assume that the same intervention would produce the same change in another place or at another time?

Table 7.1 lists common threats to internal validity (Shadish *et al.* 2002). It is all too easy to take a change to be a result of measures where that is not the case. It is also possible to overlook changes brought about by the intervention, for example where changes are made in comparison groups that lead them too to show improvements, as indicated towards the bottom of the table. Monitoring is required, thus, both in intervention groups and comparison groups to avoid falling foul of this threat.

If lesson-learning is the main purpose of evaluation, external validity is critical (Eck 2002). Knowing that a particular measure produced a particular result among a particular group at a particular place and time, thereby providing a satisfactory answer to the internal validity question, is of little value unless that tells us something about what we can expect when we do the same in another group at another place and time. The almost ubiquitous finding that effects of the 'same' measure vary from one evaluation to the next is testament to the importance of but general failure adequately to answer questions of external validity. Table 7.2 lists some threats to external validity.

Statistical problems

There is a wide range of problems in conducting statistical analysis. Sample size decisions, statistical tests of significance, measurements of effect size, indexing, finding denominators against which to measure rates and changes in rate, assessments of expected rates of revictimisation, costing interventions, monetising benefits, and time course analysis, for example, all pose substantial technical puzzles that need to be faced and solved satisfactorily to produce robust findings (see Shadish *et al.* 2002; Bowers *et al.* forthcoming).

Capturing side-effects

Previous chapters have discussed both displacement and diffusion of benefits as respectively two major negative and positive side-effects that situational crime prevention initiatives may have, and also enhancement of offender-identity labelling effects that offender-focused measures may have. It is widely recognised that

Table 7.1 Threats to internal validity

Threat to internal validity	Explanation
History	Something happens to create change that would have happened anyway, without any intervention
Maturation	Treatment subjects mature in the change direction anyway, regardless of intervention
Testing	The measurement creates the change not the intervention measure itself
Instrumentation	The measurement methods change and create the impression of real change while there is none
Statistical regression	Treatment targets begin at an extreme position and tend naturally to regress towards the mean without any need for intervention
Seasonality	Changes may be part of a regular set of rhythms unrelated to the measures put in place
Selection	Those selected for treatment are atypical and especially susceptible to influence
Mortality	Drop outs may be different from those staying the course, and these latter may change anyway
Interactions with selection	Selection biases may interact with other threats to internal validity, for example selection-maturation
Ambiguity about direction of causality	Apparent effects may be associated with treatments but it may be the effect causing the treatment
Diffusion or imitation of treatments	Those not treated or those areas not treated (for comparison purposes) may adopt the intervention measure themselves
Compensatory equalisation of treatments	Those not treated (and used for comparison purposes) may be given additional services to compensate for missing out on the treatment given to the target group
Compensatory rivalry by respondents receiving less desirable treatments	Those not treated (and used for comparison purposes) may work especially hard to equal or outperform the treatment group or area
Resentful demoralisation of respondents receiving less desirable treatments	Those not receiving treatments (and used for comparison purposes) may under-perform because they feel neglected and resentful

Table 7.2 Threats to external validity

Threat to external validity	Explanation
Place attributes	Places are never exactly the same, and the details may be important to the effects brought about
Victim attributes	Patterns of victim attributes will vary from one site to another, and the details may be important to the effects brought about
Offender/likely offender attributes	Patterns of offender/likely offender attributes will vary from one site to another, and the details may be important to the effects brought about
Intervenor attributes	Who is involved in delivering the intervention, in terms of leader, front-line worker, or agency will vary from site to site, and the details may be important to the effects brought about
Community/family/ peer group attributes	The patterns of social relationships in which offenders and victims are embedded will vary from site to site, and the details may be important to the effects brought about
Intervention attributes	What is done can never be duplicated exactly, and the details may be important to the effects brought about
Non-crime options	Other non-crime behaviours available to those who would otherwise commit an offence will vary from site to site, and the details may be important to the effects brought about
Crime options	Different crime possibilities available to those who would otherwise commit some particular type of offence will vary from site to site, and the details may be important to the effects brought about
Dosage	Intensity of intervention in relation to target people, places or crime problems varies from site to site, and the level may be important to the effects brought about

the effects of measures can outstrip the intentions of those putting them in place. The metaphor of the flapping butterfly's wing on one side of the world leading ultimately to the tornado on the other, beloved of 'chaos theorists', highlights the potential for amplified, wide-ranging and ramifying consequences to be spun out from seemingly trivial events taking place in complex systems. While it might be unrealistic for an evaluation to try to capture all the effects of all interventions, crime-related unintended consequences are of clear interest. Without getting a fix on them the net effects of interventions cannot be estimated. Yet they are very difficult to measure with precision.

Options in evaluation

The difficulties listed in the previous section would be well-known to most competent social scientists. They would take them into account in their designs for evaluation studies, trying to deal with them as well as possible. They would also provide explicit caveats to findings where they concluded that there were remaining uncertainties. Almost without exception they would share recognition that there can be no 'proof' of the effects produced. There can only be weaker or stronger and sometimes compelling evidence, though ultimately it is always fallible. Non-social scientists or neophyte-social scientists are likely to overlook many or all of the problems listed. They may claim to have proven that interventions have been effective or ineffective. Policy-makers or politicians reading evaluations will, unsurprisingly, want certainty and even be impatient when the social scientist evaluator insists that qualifications need to be made and that uncertainties inevitably remain. Able, experienced evaluators will not be drawn into saying more (or less) than can be said on the basis of their research.

So much for agreement within the experienced and competent social scientist evaluator community: there is still a great deal of scope for variation in approach and for disagreements about their adequacy and appropriateness. The following lists some commonly adopted approaches, the strengths and weaknesses of each and the relationship between them.

Randomised controlled trials (RCTs)

RCTs are widely used in medicine, where 'RCT' sometimes refers to randomised clinical trial. The basic logic is clear. Potential subjects are randomly allocated to treatment and control conditions, so that the groups are equivalent to one another in their attributes. Measurements are made before and after treatment: any differences in difference that are found in the before and after measurements between the groups are attributable to the treatment. In some cases the control condition will involve no treatment at all, in some cases the provision of a placebo, in some cases conventional treatments and in some cases there will be a mix of various control conditions. In some cases there will also be an after only measurement group, to control for any effects that conducting measurements may have had in the non-treatment before-and-after measurement control group. Ideally, the recipient of the treatment, the provider of the treatment, the person making before and after measurements, and the statistical analyst are all 'blind'. That is, the recipients and non-recipients of the treatment of interest do not know which group they belong to, treatment providers do not know which treatment they are applying, testers don't know the group to which those being tested belong, and statisticians don't know to which groups the treatment codes refer. This 'blinding' prevents expectations affecting the response of those treated, the quality of treatment application, the reading of measurements, or the pursuit of effect estimates during statistical analysis. The ideal RCT is set up to try to let findings speak for themselves, by excluding extraneous factors beyond the biochemical action of the treatments from having any influence on the outcome of the trial. The rationale for RCTs is both to find out whether treatments have their intended and expected benefits, but also to check whether they may also unintentionally be producing unwanted negative side-effects. A cardinal principle of RCTs is that they contribute to harm minimisation: they reduce the risk that treatments make matters worse not better.

Though medicine is the classic site for RCTs, treatment subjects can in principle be of any kind: they may be classrooms, fields, plants, gangs, rats, pigeons, communities or cities. Numbers will need to be large enough to provide an adequate test of the hypothesis built into the treatment. That is an expected effect size is required to determine how many units of treatment need to be allocated to treatment and control conditions to elicit findings that are statistically robust.

RCTs are attractive in that they are designed to reduce or remove most of the threats to internal validity that are listed in Table 7.1. They also produce a measurement of 'effect size' that is useful in cost-benefit analysis. The number of problem-cases prevented can be estimated and if the costs of treatment and of the problems can also be estimated returns on expenditure can be calculated and improved decisions on use of public finances made. An additional advantage is that their strengths are well-recognised and findings using them have relatively high credibility. There are, however, also several downsides:

1 RCTs are much weaker on external than internal validity. The populations from which cases are randomly assigned are always, and inevitably, spatio-temporally specific. It cannot logically be concluded that just because an effect is produced among one group at one place and time, it will be experienced in another group at another place and time. This may not matter, in practice, where groups can be assumed to be invariant in relevant respects. But it does matter if this assumption cannot plausibly be made. In relation to offenders, victims and offending the assumption of invariance is, at best, highly contestable!

2 RCTs often begin with volunteers. Generalisations can only be made to the populations from which the random assignment is made, and volunteers may not be representative of a wider population of potential treatment recipients.

3 Where treatments are to larger entities such as countries, cities, or communities, random allocation to treatment and non-treatment conditions can be impractical.

4 Blinding procedures are not possible for most social programmes, including those concerned with crime reduction.

5 The specific intention of medical trials is to rule out treatment recipients' understandings of interventions as influences on outcomes. Such understandings, however, comprise one of the major ways in which effects are produced in most social programmes, including those aimed at crime prevention. In this sense blinding makes much less sense for social programmes than for medical trials.

6 In practice the constituents of crime prevention programmes are rather lumpy, changing and idiosyncratic in delivery. They characteristically include multiple interventions, which are sometimes interlocking and sometimes discrete. RCTs are well-suited to simple, single measures implemented in standard ways to well-defined populations. Crime reduction programmes rarely have these attributes. Where interventions are complex RCTs cannot identify active and inactive ingredients.

7 RCTs are strong on estimating net-effects. If measures act in different directions in different subgroups (as they often do) then these are missed.

8 Finally, ethical problems are sometimes raised where non-recipients of treatment are denied the potential benefits provided for those randomly allocated to the experimental group, although this is largely a misplaced criticism where outcomes cannot be

known in advance, and may turn out to be negative as well as positive.

Non-RCT control/treatment group comparison designs

Largely because of the high costs and practical difficulties encountered in putting RCTs in place for some interventions, evaluation designs which fall short of the supposed RCT gold standard are sometimes used. This is the case especially where the unit of treatment is not the individual, but something larger such as a neighbourhood. These evaluation designs involve identifying one or more groups or communities to act as controls against which changes in the implementation area or group can be compared. The difference in differences between before and after measurements of intervention and control cases is again used, as with RCTs, to gauge effect sizes. Generally crime prevention control sites are selected for their similarity in terms of attributes to do with demography, housing style, class-composition and deprivation level. Most plausibly the crime patterns of interest in the control settings will have tracked those in the intervention setting, though in practice this is often not established. It is very often the case that the treatment area is decided before the comparison area is identified. Randomised allocation clearly then does not take place. The choice in advance of the treatment site is often a function of finding individuals, agencies and communities that are willing or interested or have obtained the resources to host a project. Non-RCT control/ treatment group comparison designs have the same downsides as RCTs, supplemented by a few further difficulties:

1 The blinding achieved in the most advanced RCTs does not take place.
2 There is rarely random allocation.
3 Comparison areas or groups are selected opportunistically and the assumption that they act as an adequate benchmark for the intervention area or group is not secure.
4 There can be no certainty that those working in control areas, or with control groups, do not adapt their behaviour to the status they have been allocated, involving the last three threats to internal validity listed in Table 7.1.
5 Those areas or groups selected for treatment may have been chosen because they are experiencing abnormally high levels of crime problem, risking regression to the mean.

6 Areas and groups agreeing to interventions or to co-operate in the delivery of interventions may, on that account, be distinctive or atypical, undermining the validity of comparison areas that do not need to be willing to take part in an initiative.
7 Areas or groups, where interventions are foisted on unwilling hosts, may, on that account, resist, shun or undermine initiatives in ways that render them less likely to have an effect than in other settings with willing participants.
8 Most areas and groups into which crime prevention initiatives are introduced are subject to a continuous flow of changes, both in terms of what is being done to them and in terms of who is doing it. Thus, even if comparison areas or groups begin by being similar in relevant respects, any assumption that the intervention of evaluation interest alone could be the distinguishing variable explaining any difference in crime trajectory between them, is undermined.
9 Small areas, as either intervention or comparison sites, generally have crime levels that fluctuate widely over the short to medium term. This undermines the validity of comparisons between the two for evaluation purposes.

Simple before/after and time course designs

Simple before/after designs make measurements within groups or areas before and after an initiative is put in place and compare scores. 'Interrupted time series' designs chart trends within programme areas or groups to see whether the point at which an intervention is put in place marks a change in direction. Both clearly avoid the problems of finding and making comparisons with either deliberately chosen or randomly selected groups. They do, however, bring other problems. The most obvious is that the observed change in the problem-level may have taken place anyway, regardless of the intervention. These designs, thus, fail to remove some of the major threats to internal validity that designs involving finding and using and equivalent control group or area, try to avoid.

After only designs

After only designs make measurements after an initiative has been put in place, but not before. They clearly beg the question of change. They have, however, sometimes been used to assess efforts to reduce fear of crime, where recipients of treatment are asked whether they feel less afraid after some intervention has been put in place or to assess satisfaction with a service.

Realist evaluation

The evaluation approaches discussed in this chapter so far have all been concerned to ask whether a particular initiative works. They address the 'What works?' agenda. The intervention is made and the evaluation questions relate to whether on balance it produced positive or negative effects and to the size of those effects. Realist evaluation asks a rather different question: 'what works for whom in what circumstances, and how?' (Pawson and Tilley 1997). The task of evaluation becomes that of tracing the ways in which interventions produce effects in different places and within different subgroups. The issue of *how* the initiative in question brought about its positive and negative effects among varying groups then becomes critical.

Realist evaluation is 'theory-driven'. It aims at the formulation and test of 'context-mechanism-outcome pattern configurations' (CMOCs). These assume that the same measure works differently among different groups by activating different 'causal mechanisms'. Causal mechanisms describe the ways in which effects are brought about. They are often 'invisible', as are the causal mechanisms used in explanation in the natural sciences, for example gravity, natural selection, or magnetism. Causal mechanisms in social programmes normally include the reasoning and resources introduced (or subtracted) as individuals and groups interact with the programme interventions. Realist evaluation involves the articulation and testing of the pathways through programmes wherein particular mechanisms are activated among specific sub-groups to produce well-defined expected outcome patterns that can be compared to those found when these sub-groups are compared. The theories may derive from programme designers, practitioners delivering the programme, past evaluations, social science or hard thinking. It will never be possible comprehensively to state and test all theories that may be relevant to any programme. It will always be crucial to select for and test the most promising, important or widely held theories.

The downside of realist evaluation is that it does not, cannot and steadfastly refuses to promise simple effect-size measurements. Yet it is these that are demanded for the cost-benefit analysis that will be considered later in this chapter, on the basis of which evidence-based decisions about resource-allocation can be made.

An example

The discussion of evaluation designs so far has been rather abstract. Let us make it more concrete by briefly considering an example. Take police arrest for domestic violence where an incident being attended has not led to serious bodily harm. Traditionally the police have exercised discretion, often choosing not to arrest the alleged perpetrator. We know that domestic violence incidents tend to repeat. They are seldom one-off occasions. A scheme is contemplated in which police discretion is taken away and arrest is mandated. How might it be evaluated?

The first RCT that was undertaken, in Minneapolis, randomly allocated cases to arrest and other responses and compared rates of repeat incident to see whether the arrest response produced a lower rate of repeat incident than other treatments in the ensuing six months (Sherman and Berk 1984). Discretion was removed from the officers and they were told what to do in individual cases on a randomised basis. What mattered for this trial was that the measures were implemented as required case-by-case. The data could then speak for themselves. It was not necessary to have any notion of what it is about arrest that might affect the likelihood of repeat incidents. The arrest response outperformed the other responses. Arrest seemed to work. Moreover it was possible to gauge by how much it worked – that is to estimate the effect size. Based on police records ten per cent of those arrested committed repeat violence over the following six months compared to nineteen per cent for those advised and 24 per cent for those where the suspect was simply sent away. Victim reports produced different details but much the same picture with figures of nineteen per cent, 37 per cent and 33 per cent respectively for repeat violence for arrest, advice and sending suspect away. Later studies replicating the Minneapolis experiment came out with different findings (Sherman 1992b). Arrest did not outperform other responses. Indeed it seemed sometimes to make matters worse. Whatever internal validity the original Minneapolis-St Paul study may have had, it lacked external validity. The reason it necessarily lacked external validity is that the random allocation was (as it had to be) from a specific population. It could not be of all populations in all places at all times. Random allocations to varying treatments from different populations produced different outcome patterns. If we find that arrest has an effect but we cannot be certain in any community what the direction of the effect will be, we clearly have problems in lesson-learning!

An alternative design for evaluating the arrest policies could be a non-RCT treatment/control group or area comparison. The apparent variations in the effects as measured through the RCTs bring out the practical problem in this. Unless one knew in advance what kinds of differences in condition would lead to variations in the effects of the arrest measure, one would not know on what basis adequate similarity for measuring effectiveness could be determined. The findings of a well-executed evaluation are needed in order properly to design the evaluation! Without that information one could come to highly misleading conclusions about the potential of the measure. Moreover in hindsight it seems highly likely that one area might have just that balance of members that an apparent effect could mask two contrary directions of impact.

A third evaluation design would measure rates of repeat incidents before and after the introduction of the arrest policy. The problem here is that other events may have occurred in the interim, for example publicity campaigns or inadvertent publicity of a prominent case that might affect relevant behaviour independently of the arrest policies.

Measurements of rates of repeat incidents only after the introduction of the arrest measure, without any comparison areas or cases, represents a fourth evaluation design possibility. Clearly in the absence of any data on what the rates had been previously, it would not be possible to tell whether any decline had been achieved. Of course victims and their partners could be asked to reflect retrospectively on their experience of the interventions put in place, but here problems in the reliability of recall arise.

Realist evaluation would begin with theory, with the formulation of CMOC hypotheses that differentiate between sub-groups in terms of the expected mechanisms relevant to repeat reports of domestic violence incidents that would be activated by arrest responses. Table 7.3 shows a slew of such hypotheses. The first column lists a range of potential mechanisms, the second contexts relevant to the activation of these mechanisms and the third patterns that might be looked for in an evaluation study to test each hypothesis. In realist evaluation the method selected and the data collected comprises those which are most appropriate to the evaluation hypothesis being tested. There is no *a priori* commitment to one technique or another.

One post hoc explanation for the variations on outcome by area found in the RCTs evaluating the effectiveness of arrests responses to misdemeanor domestic violence are those shown as 7 and 8 in

Table 7.3 Realist hypotheses relating to mandatory arrest for relatively low injury domestic violence*

Mechanism	Context	Data to test expected outcome pattern
1 Women's shame	Membership of 'respectable' knowing community	Reduced level of reporting of incidents among those with close attachments to communities valuing traditional family life
2 Women's fear of recrimination	History of violence; culturally supported violence; alcoholism of offender	Reduced levels of reporting incidents among chronically victimised
3 Women's fear of loss of partner	Emotional or financial dependency on partner	Reduced level of reporting among poorer and emotionally weaker women
4 Women's fear of children being taken into care	Pattern of general domestic violence against whole family	Reduced level of reporting among families known to social services
5 Women's empowerment	Availability of refuges; support for women; financial resources of women	Increased levels of separation where support and alternative living arrangements available
6 Incapacitation of offender	Length of time held	Short-term reductions in repeat incidents
7 Offender shame	Membership of 'respectable' knowing community	Reduced domestic violence within 'respectable' communities
8 Offender anger	Cultural acceptability of male violence to women; what man has to lose from brushes with the law	Increased levels of violence among those violence-sanctioning communities marginal to mainstream society
9 Offender shock	Offender attachment to partner; self-image as law-abiding respectable person	Reduced levels of violence, and help-seeking behaviour among short-tempered 'respectable' men
10 Changed norms about propriety of domestic violence	Positive publicity	Reduced levels of reported and unreported domestic violence

* These hypotheses clearly relate to domestic violence where a man is the perpetrator and a woman the victim
Source: Tilley (2002a: 106).

Table 7.3. These are not the only promising hypotheses that might be tested. Moreover, to explore them within an RCT would involve the collection and analysis of data that are relevant to individual cases in each city. This was not the strategy adopted, which was concerned instead with evaluating the aggregate effect of the policy rather than with how it worked in relation to differing groups of cases – the primary interest of realist evaluation. Instead of aiming at generalisable estimates of net effects, realist evaluation focuses on identifying and formalising a range of sub-group CMOC hypotheses and trying to collect data that will provide a basis for their rejection, tentative acceptance or refinement.

Systematic review

Over the years and across jurisdictions an enormous volume of research on crime prevention has been undertaken, including many evaluations of initiatives of various kinds. Rather than undertaking yet more primary research it may sometimes be quicker, cheaper and more informative to review what has already been found. Moreover, if planning a new study its precise focus might also be improved by reviewing existing research and working out where there are gaps in understanding.

The Campbell Collaboration has emerged as an international organisation of scholars who undertake systematic reviews in social policy. It took its inspiration from the Cochrane Collaboration that does the same for health. The Campbell Collaboration is transparent in its methods of searching for and sifting through studies that are included in its reviews. It attempts to cast its net as widely as possible in identifying studies, in part because of a 'publication bias' whereby those that come out with positive findings are more likely to be published in journals than those with negative findings. If we want a balanced judgement then all competent studies should be included. The studies included are those that meet minimum methodological standards. Preference is attached to RCTs and those that closely resemble them through the use of comparison sites and groups. Typically a Campbell Review will begin with a relatively large number of studies that look as if they might be included, but fetch up with a small number that meet the methodological requirements. Its concern is to distil a dependable estimate of the range of effect sizes that can be expected within specified confidence limits.

In relation to a Campbell Collaboration review of initiatives that took delinquents or pre-delinquents on prison visits to try to frighten them away from criminal behaviour, that is to scare them straight, the reviewers began with 487 pieces of literature. Of these 487, 30 comprised evaluation studies, but only eleven met the required methodological standards. Two of the eleven had then to be withdrawn from consideration because the data were not available. In all, then, more than 98 per cent of the items of the literature discovered were not used. The conclusion drawn from the nine studies that survived the sifting process was that efforts to scare young people straight had not worked. There is no account of, or interest in, why the initiatives had failed or whether there were subgroups among which it had produced beneficial effects, balanced by those where the effects had been deleterious.

Figure 7.1 shows the typical format for findings of Campbell Collaboration reviews, in this case of initiatives that aimed to scare young people straight. The 'forest' diagram shows that the control groups consistently outperformed the experimental groups in terms of levels of recidivism.

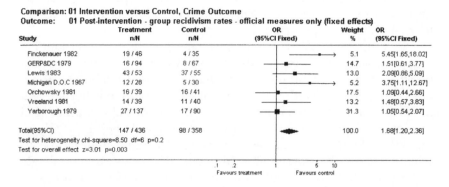

Figure 7.1 Campbell Collaboration Review findings about scared straight

Source: Petrosino *et al.* (2002).

Realist synthesis differs from Campbell Collaboration reviews in both method and purpose. Realist synthesis attempts to distil what can be learned from the body of evidence that has been assembled, about context mechanism outcome patterns (Pawson 2006). Realist synthesis will even countenance drawing on poor research. It hoovers up evidence of diverse kinds from a wide range of policy domains to construct, test and refine evidence-based middle-range theories about what kinds of programme work for whom in what circumstances.

In crime prevention, the series of Community-oriented Policing Services, Problem-Oriented Guides for Police series exemplifies a broadly realist approach. Rather than aiming to certify the efficacy of specific interventions that can be expected to generate a given effect-size, these guides review evidence to help practitioners determine what might work within their particular problem contexts. The evidence is reviewed and a table produced. Table 7.4 comprises an example.

Table 7.4 Sample findings for dealing with theft of and from cars in parking facilities, using an approach consistent with realism

Response	How it works (mechanism)	Works best if . . . (context)	Considerations
Hiring parking attendants	Improves surveillance of facilities, especially at entrances and exits	. . . the facility's perimeter is secure, so those who enter and exit must pass the attendant, and the attendant booth is designed to facilitate surveillance	Expensive; usually justified only in large facilities; effective in reducing theft of cars – less so theft from cars
Improving surveillance at deck and lot entrances/exits	Increases thieves' risk of detection entering and leaving	. . . the facility's perimeter is secure	Methods include improving the lighting, removing signs and other obstructions, and encouraging vendors to set up shop near entrances and exits

Source: Clarke (2002).

The Campbell Collaboration review methods may be more appropriate where a universal national or regional policy is being considered and the realist where local discretion is being informed.

Action research

There is a strong tradition of action research in crime prevention, where members of the same team are involved in designing, implementing and evaluating an initiative. Both situational crime prevention and problem-oriented policing have action research at their heart, as indicated in Chapter 5. They call for careful analysis of crime and disorder problems, on the basis of which tactics and strategies are decided. These tactics and strategies are monitored and adjusted in the light of experience. The outcomes are then estimated. There are built-in feedback loops as the initiative proceeds as researchers, policy-makers and practitioners work alongside one another. The advantage is that initiatives learn as they go and thereby have a better chance of successful implementation and outcome. The disadvantages are that the measures put in place may change over time, and that, consciously or otherwise, biases enter into the evaluation when those who have played a part in designing the intervention also estimate its effects.

Some of the most fertile and informative crime prevention literature has emerged from action research. For example in the US the Boston gun project, which evidently led to a massive fall in the numbers of fatal shootings in Boston and has also stimulated a much broader reconceptualisation of the potential for deterrence in crime prevention, was an action research project. Here Harvard University academics worked with practitioners to develop the initiative and also evaluated its impact (Kennedy *et al.* 2001). In Britain the Kirkholt Burglary Prevention Project, which led to a dramatic fall in the number of domestic burglaries on the Kirkholt Housing Estate in Rochdale and also kick-started a major programme of research on repeat victimisation and its potential as a focus for crime prevention efforts, was again an action research project (Forrester *et al.* 1988, 1990). Here Manchester University academics worked with a range of practitioners to develop the project and also evaluated its impact.

Action research findings are not necessarily compromised through bias, though the risks have to be acknowledged. Technical skills among the academics and sufficient independence from the interests of the practitioner community reduce the risks that misleading conclusions are drawn.

Economic evaluation

There is a strong and altogether understandable demand for economic evaluation. Those with responsibility for making use of scarce resources call on evaluation findings to help them determine where most can be got from investments of effort, time and money. If more utility can be gained from changed uses of resources then they should be switched. Evaluations may be undertaken to improve estimates of expected utility from differing uses of scarce resources.

Two forms of economic evaluation can be distinguished: cost-effectiveness analysis (CEA) and cost-benefit analysis (CBA) (Stockdale *et al.* 1999; Stockdale and Whitehead 2003; Roman and Farrell 2002).

CEA estimates the unit cost of output or outcome. How much, for example, did it cost for each installed alarm? Or how much did it cost to prevent each burglary? The calculation of costs is a little more complex, for many social programmes, than may seem to be the case at first sight. The marginal cost per unit of output or outcome describes the additional costs that are incurred (and will disregard fixed costs). The average cost per unit of output or outcome describes the mean of all the costs incurred in producing the output or outcome. 'Diminishing marginal costs' mean that generally speaking the more output that is generated the lower the unit output cost, although less discriminating allocation of those outputs may also mean that there are increasing marginal costs in relation to the units of output to produce a given unit of outcome. More concretely, installing 1,000 alarms is generally cheaper per alarm than installing ten. If ten are installed they can be allocated to those in most obvious need (perhaps because of prior victimisation), whereas 1,000 are likely also to be installed where their preventive prospects are much lower. Estimating costs of interventions can also be tricky. Economic analysis, in its concern with uses to which the resources might otherwise be put, tends to favour attaching costs even to inputs that may appear to be free to those involved in an initiative, for example volunteer labour or contributions in kind such as vehicles or office space. In practice, standard costings tend to be used in order to make comparisons across different initiatives possible. These conventions can seem bizarre to some policy-makers and practitioners, who are trying to deliver more for less by maximising volunteer contributions from third parties.

CBA is more complex than CEA. It involves not only estimating the costs of initiatives but also the benefits. Benefits have to be put into the same unit of account as costs so that levels of cost and benefit can be compared. The common unit of account is normally money. What monetary value do we attach to a crime and what savings can we then impute to one that is prevented? Direct and indirect financial losses are fairly straightforward to estimate: What was lost? What damage was incurred at what repair costs? How many days labour were lost? Monetising non-financial losses is much trickier and more contentious. Non-financial losses include emotional harms of various kinds: for example, the trauma of rape, the distress following loss of a murdered loved one, or the fear of leaving one's home following a burglary. Two techniques are commonly used for monetising the non-financial losses: 'willing to pay' (WTP) and 'willing to accept' (WTA) neither of which is fully adequate.

WTP refers to estimates, in monetary terms, of what those who might suffer emotional harms from a crime would be prepared to pay to prevent it. WTA refers to estimates of what, in monetary terms, those suffering emotional harms from a crime would be prepared to accept in recompense for it. The problems are obvious (see Adams 1995). WTA will for many become infinite for some offences, for example rape and murder. Infinite sums cannot be entered into cost benefit equations. WTP depends on the resources at the disposal of potential victims. These will not remain constant. Also, WTP estimates involve invidious variations in costs of serious crimes in relation to the resources held by different groups, who could afford varying sums to prevent the same harm.

CBA and outcome related CEA depend on a reliable method of measuring numbers of crimes prevented. This makes RCTs and their near counterparts very popular among economic analysts, but their popularity and utility in economic evaluation does not, of course, make findings any the more valid. Realist evaluations may produce more valid findings that are also of more immediate use to practitioners and local policy-makers. They fail, however, to feed the perfectly understandable appetite for effect-size measurement for comparative cost-benefit analyses, that are designed to inform the efficient, utility-maximising distribution of limited resources.

Finally, evaluation is itself not a cost-free activity. The potential benefits from investment in it therefore need also to be considered. Assigning substantial evaluation resources, whatever methodology is used, to examine thoroughly a small-scale one-off project, with little or no chance of lessons for the future being drawn, would clearly produce rather low returns.

Conclusion

Evaluation is technically difficult. It is easy for the unwary to produce misleading findings. Equally it is easy for the unscrupulous to do so in the interests of promoting themselves or pleasing their paymasters. Yet there are dangers in disseminating false success claims. At best this may draw others into wasting their resources. At worst, where net negative effects are produced, it may contribute to the creation of harms.

Just as there are ethical issues at work in decisions about crime prevention activities there are also ethical issues at stake in the conduct and publication of evaluation findings. Knowingly producing or publishing false findings runs strongly counter to basic research ethics. Putting pressure on those who are undertaking or writing up evaluations may be tempting but is equally unethical. Adopting methodologies believed in advance to produce invalid conclusions, perhaps because of external pressures by those with a poor understanding of the strengths and weaknesses of alternative possibilities, involves bad faith on the part of the responsible researcher.

There are also more general research ethics that relate to the work of evaluators in particular, in terms of their responsibilities to their subjects and those commissioning work, and most national evaluation associations publish these[1]. All stress the fundamental need not to do violence to findings.

Exercises

1 Take any recently announced large or small crime prevention initiative and devise two outline evaluation plans, one that is realist and the other that is as close to a randomised controlled trial as is practicable. Compare them. Which would you choose and why?

2 Hunt down any crime prevention evaluation. Subject it to critical scrutiny. Then try to work out a better research design.

3 Take any crime prevention measure. Look for five items of literature that would be used in a Campbell review. Look for a further five items of literature that would be included in a realist review but not a Campbell one. Use the material you have collected to produce draft realist and Campbell syntheses. Compare findings. What do you conclude about their respective strengths and weaknesses?

Further reading

A good general discussion of evaluation and crime prevention is Eck, J. (2005) 'Evaluation for lesson-learning', in N. Tilley (ed.) *Handbook of Crime Prevention and Community Safety*. Cullompton: Willan Publishing.

For a collection of essays on evaluation for crime prevention, see Tilley, N. (ed.) (2002) *Evaluation for Crime Prevention*. Crime Prevention Studies Volume 14. Monsey, NY: Criminal Justice Press.

For material relating to experimental evaluations and Campbell reviews, go to http://www.campbellcollaboration.org/CCJG/

Notes

1 The following web sites provide examples – Australasia: http://www.aes. asn.au/about/Documents%20-%20ongoing/code_of_ethics.pdf; US: http:// ethics.iit.edu/codes/coe/amer.eval.assoc.task.force.html; UK: http://www. evaluation.org.uk/Pub_library/Good_Practice.htm; Canada: http://www. evaluationcanada.ca/site.cgi?s=5&ss=4&_lang=EN

Chapter 8

Conclusion: what's to be done to improve crime prevention?

Crime is a perennial hot topic for the mass media, politicians and the general public. One moral panic succeeds another: exaggerated impressions of crime waves take hold, groups are demonised (Cohen 1973), there is a good deal of hand-wringing about how society has gone wrong and scapegoats are identified. Policies and programmes are put in place in haste, implementation is weak, interest wanes, and when they appear evaluation results are either self-serving or equivocal. Findings are forgotten and a new round begins. There are exceptions, of course, but this is the normal pattern (see Gest 2001).

Ill-informed common sense, moral panic and opportunism may be common in popular political discourse, but they are not likely to lead to sensible, effective, or ethical policies and practices (Tilley and Laycock 2000). Aside from its purpose as an introductory text for students and practitioners, this book has been written in the hope that it might make a modest contribution to more informed debate on what is to be done about crime.

Some consistent messages emerge from the chapters on approaches to crime prevention. The following comprise twelve core crime prevention propositions whose acceptance might lead to improved policy and practice.

1   All crime prevention involves theory. Successful crime prevention depends on a good enough theory that is well chosen for the issue at hand.

2   All crime problems differ in their details. Successful crime prevention turns on being able to recognise relevant similarities and differences in order to work out what theory to apply.

3   Old crime problems waste away and new ones emerge with changes in products, processes and places. Successful crime prevention depends on being able to identify and adapt to those changes. Theory is needed to recognise the saliently similar and different. It is also needed to predict future problems that might be pre-empted.

4   Offenders and crime-preventers are involved in an arms race where each adapts to the other. Preventers need theory to inform efforts to anticipate offenders' countermoves. Anticipating counter-moves can help develop preventive strategies with the best prospects of sustained crime prevention effects.

5   Many conditions are needed for crimes to take place. This offers many potential points of intervention to prevent them. Not all the conditions needed for crime relate to 'root causes' of criminality. Attention to proximal causes is often effective in preventing crime.

6   No single crime prevention measure works all the time and in all circumstances. Theory-driven boutique or bespoke crime prevention efforts to prevent specific crime problems are more promising than efforts to identify 'silver bullets'.

7   Crime problems manifest themselves at varying levels, from the specific incident that may be repeated to national or international patterns. Preventive measures can be applied at any or all levels.

8   Not all theory is equally useful. Theory that is too general cannot readily be applied. Theory that is too specific is unhelpful beyond its particular focus. 'Middle range' theory, which lies between these, promises most. Moreover theory for crime prevention needs to focus on how measures produce effects and the kinds of condition needed for them to produce their outcomes.

9   Those who have traditionally been allocated responsibility for crime prevention do not include many of those most competent to prevent crime. Effective crime prevention involves persuading some of those who are competent to accept some responsibility. It also involves decisions about who can reasonably be held responsible.

10 Strong enough crime prevention theory and acceptance of responsibility by those competent to act is not enough for effective crime prevention. Measures chosen also require conscientious implementation. Good enough implementation theory is needed for implementation to be successful.

11 Crime prevention is ubiquitous. All crime prevention measures raise ethical issues. All are susceptible to moral critique. The formulation of crime prevention strategies and tactics involve ethical choices or assumptions, even when these are not made explicit. Trade-offs are inevitably involved in selecting from alternative crime prevention methods.

12 There is a great deal yet to learn about ways of preventing crime. Cumulative programmes of action research are well-suited to making progress in developing, testing and refining middle-range theory for policy and practice.

In medicine there are moves away from efforts at finding blockbuster drugs that will be adequate for all. The field of pharmacogenetics (also sometimes referred to as pharmacogenomics) is opening up the possibility of treatment orientated to what distinguishes us as well as to what we have in common (PriceWaterhouseCoopers 2005; Wolf *et al.* 2000). We do not all react the same way to particular medication. Pharmocogenetics raises the possibility of treatments that are sensitive to our variations, so that there are fewer suffering unwanted side-effects and more given the treatment that will be effective for them. Doctors in the future will, it is hoped, be better placed to advise on particular needs.

Crime problems clearly differ from medical ones in a host of ways. Crime is a social phenomenon in ways emphasised in Chapter 4. Yet the blockbusters that have been for many years the holy grail of medical trials appear even less plausible in the field of crime prevention, where crime opportunities and crime groupings are in constant flux. The internet, international terrorism, and globally organised crime are obvious large-scale emerging and fast-changing crime problem domains. At a more micro level, changes in transport networks, patterns of schooling, licensing laws, housing arrangements, taxation rules, everyday working patterns, national and international migration patterns, fashions, product designs, child care provisions, and techniques for detection, for example, all generate a continuously changing crime landscape calling for preventive attention. Locally, housing developments, new entertainment venues, changed road-layout, changes in the local employment opportunities or altered care arrangements for children may all alter crime patterns and crime prevention needs. There is devil in the detail of local crime problems and tailoring based on a good understanding of relevance in similarity and difference, which is the concern of pharmacogenetics, is even more relevant in dealing with crime. The preceding chapters have consistently found mixed results in relation to crime prevention initiatives. These should be expected in the light of the different conditions for problems. The trick is to move to improved understanding of what works for whom and how in what circumstances, and to build the capacity to deliver greater positive effects more consistently with fewer unwanted side-effects, even in apparently new circumstances.

Problem-solving approaches, operating at the international, national, regional and local levels, rooted in the propositions laid out in this chapter, are probably best suited to work out what to do, with systematic evaluation to help refine theory. At all levels this is liable most effectively to be achieved by informed cool-headed analysis able to influence policy and practice and assess outcomes across a range of agencies and organisations. There would be benefits in delivering this in the context of an arm's length relationship with individual agencies, especially those under political control. This would comprise a strategy to reduce the risks of repeatedly launching headline-grabbing but otherwise unpropitious short-term responses to crime issues.

Exercises

1 Critically evaluate the twelve core propositions laid out in this chapter.

2 Assuming that the propositions advanced in this chapter are valid, in what ways would you alter current national and/or frameworks for crime prevention in the interests of effective and ethical policy and practice?

Annex: Norman Storey (1946–2008)

Norman was normal and this is his story. It is also history, at least of a sort. Norman's life of crime and crime prevention is in part his own unique biography, in part a tale of his time, but also in part archetypal.

Norman was born just after the Second World War, part of the baby boom. He was brought up in rural Kent. His father a clerical worker and his mother a housewife. He was the second of three children, with one brother and one sister. After secondary school he started work for an insurance company. He continued with it for the rest of his working life. He married Norma in 1970 and had two children. He retired in 2006 and died in 2008.

Norman was unremarkable. Few of you will know Norman, but most of you will recognise his type: a hard working pillar of the community. The crime prism through which we'll look at Norman's life here is not the usual one, certainly not the one used in his obituary, which appeared in the newsletter of the Cricket Club of which Norman was president for many years. Most of Norman's life of crime has been neither known nor noticed.

Like most of his friends, Norman was little supervised as a child. He caught the bus to school with his brother or sister. In the evenings he came home on his own. In summer he was free to go out to play in the evenings with village friends. At the weekends he could do so all year round. He had only to be home for tea.

When he was ten, Norman committed his first significant crime while out with his best friend, George. There was an abandoned, but fenced bandstand in the local park. Norman and George enjoyed throwing stones. They liked to throw them as accurately as they could. They found that they could just reach the bandstand and they found the sound of breaking glass a rich reward for their efforts. It was a measure of achievement and their relative performance could be gauged with some confidence. When the derelict bandstand was eventually removed Norman and George found another target that was harder to reach and slightly less rewarding: street lights. They made a smaller, more difficult target. Success came very rarely, certainly too infrequently for a competition to make any sense.

Norman continued criminal damage on an occasional basis for the next eight years. When George and Norman were eleven they bought catapults to increase the distance and accuracy with which they could project stones. When he was twelve Norman was given an air rifle that too could be used. The catapults and air rifle were not, of course, only used for criminal damage but that was one of their uses.

Norman and George's most dramatic case of criminal damage (if that is what it was) came when Norman was twelve. They set fire to a range of wooden barns. They were playing with fire. Norman's most stupid offence involved trespass on the flat roof of a school. His friends decided that they would walk across the building with their eyes shut. Norman did so, fell off and broke his arm. He subsequently felt so stupid and ashamed he told his parents he had broken his arm falling off his bicycle.

Norman was never convicted of any offence of criminal damage. George left the village in which he had been raised when both he and Norman were fifteen and they lost contact. They had wanted to commit rather more serious crime together than they managed in practice. They dreamed of being rich, with fast cars, yachts and big houses. They tried to figure out how to break into a bank: banks produced nothing and made massive profits, so if they stole a very large sum of money they felt that non-one in particular would lose out.

At his all-boys high school Norman had a group of friends, but they didn't get on with other groups. Norman sometimes got involved in fights with members of these other groups. Onlookers chanted, 'Blood! Blood! Blood! Blood!' in order to provoke Norman and his opponents into becoming ever more violent. No serious harm, however, was ever done.

Except for going 'scrumping', which had been a regular part of his and George's lives since they were seven, Norman committed his first acquisitive crime, shop theft, when he was eleven. The village shops were small and the goods were held behind the counter. They had to be asked for. Sweets, for example, were weighed out from jars. There was no self-service. Norman could not get at the sweets he so craved but often could not afford. His first shop theft was from Woolworths, in the local town. It involved taking sweets and small toys. Woolworths at that time laid out its goods round a central aisle. It's easy to see how Norman could commit his crime. While the shop assistant was serving a customer on one side she had her back turned, she was unable to see Norman and Norman could see that she was unable to see him. The goods were small (for example die-cast model cars), easily reached and quickly pocketed. It was, in a rather literal sense, child's play. Norman was never caught.

At seventeen Norman obtained a motor scooter. It offered freedom. It was also an entry ticket to the world of the Mods. Norman was drawn in. He liked to show off, riding round town. His scooter made a huge din.

One evening Norman was stopped by a police officer. Norman had failed to renew his insurance certificate and his MOT certificate had expired. Norman drove straight home, completely deflated. He knew his number was up. He confessed to his parents. They were quietly understanding, but suggested that he get rid of the scooter that was liable to lead to more trouble. The police prosecuted Norman. He was fined and his license was endorsed. The conviction was reported on the front page of the local paper. He spent the summer holidays working in a local café earning the money to pay his fine. It was a turning point. Norman was shaken out of his brief flirtation with collective delinquency, at least in the company of the Mods.

For a few years Norman committed no crimes. Eventually Norman and Norma bought a house together. It needed maintenance and modernisation. Workmen came and offered to do the work at a lower cost if paid in cash. Norman and Norma obliged, knowing that this was a device to reduce the workmen's tax liability. As he drove Norman often exceeded the speed limit, and was twice fined and had his licence endorsed, resenting the police time spent on this rather than 'real crime'. Norman did, however, slow down when he saw a police officer, or an accident, or a camera, or a sign saying cameras were in operation, or an illuminated reminder, or a village 'polite notice' asking drivers to pass through carefully and with consideration. Otherwise much of the time he continued to pay little regard to speed limits.

It was not until his fifties that Norman resumed relatively regular, deliberate efforts to commit crime. His work involved a great deal of rail travel. Whenever he had the opportunity Norman would re-use tickets to avoid the fares. He did so because he believed that the rail company provided such a poor service, with delayed, dirty and overcrowded trains, but charged outrageous peak-time fares. Non-payment when he could avoid it was his way of 'punishing' the train company. Norman was never caught.

Norman felt like committing other crimes from time to time. He would have liked, for example, to assault persistently noisy neighbours, a pair of youngsters who robbed Norma, and a garage proprietor who sold him a seriously defective car. He never acted on any of these feelings, which were, from time to time, very strong indeed. He couldn't get to the targets, he didn't know exactly who they should be, the violent sentiments faded quite quickly, he was frightened of the violence, Norma calmed him down, and the prospective reward was not enough to compensate for the costs Norman would incur if he was subsequently charged and taken to court.

Norman committed many offences over his lifetime. But there were clearly many types of crime he did not commit. It would not have occurred to him ever, for example, to commit burglary, theft from a vehicle, theft of a vehicle or personal theft. He would never have defrauded his employees or the tax authorities though he had ample opportunities to do so. Once an adult he never again contemplated criminal damage or shop theft. While Norman's dreams of bank robbery never quite left him, he never committed one. Norman's uncommitted (prevented) crimes are clearly much more numerous than the quite large number he did commit. Some (such as domestic burglary) never entered his head, some (such as murder) he found morally repugnant, some (such as bank robbery) he was simply unable to commit, some (such as assaults on rail company staff) he did not commit for fear of the legal consequences, and some (such as major corporate fraud) were irrelevant to the world Norman occupied. Norman did not commit many crimes for several reasons any of which would have been sufficient to stop it. These went from the very serious, such as murder and rape, to the relatively trivial, such as TV license fee evasion and littering.

Norman's story is norm and story. It illustrates most, though not quite all, of the ways in which crime occurs and is prevented.

Norman's crime life is outlined here to convey its ordinariness. Both what he did and what he did not do should be recognisable by all male readers, although it is possible that some female readers may be shocked to think that this is how many normal boys behave. Of course Norman was unique. The details of his life are those of no other. But this too is true of us all, even though there are marked aggregate patterns and important general lessons to be learned. Norman was certainly a man of his time and of his social and spatial place.

Growing up in the 1950s in a lower-middle class family while living in a village provide rather particular conditions for crime and its prevention. This contributes to the particularity of Norman's crime career, but the variability for settings for crime patterns is again an important general matter that emerges throughout this book.

The patient reader might like to construct a crime life of their own and to use that as a reference point as they read. If you do this try to talk to someone who will be absolutely frank with you, neither holding back what may be painful or embarrassing, nor embroidering on exploits in the interests of impressing you with their derring-do. Alternatively, the older reader in particular might like to look back on their own crime life with the same sober honesty I like to think Norman displayed as he told me his crime story.

References

Adams, J. (1995) *Risk*. London: UCL Press.
Audit Commission (2002) *Changing Habits: The Commissioning and Management of Community Drug Treatment Services for Adults*. London: Audit Commission.
Audit Commission (2007) *Police Data Quality 2006/7*. London: Audit Commission.

Bemelmans-Videc, M., Rist, R. and Vedung, E. (1998) *Carrots, Sticks and Sermons: Policy Instruments and Evaluation*. New Brunswick, NJ: Transaction.
Bottoms, A., Claytor, A. and Wiles, P. (1992) 'Housing markets and residential community crime careers', in D. Evans, N. Fyfe and D. Herbert (eds) *Crime, Policing and Place: Essays in Environmental Criminology*. London: Routledge.
Bottoms, A. and Wiles, P. (1986) 'Housing tenure and residential community crime careers in Britain', in A. Reiss and M. Tonry (eds) *Communities and Crime*, Crime and Justice Volume 8. Chicago: University of Chicago Press.
Bottoms, A. and Wiles, P. (1997) 'Environmental criminology', in M. Maguire, R. Morgan and R. Reiner (eds) *The Oxford Handbook of Criminology*, 2nd edn. Oxford: Oxford University Press.
Bowers, K. and Johnson, S. (2003a) 'Measuring the geographical displacement and diffusion of benefit effects of crime prevention activity', *Journal of Quantitative Criminology*, 19(3): 275–301.
Bowers, K. and Johnson, S. (2003b) *Reducing Burglary Initiative: The Role of Publicity in Crime Prevention*. Home Office Research Study 272. London: Home Office.
Bowers, K. and Johnson, S. (2005) 'Domestic burglary repeats and space-time clusters', *European Journal of Criminology*, 2(1): 67–92.
Bowers, K., Johnson, S. and Pease, K. (2005) 'Victimisation and revictimisation risk, housing type and area: a study of interactions', *Crime Prevention and Community Safety: An International Journal*, 7(1): 7–17.
Bowers, K., Sidebottom, A. and Ekblom, P. (Forthcoming) 'CRITIC: a prospective

planning tool for crime prevention evaluation designs', *Crime Prevention and Community Safety: An International Journal.*

Box, S. (1971) *Deviance, Reality and Society.* London: Holt Rinehart and Winston.

Bradbury, A. (2001) *Juvenile Referral Scheme.* Blackburn: Lancashire Constabulary. Tilley Award Entry available online at: http://www.popcenter.org/library/awards/tilley/2001/01-36.pdf

Braithwaite, J. (1989) *Crime, Shame and Reintegration.* Cambridge: Cambridge University Press.

Brantingham, P. and Brantingham, P. (1981) 'Notes on the geometry of crime', in P. Brantingham and P. Brantingham (eds) *Environmental Criminology.* Beverly Hills, CA: Sage.

Brantingham, P. and Brantingham, P. (1984) *Patterns in Crime.* New York: Macmillan.

Brantingham, P. and Brantingham, P. (1995) 'Criminality of place: crime generators and crime attractors', *European Journal of Criminal Policy and Research,* 3(3): 5–26.

Brantingham, P. and Brantingham, P. (2008) 'Crime pattern theory', in R. Wortley and L. Mazerolle (eds) *Environmental Criminology and Crime Analysis.* Cullompton: Willan Publishing.

Brown, R. (2004) 'The effectiveness of electronic immobilisation: changing patterns of temporary and permanent vehicle theft', in M. Maxfield and R. Clarke (eds) *Understanding and Preventing Car Theft.* Crime Prevention Studies Volume 17. Monsey, NY: Criminal Justice Press.

Budd, T., Sharp, C. and Mayhew, P. (2004) *Offending in England and Wales: First Results from the 2003 Crime and Justice Survey.* Home Office Research Study 275. London: Home Office.

Bullock, K. (2007) *Lost in Translation.* Unpublished PhD Thesis. University College London.

Bullock, K., Erol, R. and Tilley, N. (2006) *Problem-Oriented Policing and Partnerships: Implementing an Evidence-Based Approach to Crime Reduction.* Cullompton: Willan Publishing.

Bullock, K., Moss, K. and Smith, J. (2000) *Anticipating the Impact of Section 17 of the Crime and Disorder Act.* Briefing Note 11/00. London: Home Office.

Bullock, K. and Tilley, N. (2002) *Gangs, Guns and Violent Incidents in Manchester: Developing a Crime Reduction Strategy.* Crime Reduction Research Series 13. London: Home Office.

Bullock, K. and Tilley, N. (2003a) 'From strategy to action: the development and implementation of problem-oriented projects', in K. Bullock and N. Tilley (eds) *Crime Reduction and Problem-Oriented Policing.* Cullompton: Willan Publishing.

Bullock, K. and Tilley, N. (2003b) *Crime Reduction and Problem-Oriented Policing.* Cullompton: Willan Publishing.

Bullock, K. and Tilley, N. (2008) 'Understanding and tackling gang violence', *Crime Prevention and Community Safety,* 10(1): 36–47.

Burrows, J., Tarling, R., Mackie, A., Lewis, R. and Taylor, G. (2000) *Review of Police Forces' Crime Recording Practices.* Home Office Research Study 204. London: Home Office.

Chenery, S., Holt, J. and Pease, K. (1997) *Biting Back II: Reducing Repeat Victimisation in Huddersfield*. Crime Detection and Prevention Paper 82. London. Home Office.

Clarke, R. (1992) *Situational Crime Prevention: Successful Case Studies*, 1st edn. New York: Harrow and Heston.

Clarke, R. (1995) 'Situational crime prevention', in M. Tonry and D. Farrington (eds) *Building a Safer Society*, Crime and Justice Volume 19. Chicago: University of Chicago Press.

Clarke, R. (1997) 'Introduction', in R. Clarke (ed.) *Situational Crime Prevention: Successful Case Studies*, 2nd edn. New York: Harrow and Heston.

Clarke, R. (2002a) 'Introduction', in R. Clarke (ed.) *Situational Crime Prevention: Successful Case Studies*, 1st edn. New York: Harrow and Heston.

Clarke, R. (2002b) *Thefts of and From Cars in Parking Facilities*. Problem-Oriented Guides for Police Series Number 11. Washington DC: US Department of Justice Office of Community-Oriented Policing Services.

Clarke, R. (2005) 'Seven misconceptions of situational crime prevention', in N. Tilley (ed.) *Handbook of Crime Prevention and Community Safety*. Cullompton: Willan Publishing.

Clarke, R. and Eck, J. (2003) *Become a Problem-Solving Crime Analyst: In 55 Small Steps*. London: Jill Dando Institute of Crime Science.

Clarke, R. and Goldstein, H. (2003a) *Reducing Thefts at Construction Sites: Lessons from a Problem-oriented Project*. Washington, DC: US Department of Justice, Office of Community-Oriented Policing Services. Accessible at: http://www.popcenter.org/Library/RecommendedReadings/ConstructionTheft.pdf

Clarke, R. and Goldstein, H. (2003b) *Theft from Cars in City Center Parking Facilities – A Case Study*. Washington, DC: US Department of Justice, Office of Community-Oriented Policing Services. Accessible at: http://www.popcenter.org/Problems/Supplemental_Material/Car%20Thefts/clarkegold.pdf

Clarke, R. and Hough, M. (1984) *Crime and Police Effectiveness*. Home Office Research Study 79. London: HMSO.

Clarke, R. and Mayhew, P. (1988) 'The British Gas suicide story and its criminological implications', in M. Tonry and N. Morris (eds) *Crime and Justice: A Review of Research*, Volume 10. Chicago, IL: University of Chicago Press.

Cohen, L. and Felson M. (1979) 'Social change and crime rate trends: a routine activity approach', *American Sociological Review*, 44: 588–608.

Cohen, S. (1973) *Folk Devils and Moral Panics*. St Albans: Paladin.

Coleman, A. (1990) *Utopia on Trial*. London: Hilary Shipman Ltd.

Cornish, D. (1994) 'The procedural analysis of offending and its relevance to for situational prevention', in R. Clarke (ed.) *Crime Prevention Studies*, Volume 3. Monsey, NY: Criminal Justice Press.

Cornish, D. and Clarke, R. (2003) 'Opportunities, precipitators and criminal decisions: a reply to Wortley's critique of situational crime prevention', in M. Smith and D. Cornish (eds) *Theory and Practice in Situational Crime Prevention*. Crime Prevention Studies Volume 16. Monsey, NY: Criminal Justice Press.

Cornish, D. and Clarke, R. (2008) 'The rational choice perspective', in R.

Wortley and L. Mazerolle (eds) *Environmental Criminology and Crime Analysis*. Cullompton: Willan Publishing.

Cornish, D. and Clarke, R. (1986) *The Reasoning Criminal: Rational Choice Perspectives on Offending*. New York: Springer-Verlag.

Crawford, A. (1998) *Crime Prevention and Community Safety*. Harlow: Longman.

Curra J. (2000) *The Relativity of Deviance*. Thousand Oaks, CA: Sage.

Eck, J. (2002) 'Learning from experience in problem-oriented policing and situational crime prevention: the positive functions of weak evaluations and the negative functions of strong ones', in N. Tilley (ed.) *Evaluation for Crime Prevention*. Crime Prevention Studies Volume 14. Monsey, NY: Criminal Justice Press.

Eck, J. (2005) 'Evaluation for lesson-learning', in N. Tilley (ed.) *Handbook of Crime Prevention and Community Safety*. Cullompton: Willan Publishing.

Eck, J. and Spelman, W. (1987) *Problem-Solving: Problem-Oriented Policing in Newport News*. Washington, DC: Police Executive Research Forum.

Edge, S. (2007) 'The good neighbours who fought back', *Daily Express*, 24 February.

Ekblom, P. (1988) *Getting the Best out of Crime Analysis*. Crime Prevention Unit Paper 10. London: Home Office.

Ekblom, P. (1997) 'Gearing up against crime: a dynamic framework to help designers keep up with the adaptive criminal in a changing world', *International Journal of Risk, Security and Crime Prevention*, 2(4): 249–65.

Ekblom, P. (2005) 'Designing products against crime', in N. Tilley (ed.) *Handbook of Crime Prevention and Community Safety*. Cullompton: Willan Publishing.

Ekblom, P. and Pease, K. (1995) 'Evaluating crime prevention', in M. Tonry and D. Farrington (eds) *Building a Safer Society*. Crime and Justice Volume 19. Chicago: University of Chicago Press.

Ekblom, P. and Tilley, N. (2000) 'Going equipped: criminology, situational crime prevention and the resourceful offender', *British Journal of Criminology*, 40(3): 375–98.

Engstad, P. and Evans, H. (1980) 'Responsibility, competence and police effectiveness in crime control', in R. Clarke and M. Hough (eds) *The Effectiveness of Policing*. Farnborough: Gower.

Farrell, G., Chenery, S. and Pease, K. (1998) *Consolidating Police Crackdowns: Findings from an Anti-Burglary Project*. Police Research Series Paper 113. London: Home Office.

Farrell, G. and Pease, K. (1993) *Once Bitten, Twice Bitten: Repeat Victimisation and the Implications or Crime Prevention*. Crime Prevention Unit Paper 46. London: Home Office.

Farrington, D. (1996) 'The explanation and prevention of youthful offending', in J. David Hawkins (ed.) *Delinquency and Crime*. Cambridge: Cambridge University Press.

Farrington, D. (2007) 'Childhood risk factors and risk-focused prevention', in M. Maguire, R. Morgan and R. Reiner (eds) *The Oxford Handbook of Criminology*, 4th edn. Oxford: Oxford University Press.

Farrington, D., Coid, J., Harnett, L., Jolliffe, D., Soteriou, N., Turner, R. and

West, D. (2006) *Criminal Careers up to Age 50 and Life Success up to Age 48: New Findings from the Cambridge Study in Delinquent Development.* Home Office Research Study 299. London: Home Office.

Felson, M. (1986) 'Linking criminal choices, routine activities, informal control, and criminal outcomes', in D. Cornish and R. Clarke (eds) *The Reasoning Criminal: Rational Choice Perspectives on Offending.* New York: Springer.

Felson, M. (2002) *Crime and Everyday Life.* Thousand Oaks, CA: Sage.

Felson, M. (2006) *The Ecosystem for Organised Crime.* HEUNI Paper Number 26. Helsinki: The European Institute for Crime Prevention and Control.

Felson, M. and Clarke, R. (1998) *Opportunity Makes the Thief.* Police Research Series Paper 98. London: Home Office.

Fisher, H., Gardner F. and Montgomery P. (2008) 'Cognitive-behavioural interventions for preventing youth gang involvement for children and young people (7-16)', *Cochrane Database of Systematic Reviews 2008,* Issue 2.

Flood-Page, C., Campbell, C., Harrington, V. and Miller, J. (2000) *Youth Crime: Findings from the 1998/99 Youth Lifestyles Survey.* Home Office Research Study 209. London: Home Office.

Forrest, S., Myhill, A. and Tilley, N. (2005) *Practical Lessons for Involving the Community in Crime and Disorder Problem-Solving.* Home Office Development and Practice Report 43. London: Home Office.

Forrester, D., Chatterton, M. and Pease, K. with the assistance of Brown, R. (1988) *The Kirkholt Burglary Prevention Project, Rochdale.* Crime Prevention Unit Paper 13. London: Home Office.

Forrester, D., Frenz, S., O'Connell, M. and Pease, K. (1990) *The Kirkholt Burglary Prevention Project, Phase II.* Crime Prevention Unit Paper 23. London: Home Office.

Friendship, C. and Debidin, M. (2006) 'Probation and prison interventions', in A. Perry, C. McDougall and D. Farrington (eds) *Reducing Crime: The Effectiveness of Criminal Justice Interventions.* Chichester: Wiley.

Frisher, M. and Beckett, H. (2006) 'Drug use desistance', *Criminology and Criminal Justice,* 6(1): 127–45.

Furedi, F. and Bristow, J. (2008) *Licensed to Hug.* London: Civitas.

Gabor, T. (1994) *Everybody Does It: Crime by the Public.* Toronto: University of Toronto Press.

Garland, D. (2001) *The Culture of Control.* Oxford: Oxford University Press.

Gest, T. (2001) *Crime and Politics.* Oxford: Oxford University Press.

Gilling, D. (1997) *Crime Prevention.* London: UCL Press.

Goldblatt, P. and Lewis, C. (1998) *Reducing Offending: An Assessment of the Research Evidence on Ways of Dealing with Offending Behaviour.* Home Office Research Study 187. London: Home Office.

Goldstein, H. (1979) 'Improving policing: a problem-oriented approach', *Crime and Delinquency,* 25: 236–258.

Goldstein, H. (1990) *Problem-Oriented Policing.* New York: McGraw-Hill.

Gouldner, A. (1959) 'Reciprocity and autonomy in functional theory', in L. Gross (ed.) *Symposium on Sociological Theory.* Evanston, IL: Row. Peterson.

Gouldner, A. (1960) 'The norm of reciprocity: a preliminary statement', *American Sociological Review,* 25:161–78.

Green, S. (2007) '"Victims movement" and restorative justice', in G. Johnstone and D. Van Ness (eds) *Handbook of Restorative Justice*. Cullompton: Willan Publishing.

Greene, J. (2000) 'Community policing in America: changing the nature, structure, and function of the police', in J. Horney (ed.) *Policies, Processes and Decisions of the Criminal Justice System. Criminal Justice 2000*. Washington, DC: US Department of Justice Office of Justice Programs.

Guerette, R. (2008) *The Pull, Push, and Expansion of Situational Crime Prevention Evaluation: An Appraisal of Thirty-Seven Years of Research*. Presented at Stavern, May 2008.

Hanmer, J. (2003) 'Mainstreaming solutions to major problems: reducing repeat domestic violence', in K. Bullock and N. Tilley (eds) *Crime Reduction and Problem-Oriented Policing*. Cullompton: Willan Publishing.

Hanmer, J., Griffiths, S. and Jerwood, D. (1999) *Arresting Evidence: Domestic Violence and Repeat Victimisation*. Policing Research Series Paper 104. Home Office: London.

Hardie, J. and Hobbs, B. (2005) 'Partners against crime: the role of the corporate sector in tackling crime', in R. Clarke and G. Newman (eds) *Designing Out Crime from Products and Systems*. Crime Prevention Studies Volume 18. Monsey, NY: Criminal Justice Press.

Harper, C. and Chitty, C. (2005) *The Impact of Corrections on Reoffending: A Review of 'What Works'*. Home Office Research Study 291, 3rd edn. London: Home Office.

Hartshorne, H. and May, M. (1928) *Studies in the Nature of Character, Volume 1, Studies in Deceit*. New York: Macmillan.

Hayes, H. (2007) 'Restorative justice and reoffending', in G. Johnstone and D. Van Ness (eds) *Handbook of Restorative Justice*. Cullompton: Willan Publishing.

Hesseling, R. (1994) 'Displacement: a review of the empirical literature', in R. Clarke (ed) *Crime Prevention Studies*, Volume 3. Monsey, NY: Criminal Justice Press.

Hirschi, T. (1969) *Causes of Delinquency*. Berkeley: University of California Press.

Hodgkinson, S. and Tilley. N. (2007) 'Travel-to-crime: homing in on the victim', *International Review of Victimology*, 14(3): 281–298.

Hollin, C., Palmer, E., McGuire, J., Hounsome, J., Hatcher, R., Bilby, C. and Clark, C. (2004) *Pathfinder Programmes in the Probation Service: A Retrospective Analysis*. Home Office Online Report 66/04. London: Home Office.

Holloway, K. and Bennett, T. (2004) *The Results of the First Two Years of the NEW-ADAM Programme*. Home Office On-Line Report 19/04. London: Home Office.

Home Office (2004) *Prolific and Other Priority Offender Strategy*. London: Home Office, Youth Justice Board and the Department for Education and Skills.

Home Office (2006) *Building Communities, Beating Crime: A Better Police Service for the 21st Century*. London: Home Office.

Homel, P., Nutley, S., Webb, B. and Tilley, N. (2004) *Investing to Deliver: Reviewing the Implementation of the UK Crime Reduction Programme*. Home Office Research Study 281. London: Home Office.

Homel, R. (1988) *Policing and Punishing the Drinking Driver: A Study of General and Specific Deterrence*. New York: Springer-Verlag.

Homel, R. (1995) 'Can the police prevent crime?', in K. Bryett and C. Lewis (eds) *Contemporary Policing: Unpeeling Tradition*. Sydney: Macmillan.

Homel, R. (2005) 'Developmental crime prevention', in N. Tilley (ed.) *Handbook of Crime Prevention and Community Safety*. Cullompton: Willan Publishing.

Homel, R., Hauritz, M., McIlwain, G., Wortley, R. and Carvolth, R. (1997) 'Preventing drunkenness and violence around nightclubs in a tourist resort', in R. Clarke (ed.) *Situational Crime Prevention: Successful Case Studies*, 2nd edn. Albany, NY: Harrow and Heston.

Hope, T. (1995) 'Community crime prevention', in M. Tonry and D. Farrington (eds) *Building a Safer Society*. Crime and Justice Volume 19. Chicago: University of Chicago Press.

Hope, T. and Murphy, J. (1983) 'Problems of implementing crime prevention', *The Howard Journal*, 23: 38–50.

Hough, M. (2004) 'Modernisation, scientific rationalism and the crime reduction programme', *Criminal Justice*, 4(3): 239–53.

Hough, M. and Maxfield, M. (2007) *Surveying Victims in the 21st Century*. Crime Prevention Studies Volume 22. Monsey, NY: Criminal Justice Press.

Hough, M. and Tilley, N. (1998) *Getting the Grease to the Squeak: Research Lessons for Crime Prevention*. Crime Prevention and Detection Series Paper 85. London: Home Office.

Houghton, G. (1992) *Car Theft in England and Wales: The Home Office Car Theft Index*. Crime Prevention Unit Paper 33. London: Home Office.

Hughes, G. (1998) *Understanding Crime Prevention*. Buckingham: Open University Press.

Hughes, G. (2007) *The Politics of Crime and Community*. Basingstoke: Palgrave.

Hughes, G., McLaughlin, E. and Muncie, J. (2002) *Crime Prevention and Community Safety*. London: Sage.

Innes, M. (2004) 'Signal crimes and signal disorders: notes on deviance as communicative action', *British Journal of Sociology*, 55(3): 335–55.

Jeffery, C. Ray (1971) *Crime Prevention Through Environmental Design*. Beverley Hills, CA: Sage.

Johnson, S. and Bowers, K. (2007) 'Burglary prediction: the role of theory, flow and friction', in G. Farrell, K. Bowers, S. Johnson and M. Townsley (eds) *Imagination for Crime Prevention: Essays in Honour of Ken Pease*. Crime Prevention Studies Volume 21. Monsey, NY: Criminal Justice Press.

Johnson, S., Bowers, K. and Pease, K. (2005) 'Predicting the future or summarising the past? crime mapping in anticipation', in M. Smith and N. Tilley (eds) *Crime Science*. Cullompton: Willan Publishing.

Johnstone, G. and Van Ness, D. (2007) *Handbook of Restorative Justice*. Cullompton: Willan Publishing.

Kelling, G. (2005) 'Community crime reduction: activating formal and informal control', in N. Tilley (ed.) *Handbook of Crime Prevention and Community Safety*. Cullompton: Willan Publishing.

Kennedy, D. (2008) *Deterrence and Crime Prevention*. London: Routledge.

Kennedy, D., Braga, A., Piehl, A. and Waring, E. (2001) *Reducing Gun Violence: The Boston's Gun Project's Operation Ceasefire: Developing and Implementing Operation Ceasefire*. Washington, DC: National Institute of Justice US Department of Justice Office of Justice Programs.

Knutsson, J. (2004) *Problem-Oriented Policing: From Innovation to Mainstream*. Crime Prevention Studies Volume 15. Monsey, NY: Criminal Justice Press.

Koch, B. (1998) *The Politics of Crime Prevention*. Aldershot: Ashgate.

Lancashire Constabulary (2003) *The Tower Project: Goldstein Award Entry*. Available at http://popcenter.org/library/awards/goldstein/2003/03-59(F).pdf, accessed August 2008.

Langman, J. (2005) *A Guide to Promising Approaches*, 2nd edn. London: Communities that Care.

Laub, J.H. and Sampson, R.J. (2003) *Shared Beginnings, Divergent Lives: Delinquent Boys to Age 70*. Massachusetts: Harvard University Press.

Laycock G. (1985) *Property Marking: A Deterrent to Domestic Burglary?* Crime Prevention Unit Paper 3. London: Home Office.

Laycock, G. (1997) 'Operation Identification, or the power of publicity?', in R. Clarke (ed.) *Situational Crime Prevention: Successful Case Studies*, 2nd edn. New York. Harrow and Heston

Laycock, G. (2004) 'The UK car theft index: an example of government leverage', in M. Maxfield and R. Clarke (eds) *Understanding and Preventing Car Theft*. Crime Prevention Studies Volume 17. Monsey, NY: Criminal Justice Press.

Laycock, G. and Tilley, N. (1995a) *Policing and Neighbourhood Watch*. Crime Prevention and Detection Series Paper 60. London: Home Office.

Laycock, G. and Tilley, N. (1995b) 'Implementing crime prevention', in M. Tonry and D. Farrington (eds) *Building a Safer Society: Strategic Approaches to Crime Prevention*. Crime and Justice volume 19. Chicago: University of Chicago Press.

Laycock, G. and Webb, B. (2000) 'Making it happen', in S. Ballintyne, K. Pease and V. McLaren (eds) *Secure Foundations*. London: IPPR.

Laycock, G. and Webb, B. (2003) 'Conclusion: the role of the centre', in K. Bullock and N. Tilley (eds) *Crime Reduction and Problem-Oriented Policing*. Cullompton: Willan Publishing.

Lemert, E. (1972) *Human Deviance, Social Problems and Social Control*. Englewood Cliffs, NJ: Prentice-Hall.

Lewin, K. (1951) 'Field theory in social science', in D. Cartwright (ed.) New York: Harper & Row.

Lipsky, M. (1980) *Street-Level Bureaucracy*. New York: Russell Sage Foundation.

Loeber, R., Wim Slot, N. and Stouthamer-Loeber, M. (2006) 'A three-dimensional, cumulative, developmental model of serious delinquency', in P-O. Wikström and R. Sampson (eds) *The Explanation of Crime*. Cambridge: Cambridge University Press.

Maguire, J., edited by Furniss, M. Jane. (2000) *Cognitive Behavioural Approaches: An Introduction to Theory and Research*. Available at: http://inspectorates. homeoffice.gov.uk/hmiprobation/docs/cogbeh1.pdf?view=Binary, accessed June 2008.

Maguire, M. (2004) 'The crime reduction programme in England and Wales', *Criminal Justice*, 4(3): 213–37.

Makkai, T. and Payne, J. (2003) *Key Issues from the Drug Use Careers of Offenders (DUCO) Study*. Trends and Issues Number 267. Canberra: Australian Institute of Criminology.

Marsden, J. and Farrell, M. (2002) 'Research on what works to reduce illegal drug misuse', Appendix Five to Audit Commission, *Changing Habits: The Commissioning and Management of Community Drug Treatment Services for Adults*. London: Audit Commission.

Martin, J. and Webster, D. (1994) *Probation Motor Projects in England and Wales*. London: Home Office.

Mayhew, P., Clarke, R., Sturman, A. and Hough, M. (1976) *Crime as Opportunity*. Home Office Research Study 34. London: HMSO.

McDougall, C., Perry, A. and Farrington D. (2006) 'Overview of effectiveness of criminal justice interventions in the UK', in A. Perry, C. McDougall and D. Farrington (eds) *Reducing Crime: The Effectiveness of Criminal Justice Interventions*. Chichester: Wiley.

McSweeney, T. and Hough, M. (2005) 'Drugs and alcohol', in N. Tilley (ed.) *Handbook of Crime Prevention and Community Safety*. Cullompton: Willan Publishing.

Mistry, D. (2006) *A Process Evaluation of a Pilot Community Engagement Project*. Unpublished Report to the Home Office.

Mistry, D. (2007) *Community Engagement: Practical Lessons from a Pilot Project*. Development and Practice Report 48. London: Home Office.

Moffitt, T. (1993) '"Adolescent-limited" and "Life-course-persistent" antisocial behavior: a developmental taxonomy', *Psychological Review*, 100(4): 674–701.

National Institute on Drug Abuse (NIDA) (2006) *Principles of Drug Abuse Treatment for Criminal Justice Populations: A Research-Based Guide*. National Institutes of Health. US Department of Health and Human Services.

Newburn, T. and Hayman, S. (2002) *Policing, Surveillance and Social Control*. Cullompton: Willan Publishing.

Newman, O. (1972) *Defensible Space*. New York: Macmillan.

Nicholas, S., Kershaw, C. and Walker, A. (2007) *Crime in England and Wales 2006/7*. Home Office Statistical Bulletin 11/07. London: Home Office.

Office of National Drug Control Policy (ONDCP) (2000) *Drug-Related Crime*. Washington: Office of National Drug Control Policy.

Pawson, R. (2006) *Evidence-Based Policy: A Realist Perspective*. London: Sage.

Pawson, R. and Tilley, N. (1997) *Realistic Evaluation*. London: Sage.

Pawson, R. and Tilley, N. (2005) 'Realist evaluation', in S. Mathison (ed.) *Encyclopedia of Evaluation*. Thousand Oaks, CA: Sage.

Pease, K. (1997) 'Predicting the future: the roles of Routine Activity Theory and Rational Choice Theory', in G. Newman, R. Clarke and S. Giora Shoham (eds) *Rational Choice and Situational Crime Prevention*. Aldershot: Ashgate.

Peck, E. and 6, P. (2006) *Beyond Delivery*. Basingstoke: Palgrave.

Perry, A., McDougall, C. and Farrington, D (2006) *Reducing Crime: The Effectiveness of Criminal Justice Interventions*. Chichester: Wiley.

Petrosino, A., Turpin-Petrosino, C. and Buehler, J. (2002) '"Scared Straight" and other juvenile awareness programs for preventing juvenile delinquency', in *The Campbell Collaboration Reviews of Intervention and Policy Evaluations (C2-RIPE)*. Philadelphia, PA: Campbell Collaboration.

Povey, K. (2000) *On the Record*. London: Her Majesty's Inspectorate of Constabulary.

Poyner, B. (2002) 'Situational crime prevention in two parking facilities', in R. Clarke (ed.) *Situational Crime Prevention: Successful Case Studies*, 2nd edn. New York. Harrow & Heston.

Pressman, J. and Wildavsky, A. (1973) *Implementation*. Berkley, CA: University of California Press.

PricewaterhouseCoopers (2005) *Personalized Medicine: The Emerging Pharmacogenomics Revolution*. Global Research Centre Health Research Institute.

Quinton, P. and Morris, J. (2008) *Neighbourhood Policing: The Impact of Piloting and Early National Implementation*. Home Office Online Report 01/08. London: Home Office.

Ratcliffe, J. (2008) *Intelligence-Led Policing*. Cullompton: Willan Publishing.

Rawlings, P. (2003) 'Policing before the police', in T. Newburn (ed.) *Handbook of Policing*. Cullompton: Willan Publishing.

Read, T. and Tilley, N. (2000) *Not Rocket Science: Problem-Solving and Crime Reduction*. Crime Reduction Research Series 6. London: Home Office.

Reppetto, T. (1976) 'Crime prevention and the displacement phenomenon', *Crime and Delinquency*, 22: 166–77.

Rodriguez, M. (1993) *Together We Can*. Chicago, IL: Chicago Police Department.

Roman, J. and Farrell, G. (2002) 'Cost-benefit analysis for crime prevention: opportunity costs, routine savings and crime externalities', in N. Tilley (ed.) *Evaluation for Crime Prevention*. Crime Prevention Studies Volume 14. Monsey, NY: Criminal Justice Press.

Royal Academy of Engineering (2007) *Dilemmas of Privacy and Surveillance: Challenges of Technological Change*. London: Royal Academy of Engineering.

Sampson, R., Raudenbush, S. and Earls, F. (1997) 'Neighborhoods and violent crime: a multilevel study of collective efficacy', *Science*, 277: 918–24.

Scarman, L. (1982) *The Scarman Report: The Brixton Disorders 10–12 April 1981*. Harmondsworth: Penguin.

Scott, M. (2000) *Problem-Oriented Policing: Reflections of the First Twenty Years*. Washington, DC: Department of Justice Office of Community-Oriented Policing Services.

Scott, M. (2005) 'Shifting and sharing police responsibility to address public safety issues', in N. Tilley (ed.) *Handbook of Crime Prevention and Community Safety*. Cullompton: Willan Publishing.

Scott, M. and Goldstein, H. (2005) *Shifting and Sharing Responsibility for Public Safety Problems*. Problem-Oriented Guides for Police Response Guide Series Number 3. Washington, DC: Department of Justice Office of Community-Oriented Policing Services.

Seddon, T. (2007) 'Coerced drug treatment in the criminal justice system: conceptual, criminological and ethical issues', *Criminology and Criminal Justice*, 7(3): 269–6.

Shadish, W., Cook, T. and Campbell, D. (2002) *Experimental and Quasi-Experimental Designs for Generalised Causal Inference*. Boston: Houghton Mifflin.

Sherman, L. (1990) 'Police crackdowns: initial and residual deterrence', in M. Tonry and N. Morris (eds) *Crime and Justice*, Volume 12. Chicago: University of Chicago Press.

Sherman, L. (1992a) 'Attacking crime: police and crime control', in M. Tonry and N. Morris (eds) *Modern Policing. Crime and Justice: A Review of Research*, Volume 15. Chicago: University of Chicago Press.

Sherman, L. (1992b) *Policing Domestic Violence*. New York: Free Press.

Sherman, L. and Berk, R. (1984) *The Minneapolis Domestic Violence Experiment*. Washington, DC: Police Foundation.

Sherman, L., Gottfredson, D., MacKenzie, D., Eck, J., Reuter, P. and Bushway, S. (1997) *Preventing Crime: What Works, What Doesn't, What's Promising*. Washington, DC: US Department of Justice, Office of Justice Programs.

Sims, L. (2001) *Neighbourhood Watch: Findings from the 2000 British Crime Survey*. Home Office Findings 150. London: Home Office.

Skodbo, S., Brown, G., Deacon, S., Cooper, C., Hall, A., Millar, T., Smith, J. and Whitham, K. (2007) *The Drug Interventions Programme (DIP): Addressing Drug Use and Offending through 'Tough Choices'*. Research Report 2. London: Home Office.

Skogan, W. (2004) *Community Policing: Can it Work?* Belmont, CA: Thomson Wadsworth.

Skogan, W. (2006) *Policing and Community in Chicago*. Oxford: Oxford University Press.

Skogan, W. and Hartnett, S. (1997) *Community Policing: Chicago Style*. Oxford: Oxford University Press.

Smith, M. (2004) *Routine Precautions Used by Taxi-drivers: A Situational Crime Prevention Approach*. Presented at the American Society of Criminology Meeting, Nashville, Tennessee, November 2004.

Smith, M., Clarke, R. and Pease, K. (2002) 'Anticipatory benefits in crime prevention', in N. Tilley (ed.) *Analysis for Crime Prevention*. Crime Prevention Studies Volume 13. Monsey, NY: Criminal Justice Press.

Stockdale, J. and Whitehead, C. (2003) 'Assessing cost-effectiveness', in K. Bullock and N. Tilley (eds) *Crime Reduction and Problem-Oriented Policing*. Cullompton: Willan Publishing.

Stockdale, J., Whitehead, C. and Gresham, P. (1999) *Applying Economic Evaluation in Policing Activity*. Police Research Series Paper 103. London: Home Office.

Sutton, M. (1998) *Handling Stolen Goods and Theft: A Market Reduction Approach*. Home Office Research Study 178. London. Home Office.

Sutton, M., Schneider, J. and Hetherington, S. (2001) *Tackling Theft with the Market Reduction Approach*. Home Office Crime Reduction Series Paper 8. London: Home Office.

Tarling, R. (1993) *Analysing Offending: Data, Models and Interpretations*. London: HMSO.

Tilley, J. and Webb, J. (1994) *Burglary Reduction: Findings from the Safer Cities Programme*. Crime Prevention Unit Series Paper 51. London: Home Office.

Tilley, N. (1993a) 'Crime prevention and the Safer Cities story', *The Howard Journal*, 32(1): 40–57.

Tilley, N. (1993b) *After Kirkholt: Theory, Methods and Results of Replication Evaluations*. Crime Prevention Unit Paper 47. London: Home Office.

Tilley, N. (1993c) *The Prevention of Crime Against Small Businesses: The Safer Cities Experience*. Crime Prevention Unit Series Paper 45. London: Home Office.

Tilley, N. (1996) 'Demonstration, exemplification, duplication and replication in evaluation research', *Evaluation*, 2(1): 35–50.

Tilley, N. (2000a) 'Doing realistic evaluation of criminal justice', in V. Jupp, P. Davies and P. Francis (eds) *Doing Criminological Research*. London: Sage.

Tilley, N. (2000b) 'The evaluation jungle', in S. Ballintyne, K. Pease and V. McLaren (eds) *Secure Foundations: Key Issues in Crime Prevention, Crime Reduction and Community Safety*. London: IPPR.

Tilley, N. (2003) 'Community policing, problem-oriented policing and intelligence-led policing', in T. Newburn (ed.) *Handbook of Policing*. Cullompton: Willan Publishing.

Tilley, N. (2004a) 'Applying theory-driven evaluation to the British Crime Reduction Programme', *Criminal Justice*, 4(3): 255–76.

Tilley, N. (2004b) 'Using crackdowns constructively', in R. Hopkins Burke (ed.) *Hard Cop, Soft Cop*. Cullompton: Willan Publishing.

Tilley, N. (2004c) 'Karl Popper: a philosopher for Ronald Clarke's situational crime prevention', in S. Shoham and P. Knepper (eds) *Tradition and Innovation in Crime and Justice*. Willowdale, ON: de Sitter.

Tilley, N. (2005) 'Crime reduction: a quarter century review', *Public Money and Management*, 25(5): 267–74.

Tilley, N. (2006) 'Asking the right questions in criminal justice evaluations', *Criminal Justice Matters*, 62: 12–13.

Tilley, N. (2008) 'The development of community policing in England: networks, knowledge and neighbourhoods', in T. Williamson (ed.) *The Handbook of Knowledge-Based Policing*. Chichester: Wiley.

Tilley, N. and Laycock, G. (2000) 'Joining up research, policy and practice about crime', *Policy Studies*, 21(3): 213–227.

Tilley, N. and Webb, J. (1994) *Burglary Reduction: Findings from Safer Cities Schemes*. Crime Prevention Unit Series Paper 51, London: Home Office.

Tillyer, M. and Kennedy, D. (2008) 'Locating focused deterrence within a situational crime prevention framework', *Crime Prevention and Community Safety*, 10(2): 75–84.

Tseloni, A., Osborn, D., Trickett, A. and Pease, K. (2002) 'Modelling crime using the British Crime Survey: what have we learnt?', *British Journal of Criminology*, 42(1): 109–28.

Tuffin, R., Morris, J. and Poole, A. (2006) *An Evaluation of the National Reassurance Policing Programme*. Home Office Research Study 296. London: Home Office.

van Dijk, J., van Kesteran, J. and Smit, P. (2007) *Criminal Victimisation in International Perspective: Key Findings from the 2004-2005 ICVS and the EU ICS*. The Hague: Boom Juridische Uitgevers.

Webb, B. (2005) 'Preventing vehicle crime', in N. Tilley (ed.) *Handbook of Crime Prevention and Community Safety*. Cullompton: Willan Publishing.

Webb, B., Smith, M. and Laycock, G. (2004) 'Designing out crime through vehicle licensing and registration systems', in M. Maxfield and R. Clarke (eds) *Understanding and Preventing Car Theft*. Crime Prevention Studies Volume 17. Monsey, NY: Criminal Justice Press.

Wikström, P-O. (2006) 'Individuals, settings and acts of crime: situational mechanisms and the explanation of crime', in P-O. Wikström and R. Sampson (eds) *The Explanation of Crime*. Cambridge: Cambridge University Press.

Wikström, P-O. (Forthcoming) 'Situational action theory', in B. Fisher and S. Lab (eds) *Encyclopedia of Victimology and Crime Prevention*. Thousand Oaks, CA: Sage.

Wilkins, L. (1964) *Social Deviance*. London: Tavistock.

Wilson, J. and Kelling, G. (1982) 'Broken windows', *Atlantic Monthly*, March: 29–38.

Wilson, W. (1987) *The Truly Disadvantaged*. Chicago: University of Chicago Press.

Wolf, C., Smith, C. and Smith, R. (2000) 'Science, medicine and the future: pharmacogenetics', *British Medical Journal*, 329: 987–90.

Wortley, R. (2001) 'A classification of techniques for controlling situational precipitators of crime', *Security Journal*, 14: 63–82.

Wortley, R. and Mazerolle, L. (2008) *Environmental Criminology and Crime Analysis*. Cullompton: Willan Publishing.

Young, J. (1991) 'Left realism and the priorities of crime control', in K. Stenson and D. Cowell (eds) *The Politics of Crime Control*. London: Sage.

Young, J. (1999) *The Exclusive Society*. London: Sage.

Zimring, F. and Hawkins, G. (1995) *Incapacitation: Penal Confinement and the Restraint of Crime*. New York: Oxford University Press.

Index